IN PRAISE OF *SPELLBINDING SENTENCES*

Spellbinding Sentences is a wonderfully clear, thoughtful and practical guide for any writer who wants to master the basic unit of our craft: the sentence. Barbara Baig explains the building-blocks of our language and the different ways they can be fitted together to create the effects that you want. This book will help any writer to move well beyond mere correctness, towards writing which is not just clear and accurate in meaning, but full of style and music as well.

—Emma Darwin, prize-winning UK author
A Secret Alchemy and The Mathematics of Love

Barbara Baig's exposition of "sentence craft" is a wonderful and useful treatment for writers young and old, fiction and nonfiction, practical and personal. Here teachers and students will find a handy toolkit for developing the "word mind," whose achievement is the beginning of distinctive, effective prose.

—Mark Bauerlein, Professor of English, Emory University,
former Director of Research and Analysis at the National
Endowment for the Arts, and author of the award-winning
*The Dumbest Generation: How the Digital Age Stupefies
Young Americans and Jeopardizes Our Future*

When it comes to creating compelling prose, Barbara Baig's *Spellbinding Sentences* is a great place to start.

—Nancy Lamb, author of *The Art and Craft of Storytelling*

Barbara Baig knows that mastery comes from practice, and that practice yields power—a message sorely neglected in the writing world today. I recommend her *Spellbinding Sentences* to beginning and experienced writers alike.

—Janet Pocorobba, Assistant Director,
MFA Program in Creative Writing, Lesley University

Barbara Baig's new book is a master course in the most fundamental of a writer's skills—how to build sentences that readers want to read. She goes well beyond the basics, teaching elegance and grace as much as grammar, and offering exercises that are essential to true mastery of the craft. Barbara Baig loves writing, and it shows.

Learning to write, like learning to build, begins with understanding the fundamentals. Master them and you can create anything from a wall to a soaring cathedral. *Spellbinding Sentences* will take you far on your journey to mastery.

Barbara Baig has done something that needed to be done: break down the craft of writing into understandable and digestible sub-skills that can be mastered one step at a time. Working with her book is like hiring a great tennis coach, one who guides you to ever-better performance and who evinces equal passion for the game, for technique, and for the process of mastery itself. Whatever you wish to write—fiction, non-fiction, professional reports, or even memos—this book can help you improve. It's a book, not just to read, as Ms. Baig emphasizes, but to *do*. And, if you do, you will no doubt be rewarded.

Barbara's teaching method is more comprehensive than any other I've experienced. She moves beyond grammar basics and gets into the heart of writing as a craft that should be practiced, explored, played with, and enjoyed. Anyone who is serious about taking his or her writing to a deeper level will benefit from Barbara's thorough, lively lessons.

Spellbinding SENTENCES

A WRITER'S GUIDE TO ACHIEVING EXCELLENCE & CAPTIVATING READERS

Barbara Baig

WRITER'S DIGEST
BOOKS

WritersDigest.*com*
Cincinnati, Ohio

Spellbinding
SENTENCES

A WRITER'S GUIDE TO
ACHIEVING EXCELLENCE
& CAPTIVATING READERS

Barbara Baig

"Get this book and profit from it!"
—Ursula K. Le Guin

For more resources for writers, visit www.writersdigest.com.

22 21 20 19   9 8 7 6

Distributed in the U.K. and Europe by F+W Media International
Brunel House, Newton Abbot, Devon, TQ12 4PU, England
Tel: (+44) 1626-323200, Fax: (+44) 1626-323319
E-mail: postmaster@davidandcharles.co.uk

ISBN-13: 978-1-59963-915-4

Edited by *Cris Freese*
Designed by *Alexis Brown*
Production coordinated by *Debbie Thomas*

"Writing is an art: its medium is language."

—FRANCIS CHRISTENSEN

TABLE OF CONTENTS

WELCOME

So, you want to write—or to write better. Perhaps you dream of producing a novel or memoir so compelling that major publishers will fight over it. Perhaps you hope to have your poems accepted by a small press. Perhaps an essay in *The New York Times* is your goal, or perhaps you want to self-publish your work. You may be enrolled in an MFA program in writing; you may be learning to write on your own, or with the help of a writers' support group. Or perhaps you are someone who has always yearned to write but has never quite dared to take the first step. Wherever you stand now as a writer—whether you are just getting started or have been writing for some time—this book is for you.

It will provide you with something you can't get anyplace else: a focused, classroom-tested training program that will teach you to write spellbinding sentences.

"Sentences?" you may ask. "Why should I care about sentences? I'm not interested in all that boring grammar stuff!"

But this is not a grammar book; it's a book about the power of words. It will teach you—in a down-to-earth, practical way—how to make that power your own.

You may not believe you need that power. You may have been told that what really counts in writing is story, or the ability to dig deep inside yourself and be totally honest about what you uncover. You may believe that if you can only come up with a riveting plot, some editor will "fix" all the writing for you. But the truth is that story, by itself, is just not enough—and professional literary agents and editors, being busy people, would much rather work with writers who've mastered their craft.

These days, most writing instruction focuses on large-scale craft: characters, plot, setting, and so on—and, yes, you certainly need this knowledge. But if you can't *communicate* your story to readers, if you can't use language with such skill that readers *have* to keep turning the pages, then no one will spend more than a few minutes with your work. If you want to keep your readers spellbound, then you also need to learn the "small" craft of writing: the skills of choosing words and arranging them into coherent and powerful sentences. This book will teach you these skills.

As a guide to improving skills, this is not a book just to read: It's a book to *do*. You can't become a better violinist or tennis player simply by reading about those activities; you must put bow to strings or racket to ball on a regular basis. So it is with writing: If you want to develop your skills, you must practice. There's real work involved. This work doesn't require a lot of fancy equipment—not even a computer. And you don't need long stretches of empty time. What you *do* need is an eagerness to learn, and a willingness to put some attention and energy into writing practice.

In the pages that follow, I will be your writing coach. Like a violin teacher or tennis coach, I will show you how to develop your skills, provide you with exercises, and explain how to do those exercises. Like any coach, I will repeat important principles over and over, because repetition is essential to learning. Just as a tennis or baseball coach continually reminds his students, "Keep your eye on the ball!" I will tell you again and again to relax, to listen to your words and sentences, to pay attention to how professional writers use language.

When a professional writer is at work, his mind is busy making choices, choices about content—*What do I want to write about? What material shall I use? Will this piece of writing be a poem or an essay? Who is my audience?*—and choices about language—*What word do I need here? How can I make a picture so my reader will see it? Is this sentence too long?* Some of these choices are the result of conscious thought, but many of them, especially in the realm of craft, are the result of training. Training is what creates professionals. With a baseball game on the line, for example, a professional center fielder can track a fly ball perfectly and make the catch, because his mind and muscles have been trained to choose the right moves. In the same way, when an experienced writer drafts and revises a piece, her mind can come up with effective words and sentence constructions, because she has trained the mental "muscles" that make those choices.

Even more important: Because they have consciously trained themselves in the craft of making sentences, professional writers have far more choices available to them. Without that training, aspiring writers are stuck in a rut: They use the same words, the same sentence structures, over and over, without even realizing it. This book will open your mind to a world of possible word choices and sentence constructions, so that you, too, can write like a professional.

The book is organized like my workshop, The Art of the English Sentence, which I teach in an MFA in Creative Writing program. Its chapters will take you, step-by-step, through information and practices that will increase your understanding of how words and sentences work. The two main sections of the book focus, in turn, on diction (the skill of choosing words) and on syntax (the skill of arranging those words into effective sentences). Having practiced these skills, we'll then explore some more advanced compositional techniques.

My approach here is both highly specific and generously open-ended. All the practices are designed to be equally available—and helpful—to both beginning and more experienced writers. So you can use them in whatever ways you wish, and you can keep returning to them over time, as your needs and desires change.

What I offer here is not a collection of rules (that's what grammar books are for), but a selection of *basic tools* that skilled professional writers use to craft sentences. I have not included every possible technique; rather, I have tried to present this material in such a way that any interested writer, beginning or experienced, can develop a solid foundation in sentence-making skills. With this foundation in place, you can easily go on to explore more advanced or experimental approaches. At the end of the book you'll find a list of resources for further learning.

A journey towards mastery, in writing as in any other field, is a source of pleasure. To acquire expertise is to gain confidence in oneself and one's abilities, to feel a sense of power. And when you have learned how to wield that power with words, then the pleasure will not be yours alone: It will also be your reader's.

SECTION 1

The Mastery Path

....

Mastery is the mysterious process during which what is at first difficult becomes progressively easier and more pleasurable through practice.

....

—GEORGE LEONARD,
Mastery: The Keys to Success and Long-Term Fulfillment

What makes certain people really good at using language? What gives them the ability to choose just the right words, to craft pieces of writing made up of one eloquent sentence after another?

Most of us are sure we know the answer to these questions: innate talent—a natural ability so powerful that success in a particular field comes effortlessly. Whenever we encounter people who are great at what they do—be they writers or musicians, athletes or inventors—we assume they were born with their abilities. Most aspiring writers look at the work of great authors, sigh, and say, "I wish *I* had that kind of talent."

But in the scientific field of expertise studies, researchers have been demonstrating, over and over, that natural talent is a myth. They've studied chess players and writers, artists and firefighters, tennis players and violinists and nurses, and people in many other fields—and in none of these studies did they find evidence of *anyone* who was "born great" at some activity.

Professor K. Anders Ericsson, the preeminent researcher in the field of expertise studies, has spent decades studying people who achieve greatness. He concludes that genius or expertise "isn't magic, and it isn't born. It happens because some critical things line up so that a person of good intelligence can put in the sustained, focused effort it takes to achieve extraordinary mastery."[1] Those "critical things" include getting started early in life, finding great teachers—and practice, practice, practice.

Few of us have the good fortune to find our chosen path early. But no matter how old we are, we all can make use of the powerful learning tool of practice. Practice quite literally changes our brains. That's because the human brain has an important characteristic known as its "plasticity"—its "built-in capacity to become, over time, what we demand of it."[2] When we engage in practice under the guidance of a knowledgeable coach, as top musicians and athletes do, new neural connections are created in our brains; we become able to do things that we could not do before.

These days, many aspiring writers are held back from achieving their potential because they've been told, "Just keep writing. Eventually you'll get better." This simply isn't true. No amount of just swinging the bat will turn someone into a major-league baseball player. No amount of singing in the shower will make someone a professional opera singer. If you want to become great—or even just good—at an activity, you need a teacher or coach to show you the skills you need to practice—and then you must practice them, over and over, and over. In doing so, you leave the myth of innate talent far behind, and instead you set your feet on the path to mastery.

In Chapter 1, I explain how I developed my practice-based approach to writing instruction. Then I turn to what practice really is and how to get the most out of doing it. If you want to start practicing right away, Chapter 3 sets out a group of basic practices that will launch you on your learning journey.

CHAPTER 1

MASTERING THE CRAFT

. . . .

Craft enables art.

. . . .

—URSULA K. LE GUIN

Skilled professionals make what they do look easy: Think of a major-league hitter driving a ninety-six-mile-per-hour fastball over the outfield wall, or a soprano singing a high C. Think of your favorite author composing one eloquent, magical sentence after another. It can be hard to see through the apparently effortless art to the skills underneath. This is especially so with writing, where we can't get inside a writer's mind to see the choices being made as he works.

Writing instruction these days tends to focus on the finished product: In thousands of workshops and classes, drafts are "workshopped," critiqued, discussed, revised. What interests me, though, is not *what* we write, nor *why* we write, but what we are actually *doing* when we write. What skills are we using? What is it that professional writers know how to *do* that inexperienced writers do not?

These questions have preoccupied me for most of my teaching life. My breakthrough came one night many years ago when I was listening to a Boston Red Sox baseball game on the radio. I realized that hitting a baseball is a complex skill. I thought about how athletes (and musicians) train. Their coaches break down complex skills like hitting a baseball or playing an instrument into their component parts. Then they teach each one of those component skills, one at a time, until eventually the entire complex skill is mastered. So an aspiring major-league hitter might start by practicing keeping his eye on the ball, then work on the position of his feet as he swings, then add the two together. A singer might begin by practicing the pitches of the diatonic scale, then learn to articulate language sounds, then combine the two. As these thoughts went through my mind, it suddenly became clear to me that, once you can break down any complex skill into its component subskills, then—ah, then!—you can *teach* those skills. So it is with sports and music; so—I realized at that moment—it can be with writing. From that night on, I devoted myself to developing a practice-based approach to teaching writing skills, one I now call The Mastery Path for Writers.

But what *are* the component skills that make up the complex work of writing? It took me many years of teaching and thinking to come up with a satisfactory answer to that question. Naturally, others had anticipated me. One of them, the nineteenth-century English writer Matthew Arnold, described the work of writing like this: "Have something to say, and say it as well as possible." I eventually put it this way: When we write, we need two main sets of skills—"content skills" and "craft skills." Content skills are those we rely on to come up with things to say: They depend on the well-trained mental faculties of creativity, imagination, memory, curiosity, and others, as well as on our ability to establish a natural relationship with our readers. Craft skills depend, among other things, on an understanding of how to use language with precision and power.

Content and craft skills are the yin and the yang of writing: You have to have both. Every good writer must be able to come up with things to say, and must have skill with words to communicate those things. So, what are we doing when we write? We are exercising our content and craft skills ... or, at least, we're doing that if we indeed possess those skills.

Having been a writing teacher for decades, I know that many aspiring creative writers are so busy churning out pages of works-in-progress that they have never taken the time to learn and develop their skills. But if you just keep doing the same thing over and over, are you really going to get any better? There's another way—a much better way—to become a good writer.

MASTERING A WRITER'S SKILLS

If you've ever learned to play a musical instrument, or a sport, you'll remember your teacher or coach showing you the component parts of a complex skill and how to practice each one separately before putting them together. The scientific researchers studying how certain people achieve greatness have now demonstrated that this kind of teaching and learning is essential to acquiring expertise.

Just like athletes and musicians, writers can break down the complex activity of writing into its component skills; we can practice each skill on its own, then combine it with others. Our content skills can be developed through practices that train our creativity, our powers of observation and imagination and curiosity, our subconscious, our storytelling voice, our ability to be in relationship with our readers. I've provided such practices in my first book, *How to Be a Writer: Building Your Creative Skills Through Practice and Play.* When we do these practices, we don't think about our words at all; we concentrate on using whichever faculty we are trying to train.

As writers we also need practice in shaping our work. We need to know how a novel works, if we want to write one, or how a personal essay is best constructed, if that's our chosen genre. If you need skills in this area, there are plenty of how-to books available to help you.

Finally, we need to know how to use the English language, with precision and with power. Over the three decades of my teaching career, I have learned that many aspiring writers have no idea how language works or how to use it well. They may have great ideas, their minds may be filled with wonderful stories—but they can't *communicate* those ideas or stories because they don't know anything about words! They don't know that words have different qualities and histories and music; they don't know all the various ways words can be patterned. In their ignorance of their medium, they are like would-be painters blind to the difference between cadmium red and cobalt blue, or sculptors unable to feel the difference between granite and marble.

So here, in this book, I'll be inviting you to set aside all your ideas and stories, all your knowledge of genre, and to concentrate entirely on language. I'll be asking you to let go of what I call "content mind" and instead put all your energy and attention into learning to use your "word mind." I'll be showing you how to take a learning journey into the realm of what I like to call "word craft" or "sentence craft."

On this journey you'll acquire, through guided practice, expertise in two areas: choosing words (diction), and arranging words into effective sentences (syntax). You'll also get an introduction to sentence rhythm, one element of the music of language. (Although I love the whole world of verbal music, it's a subject that needs its own book.)

In order to develop the practices in this book, I had to do them many, many times, by myself and with students. I can assure you that, done faithfully and with attention, they will make you a better writer.

First, you'll vastly expand your repertoire of choices for words and sentence construction.

Second, as you experiment with making these choices during practice, you'll gradually discover the ones you prefer, the ones that sound and feel "right" to you. And by "right" I don't mean mere grammatical correctness (though that is important); I mean "right" in the sense that those choices give your writing power and let you articulate your visions, tell your stories, keep your reader spellbound … in short, "right" in the sense of making successful magic with language.

Third, over time, you'll find yourself able to make these choices while you are engaged in writing or rewriting a draft. Having trained your skills in practice, you can now use them in your work.

Fourth, as you exercise and train your craft muscles, you will also be strengthening and freeing your creativity. Contrary to a prevalent view, creativity is not simply self-expression. It is not just "going with the flow." Creativity is *making* something, bringing something into the world that did not exist before you made it, whether that "something" be a hand-knit sweater, or a handmade table, or a poem, or a sentence. It is through this making, and only through this making, that you find yourself as a writer. Pam Allen, a professional knitter and writer, tells novice knitters: "Creativity is less about being born with a friendly muse and more about putting time and effort into developing know-how. Granted, moments of inspiration can wake you up at 4:00 in the morning, but rarely do they happen unless you first lay the groundwork. ... By learning, practicing, and mastering your art and craft, you become creative."[3] Her words apply to writers as well. Through the discipline of learning the craft, through training and exercising your linguistic abilities, you free your creativity.

Fifth, the more you practice making choices in diction and syntax, the more you discover your authentic voice on the page. Like creativity, the concept of "writer's voice" has in recent years become hostage to psychology. Writers in search of voice are exhorted—sometimes even pressured—to dig deep into their psyches, to excavate their worst memories. This is nonsense. Listen instead to John Fairfax and John Moat, founders of the well-respected Arvon writers' workshops in England: Voice, they say, is a writer's "individual use of language which enables him at last to come at the material which only he can express. It is the hallmark of the accomplished writer and his or her unique *authority*."[4]

A writer's voice, then, is the result of the choices a writer makes about words and about how to put them together. Some of these choices are, naturally, unconscious. But the more you become aware of the possibilities of language open to you, the more you expand your repertoire of choices. And so, as you learn more about how to make these choices, and as you experiment with making them in different situations, you will also, inevitably, develop your own individual voice—or style—on the page.

Making these choices, let me assure you, is not a chore, once you get the hang of it. On the contrary, to exercise your skill with words is one of the great pleasures of being a writer. Think of the satisfaction a tennis player feels when his racket meets the ball at precisely the right angle and sends it just out of reach of his opponent; think of the satisfaction a vocalist feels when she hits a high note dead-on. Writers get that same sense of satisfaction when they find exactly the right word or phrase to make a sentence sing or to drive home its meaning.

If I haven't yet convinced you that mastering the craft of sentences is a worthwhile endeavor, let me add a few more benefits to the list:

1. Learning sentence craft will definitely make you a better writer. You will develop a conscious understanding of the skills you need to write well, and if you conscientiously practice, those skills will serve you every time you sit down to produce a piece of writing. If your goal as a writer is publication, mastery of sentence craft will set you apart from many other aspiring writers.
2. Learning how to craft sentences is empowering. Being able to make use of the power of words will make you a stronger and more confident person, on the page and in your life.
3. Working with words keeps your brain alive. If we don't make regular use of our language abilities—if we don't exercise and stretch those particular "muscles" in our brains—those abilities will disappear. Even if we never get published, keeping our language abilities "in shape" means that we keep our brains active and healthy.
4. Learning the craft of sentence-making is pleasurable. Just like playing tennis for fun, or singing in a choir, playing with words is an enjoyable activity. And the more we learn about how words work, the better we understand what writers we love are doing on the page—which deepens our enjoyment of their work.
5. Learning how to make powerful sentences will give you skills you can use, if you wish, to benefit others. When you know you can communicate well, you will have the confidence to speak about, and write about, matters that are important to you.
6. Learning to make skillful sentences can lead to success in work and in life. Several recent studies have shown that employers rate lack of writing skills as the number one problem with their employees. If you master the craft of sentence-making, you will provide yourself with a highly marketable skill.

WHAT YOU NEED TO MASTER SENTENCE CRAFT

Mastering the craft of making sentences requires very little in the way of equipment: a dictionary, a thesaurus, a grammar book for reference purposes, and a notebook and pen, or a computer.

What you really need are two things: a desire to learn, and a willingness to practice.

I urge you as well to consider abandoning a great deal of what you were probably taught in school about writing. Let yourself begin anew in the world of words, using only your desire to learn and your innate ability to play with words and make sentences.

One of the most wonderful things about writing is that it's never too late to begin, or to begin again. If you want to play football, or to sing opera, you might have a hard time getting started with those activities later in life. But (given good health) our language brain remains with us all our lives, and it's never too late—or too early—to wake it up and use it.

There's a lot to learn about the craft of using words; this book aims only to present some basics. At the same time, learning the basics can take you far on your journey as a writer. And to learn these basics, all you need to do is practice them.

CHAPTER 2

CLAIMING YOUR POWER: LEARNING THROUGH PRACTICE

Most people won't realize that writing is a craft. You have to take your apprenticeship in it like anything else.

—KATHERINE ANNE PORTER

Practice is not something just to read about; it's something to *do*.

That's a central theme of this book, and I repeat it here (as I will frequently in the upcoming pages) because most of us are used to learning through study, not practice. We're used to reading and taking notes, perhaps thinking about what we've read or talking about it with other people. If we're in school (in a liberal arts program), we show we've studied well by producing term papers or taking exams. Rarely, if ever, in our progress through the conventional academic system, do we *do* anything with what we've studied.

In other fields, though—sports, or music, or practical arts—learning through practice rules. Basketball players practice shooting baskets. Jazz musicians practice scales and intervals. Aspiring cooks apprentice themselves to masters to learn their skills. Even people learning a foreign language devote themselves to practice. This is a different way to learn from the one most of us are used to. Different, and—when it comes to learning how to write—much, much better.

Imagine, if you will, a group of kids who want to learn how to play baseball. The coach spends an hour with them, three times a week, and they talk about baseball. They learn its history and read about star players; they watch films of outstanding plays; they have discussions about what makes certain players great. And then they go out to play a game. How well will they play?

You may laugh at the absurdity of this example; but replace "baseball" with "writing" and you have a pretty good idea of what goes on in most literature and writing classes: People *talk about* writing; they don't *do* it. But the domain of literary analysis and theory and criticism is not the same as the domain of writing; and so, if we want to improve our writing skills, we have to exercise our writing muscles, not our ability to discuss and critique. We have to practice doing what skilled writers do.

And the truth is that real writers *do* practice: They keep notebooks and sketchbooks, just like visual artists. They write lots of pieces that they never publish, to try out ideas and techniques, to develop their skills. Since these pieces remain unpublished, we don't get to read them, so we assume that a "real writer" is somehow born being able to write well. Once we give up this assumption, though, we are free to use the powerful learning tool of practice, just as professionals do.

So, if you believe that improving your writing skills means learning how to think and talk about writing, I invite you now to abandon that idea. I encourage you, instead to focus on learning to write through practice.

WHAT IS PRACTICE?

For many people, the word *practice* means "mindless drill"—memorizing the multiplication tables or all the prefixes in the English language. But drill and practice are not the same at all.

To begin with, practice is play: It's doing something over and over again because you *want* to, because you enjoy the activity, because your mind is completely engaged. Many famous writers spent countless happy hours in childhood writing poems and stories; the Brontë sisters (and their brother), for instance, produced a number of miniature illustrated books of their own stories. Many of us, though, were not so fortunate. We learned to write in school, where our writing was almost always judged and graded; we became used to doing what I call "performance" writing, writing that *counts*. As adults, many of us continue to write under performance conditions, trying to produce something good, something others will praise. But performance conditions usually create anxiety, which interferes with our creativity and makes it hard for us to write well. After years of writing under performance conditions, it can be difficult for us, especially those of us who are adults, to allow ourselves the freedom to play with words.

But a playful attitude is, I'm convinced, essential to learning through practice. I don't mean that writing practice shouldn't be taken seriously; I mean that you'll get the most out of it if you bring to it, not the judgmental attitude of an old-fashioned English teacher—*Oh, I did that wrong!*—but the engaged curiosity of a healthy child—*I wonder what will happen if I try THIS?*

To let yourself play with writing, remember that practice is totally different from performance. Practice writing is always *private* writing. No one will ever see it unless you decide to share it. When you sit down to practice, if you find yourself tense or anxious, remember that practice writing is not for other people; it's your own private playing field where you get to fool around, experiment, and see what happens.

For some of you, though, this reminder may not be enough. After years of writing in school or at work, you may have created an internal judge, or critic, who waits inside you to criticize whatever you put on the page. I urge you to do your best to ignore this judge as you practice. (Spending time with the exercise at the end of this chapter will help.) These inner judges kill our spirit, and their criticism—*That's terrible! You can't write!*—interferes with the simple noticing of what is (or isn't) there in our words, an activity that allows us to learn and move forward. When that inner judge raises his voice, keep telling yourself *I'm only practicing.*

If you are plagued by an inner critic, or you've had unpleasant experiences with writing, or you get anxious when you write, or you'd just like to fool around with words for a while, then you may want to let your first time through some or all of the practices be guided entirely by the spirit of play.

Practice as Learning

With play as our foundation, we can use practice as a learning tool. One of the essential characteristics of a practice activity is that it is designed to be repeated, not just once but many times. That's because repetition embeds things in our brains; repetition actually changes the nature of our brains. As Daniel Coyle, author of *The Talent Code,* explains, "Every human skill, whether it's playing baseball or playing Bach, is created by chains of nerve fibers carrying a tiny electrical impulse—basically, a signal traveling through a circuit."[5] The more we practice a skill, the more we develop these circuits in our brains. One of Coyle's sources, an eminent neurologist, says, "All skills, all language, all music, all movements, are made of living circuits, and all circuits grow according to certain rules."[6] As long as our brains remain healthy, we can keep "growing" these mental circuits and keep acquiring new skills and improving the ones we have. And the more time and energy we put into practice, the more our skills (and our brains) will grow.

In centers all over the world where athletes and musicians come to develop their skills, coaches and teachers are putting the principle of learning through practice into action. They are teaching skills in a way that reflects how the brain learns best, through a process known as *chunking*; namely, breaking down a complex skill into its component parts and guiding students to learn and practice each part separately. Daniel Coyle, who visited many of these centers, says, "The instinct to slow down and break skills into their components is universal ... [and] a massive body of scientific research shows that this is precisely the way skills are built."[7] Chunking explains how professionals make a difficult task look easy. Over time, having practiced those "chunks" of skills over and over and over, they are then able to put them all together and use them with the fluency and ease that is one of the hallmarks of expertise.

So, as you do the practices in this book, I urge you not to rush through them, even if you understand the material intellectually. Let yourself slow down so that your whole brain—even your body—can participate in each practice. In that way, the particular "move" each practice is teaching will become part of you, and eventually, when you use that "move" to compose a sentence, the result will appear effortless.

In this book, I have done my best to break down the complex skill of composing sentences into its component subskills and to give you exercises to develop each subskill in turn. I have used this progression of exercises in classes over a number of years because I think the earlier practices provide a solid foundation for the later ones. But if you wish to create your own learning path through the book, you can certainly do so. One of the best ways to do that is to invent your own practices.

Deliberate Practice

Once we've become familiar with the process of learning skills through practice, we can, if we like, move on to a more strenuous form of practicing, what Professor K. Anders Ericsson calls "deliberate practice." (Coyle calls it "deep practice.") Deliberate practice is what turns amateurs into professionals. Amateurs practice, of course, but they don't engage in deliberate practice. What's the difference?

Ericsson explains: "People who play tennis once a week for years don't get any better if they do the same thing each time. Deliberate practice is about changing your performance, setting new goals and straining yourself to reach a bit higher each time. It involves you deciding to improve something and setting up training conditions to attain the skill ... Those who get better work on their weaknesses."[8]

Legendary golfer Sam Snead would have agreed with Ericsson. "It's only human nature to want to practice what you can already do well," Snead once said, "since it's a hell of a lot less work and a hell of a lot more fun." But it's the people who devote themselves to developing skills they *don't* already have who become experts. Snead also said, "When I was young, I'd play and practice all day, then practice more at night by my car's headlights. My hands bled. Nobody worked harder at golf than I did."[9]

Deliberate practice demands hard work, but hard work by itself is not enough; you also have to know *what* to work on. So deliberate practice, first of all, is highly focused. As Dr. Ericsson explains, deliberate practice is deliberate because it is "*specifically designed* to improve some aspect of an individual's target performance."[10]

Second, deliberate practice demands a change of attitude: no lackadaisical, "oh—whatever" approach works here. People engaged in deliberate practice are giving all of their attention and energy—every brain cell, every muscle—to that practice. As Ericsson points out, "For expert performers, there's always effort. Improvement is never effortless."[11] At the same time, such people are not judging what they do; instead they're *noticing* what's working and what's not working, and they are attempting to bridge the gap they perceive between what they can do and what they want to do. They bridge this gap in two ways: by getting a clearer, more detailed understanding of the action, the sound, the kind of word they want; and by taking on even more focused practice. In other words, they practice, not mindlessly or randomly, but strategically. It's practice strategy (along with good coaching, determination, and perseverance) that separates experts from amateurs in the realm of learning. When experts fail, says one psychologist who studies how people learn, "they don't blame it on luck or themselves. They have a strategy they can fix."[12]

Third, deliberate practice involves challenging yourself to move past the things you can do easily and into the realm of what you can't do, or can't do well. You have to get comfortable balancing on what I like to call your "learning edge," where you have one foot on the ground of what you already know how to do, and the other foot reaching forward into the unknown. You also have to be willing to tolerate the frustration of not being able to do a practice activity well the first or second time you try it, something many adults have difficulty with. But, as I always tell my students, "If you're not frustrated some of the time as you're learning, you're not really moving forward." People who become experts in their field have a high tolerance for that kind of frustration: Instead of giving up, as so many of us do, they use frustration as a spur to increased practice and learning.

Finally, people who engage consistently in deliberate practice eventually become their own teachers. They know where their strengths and weaknesses lie. They've become used to measuring their performance against established standards of expertise, or against their own best performances, and they have devised their own practices to improve their skills.

Athletes and musicians in training have coaches who can point out to them what they are doing well and where their skills need more work. Naturally, a book can't provide that kind of individual coaching. But skilled writers are always self-taught. Long before the invention of creative writing workshops, writers learned their skills from the masters, through intensive reading and imitation. Consequently, the practices in this book are designed, not only to help you learn, but also to show you how to identify specific techniques in the work of professional writers; once you can identify these techniques, you can imitate them and make them your own.

As you work your way through this book, you will acquire a large repertoire of practices, and you will also be encouraged to invent your own. If you wish, then, you can select from all these practices and design your own learning program, customized to your particular needs. In becoming your own teacher, you will find your own way to excellence.

The "Be a Writer" Practice
To begin our journey towards writing expertise, we start with this simple practice. What is the most basic thing that writers do? They put words on paper. So when we practice putting words on paper, we are practicing the fundamental activity of being writers.

It's essential to remember, in doing this practice, that practice writing is private writing. No one will see these words you produce; you don't even have to read them over afterwards if you don't want to. So try, as much as you can, to relax as you write. You may find it helpful, before you begin, to consciously relax your muscles, one group at a time, or to take a few deep breaths. Perhaps you want to sit up straight or stretch your fingers before you begin.

Now, sit down with a pen and paper, or at your computer. Set a timer for ten minutes, or place a clock nearby but not directly in your line of vision.

In this practice, you can write anything. You don't have to begin with a subject or an idea. If, as you write, you find a subject, you don't have to stay with it. You don't have to create a beginning, middle, and end. You don't have to write lovely, coherent sentences and paragraphs.

There's only one thing you must do: You must keep the pen (or your fingers on the keyboard) moving, *no matter what*. You must keep putting words on the page.

This means that you can't stop to think, you can't go back over what you just wrote to fix errors, you can't let your mind wander. If you have to repeat a sentence or a word in order to keep writing, that's fine. If you have to write *This is so stupid, I can't believe I'm doing it,* that's fine, too. But you *must* keep writing (though there's no need to write fast).

And now—go ahead: Take a little time to be a writer.

When your ten minutes (or more, if you like) are up, gradually bring the writing to a close.

Now, without sitting in judgment of your writing, notice that for the last ten minutes you were doing what writers do: You were practicing putting thoughts on paper using words.

You can use this exercise, known as freewriting, in many ways: to warm up before you start work on a piece of performance writing, to get ideas, to exercise your mental faculties, to vent your feelings, and more. It's great exercise for what I like to call "the content mind," the part of our minds that gives us material for pieces of writing. (If you'd like to know more about developing your content mind, see my book *How to Be a Writer*.)

Now let's turn to the other part of our mind we need in order to write: the "word mind."

TIPS FOR EFFECTIVE PRACTICING

1. **RELAX.** You can't learn when you're tense and distracted, so when you sit down to practice, take a moment or two to set aside your worries and relax your mind and body. If your mind is churning, take ten minutes to empty all your thoughts onto the page, using the freewriting technique. Afterwards, if you want to, tear up the paper or delete what you've written.

2. **FOCUS.** Make sure you know where you're going to direct your mental energy. That doesn't mean you know ahead of time how a practice will come out (you're learning, after all); it means that you remind yourself to concentrate only on the technique at hand.

3. **ASSESS.** Assessment here is not judgment; it's not praise or condemnation. It's looking at what you produced in an exercise and asking yourself, "Do I now understand how to do this technique? If not, what's not making sense to me?" Assessment enables you to become your own best teacher. Assessment also means thinking about what to do next: If you're not sure you understand a technique, what can you do? Perhaps you need to reread the explanation of the technique. Perhaps you need to consult a writing friend or a grammar book; perhaps you need to seek examples of the technique in the work of professional writers. Or perhaps you need to return to a previous technique, making certain that you understand it before once again moving forward.

4. **REPEAT.** Expertise in any activity comes with repetition; so it is with writing. If you want a technique to become second nature, you need to keep practicing it.

5. **TAKE YOUR TIME.** Building new skills doesn't happen overnight. Don't be in a rush.

6. **CHALLENGE YOURSELF.** If you are engaged in deliberate practice, find ways to combine exercises or invent new ones in order to make your mind work harder.

7. **PRACTICE "IN THE WORK."** You can do writing practice as a separate activity; you can also practice as you work on school or work assignments or on projects you choose (letters, e-mails, blog posts, stories, poems, and so on). As you work, try to expand your concentration so that you can come up with what you want to say *and* focus on using one of the craft techniques you have learned.

CHAPTER 3

THE BASIC SENTENCE CRAFT PRACTICES

....

Art begins with craft, and there is no art until craft has been mastered.

....

—ANTHONY BURGESS

Practicing with our "content mind" is great fun, and without well-developed content skills, such as imagination and curiosity, we can't come up with ideas and material for pieces of writing. From here on, though, we're going to set aside all consideration of content and focus entirely on language. We'll follow the lead of coaches in sports and music, and concentrate only on one set of skills: those needed to develop our "word mind." In this chapter I introduce you to some basic practices, beginning with one that will reacquaint you with your word mind.

BASIC PRACTICE #1: WAKING UP THE WORD MIND

Begin with freewriting, as in the exercise from Chapter 2. Get your pen moving across the page, or your fingers across the keyboard, without stopping. Remember to relax; there's no rush.

Once you feel comfortable, see if you can shift your mental focus: Turn your attention away from what you are saying to the words you are using. At first you may find this difficult; that's fine. Just keep trying to bring your mind back to words. You may also find that your writing stops making sense; that's fine, too. (If a great idea occurs to you while you work, however, by all means write it down!) You may find that you stop writing sentences altogether and move instead into listing words.

Try as best you can to keep from judging the words that come to you. There are no right or wrong answers in this practice. Instead, as you write, *listen* to your words; pay attention to what you hear. Afterwards take a moment or two to reflect, on paper if you wish, about what happened when you did the exercise.

Sometimes people fall in love with this practice right away. Other times they may say, "That was *hard!*" You, too, may find it difficult. If that's the case, don't give up! Chances are very good that you have never tried to write this way before, with an awareness of words. If your inner critic speaks up (*What boring words you have! How could* you *ever become a writer?*), just ignore it. Instead, simply notice the words you use, without judging them: *Oh, look at that* but *and that* and ... *and here's another* but ... ! Let your curiosity and sense of wonder kick in: *I wonder where the word* and *comes from, anyway?* Remember that this practice is designed simply to start you on a path of awakening to words, not to produce "great writing."

Most of the time, when we write, we are focused on what we want to say; we're using our content minds exclusively. And most of the time, when we write, our word minds are functioning on automatic. If we want to get better at using words, our first step is to bring into conscious awareness the part of our mind that gives us those words, even if we're not happy with what it gives us.

Remember, too, that writing is a dance between content and craft, between the content mind and the word mind. We need to know how to use both parts of our minds when we write and rewrite; we need to know how to move back and forth between them; we need to know how to handle those occasional ecstatic moments when both parts are working simultaneously. To engage in this dance of writing, we need to learn how to let words lead, some of the time. And to let words lead, we need, above all, to listen to them.

Waking Up Your Writer's Ear

As you do Basic Practice #1, you may find it difficult, at first, to hear the words you use. We all have to process so many written words every day that we tend to rely on speed reading, or skimming. At first, then, you may find it hard to slow down enough to notice your words.

Keep trying. If you feel that your thoughts are racing, make a conscious decision to move your pen, or your fingers, more slowly. As you do that, you will be able to bring your full attention to your words, at least once in a while.

And as you keep turning your attention deliberately to your words, an amazing thing will happen: Your writer's ear will wake up. Rather than speeding through your frantic mind, your words will linger, letting you hear and appreciate their individual qualities, their meanings, their sounds, their rhythms.

The writer's ear reminds us that words are not merely marks on a page; they are living beings with their own identities, their own characteristics; they are made of breath and sound, as well as meaning. When we wake up our writer's ear, words come alive in our minds; and when we use our writer's ear to compose sentences and paragraphs, our words will come alive in the minds of our readers. Our brains and nervous systems still work the way they did millennia ago, when our ancestors lived in oral cultures, without writing. And despite modern technology, most people retain an "inner ear" for language, even on the page. They can hear the sound of a writer's voice; sometimes they even subvocalize, moving their lips to shape the words they are reading, without making sounds. When these words come alive, full of breath and sound and energy, readers will respond to their power.

Every skilled writer has a highly trained writer's ear, whether that ear has been trained unconsciously, through reading, or through deliberate practice, or a combination of both. Our writer's ear is the organ of the word mind. Our writer's ear can be tuned into the meaning of words, as well as their music; it can tell us how best to arrange our words into sentences that will have the effect we intend on our readers. Throughout this book, I will be encouraging you to make conscious use of your writer's ear. You may want to take a few minutes now to repeat Basic Practice #1, with the intention of using your writer's ear.

BASIC PRACTICE #2: KEEPING A NOTEBOOK

Most writers keep notebooks, and you'll need one for the practices in this book. You can certainly practice on the computer, if you like, but it's still a good idea to have a small notebook to carry around with you. A portable notebook lets you practice anytime you have a few minutes to spare. A notebook, portable or not, lets you keep all your practicing in one place; a notebook makes it easy for you to read through your practicing to decide what you might want to work on right now. Most of all, a notebook gives you an easy way to collect words.

Get into the Habit of Collecting Words

If you do the waking up the word mind practice on a regular basis, you will notice that you are paying more attention to words, both the words you come up with and the words that come your way from other people. You can, if you like, make a conscious decision not only to notice these words, but to *collect* the ones that appeal to you. Any time you hear or read a word that calls to you—from conversation or radio, books or magazines or advertising, or anywhere at all—write that word down in your notebook. You have now taken the first step towards making that word your own.

As with many endeavors, this first step may be the hardest for you. It takes a little bit of extra effort—not all that much, really—to get out your notebook and write down some words. But, as with any practice, once you get into the habit of doing this, it becomes very easy. And the more you do it, the more your mind will begin to work the way the minds of skilled writers do.

Good writers are people who love language; one of the reasons they write is that it gives them the opportunity to spend a lot of time with words. So they notice and collect words all the time, exercising and strengthening their word minds in the process. You can do this, too. In the next section you'll have several opportunities to practice this collecting. For now, try this:

Practice: Use Your Notebook to Collect Words

Listen to the radio or television, or someone speaking, without paying attention to the content of the words you hear. Instead, use your writer's ear to focus on the words themselves. Write down any words that stand out for you.

BASIC PRACTICE #3: READING AS A WRITER

When we read, most of the time, we are paying attention to content. What ideas is this writer articulating? What story is she telling? What will happen next? We are engaged with the material with our content minds. But if we want to become better writers, we also have to read with our word minds. To do that, we need to slow down and savor the words on the page.

When we read more slowly, when we really *listen* to a writer's words and sentences, perhaps even taking the time to read them out loud, an amazing thing happens: Those words, those phrases, those sentence rhythms enter our ears and lodge themselves in our writer's brain. There they become part of a storehouse of language techniques we can then draw on when we write.

This process happens largely below the level of conscious thought. We can learn even more effectively, though, when we actively apprentice ourselves to a favorite writer, by copying out, word-for-word, passages from her work, or by giving some of our practice time to writing imitations of her sentences. Long before anyone ever thought of creative writing courses, aspiring writers learned their craft by choosing a published writer as a model and imitating his work.

Perhaps you think that learning this way is a form of plagiarism; I can assure you that it is not. In any field—ballet, baseball, art—people learn by finding models of excellence and imitating them. Anders Ericsson, the preeminent expertise researcher, assures us that we are all "prewired to imitate."[13] I'm quite convinced that aspiring writers often flounder in part because the practice of imitation, a learning tool of inestimable value, has been withheld from them.

So, as you read your favorite writer, I strongly encourage you to spend some time noticing how she uses language. The practices in the rest of this book will teach you some specific things to look for: what kinds of choices this writer makes about words, what choices she makes about constructing sentences. The more you develop, through practice, your understanding of how words work, the more you will be able to learn about sentence craft from the work of writers you love.

And then, take some time to imitate a sentence or two, or an entire paragraph. If you like, for every practice in the rest of this book, you can examine a passage by a favorite writer to discover the choices he made in that particular aspect of sentence-making. Then try doing the practice the way you imagine this writer might do it.

Practice: Read with Your Writer's Ear

Read a passage from a favorite writer out loud and listen to the words. What do you notice about how this writer uses language?

Practice: Imitate a Model of Excellence

Choose a writer whose work is, for you, a model of excellence. This is your choice, one that should not be dictated by current academic/literary taste or the latest bestsellers. Copy out a passage from a work by your chosen writer, and then, as best you can, imitate those sentences. You will get the most out of this exercise if you follow it with the next basic practice.

BASIC PRACTICE #4:
REFLECTING ON YOUR PRACTICE

In addition to learning through imitation, humans also learn through reflection. If you like, take time during your practice sessions to think over, in writing, what happened as you did each exercise. What did you notice? What questions are coming up for you about language and your use of it? What are you learning? Reflecting in this way gives you a place to bring to consciousness, and to preserve, what you are learning right now about words and how you want to use them.

This reflection practice also helps you stay in charge of your own learning journey. It helps you see what steps you have taken so far on your path in the world of sentence craft. It helps you ask yourself questions or articulate half-formed thoughts. And it helps you see where you might want or need to go next.

If you don't want to reflect after each practice, then try to do it at the end of a practice session. Ask yourself questions, rather than make judgments. To write *My writing stinks. I'll never learn how to do this* is to put boulders in your own way. Instead, write about what you have been learning, and what you might want to learn next. You will probably be amazed at how intelligent your learner's intuition is and what good suggestions it has for you.

I consider reflection on learning to be an essential practice, one that helps you integrate material and move forward, so at the end of each chapter you'll find a reminder to take some time to reflect.

Practice: Reflect on Your Journey

Before we turn to more specific practices, you may wish to reflect on where you are now as a writer and what you would like to learn or how you can best engage in writing practice. What are your particular strengths as a writer? What skills do you feel you most need to learn and develop?

MAKE PRACTICE PART OF YOUR LIFE

You can do the practices in this book anytime on your learning journey, and you need not set aside hours in which to do them. Think about how you can best find a place for practice in your life. If you are ready to take on the discipline of deliberate practice, then daily practicing is essential. But it's definitely possible to improve your skills, even if your circumstances don't allow you the time for rigorous daily practice. You can take ten minutes here, or fifteen minutes there; the more often you can take time, even a little bit of time, to practice, the better. And, as with other kinds of practicing, you need to give your brain a chance to assimilate your new learning. You may find that practicing before you go for a walk, or before you make dinner, gives you an opportunity for assimilation.

What matters above all is the doing of the practices, and the reflecting on them. Writing, like any other craft, is learned by doing. You can read about it, or talk about it, all you want, but your abilities will never improve if you don't exercise them.

Finding time to practice may mean choosing to give up something else. But because waking up and exercising the word mind are so inherently pleasurable, I suspect that after a while you will begin to look forward to your practice sessions, and to feel that doing writing practice is its own reward.

After all, where else in our lives do we get the chance to practice making magic?

SECTION 2

The Power of Diction: Choosing Words

That was the time when words were like magic …
A word spoken by chance
might have strange consequences.
It would suddenly come alive
and what people wanted to happen could happen.
All you had to do was say it.

—**EDWARD FIELD,** *Eskimo Songs and Stories*

In myths from cultures all over the planet, the world comes into being—
or some part of it does—through language. *Let there be light,* says the
God of the Bible—and light comes into existence. Similarly, the Inuit
of Canada tell us that once, long ago, the Earth was always in darkness.
That was a time, the story goes, "when just saying a word could make
something happen." And in that time, a fox and a hare each had a magic
word. The fox's word was *darkness*, because he wanted it to stay dark all
the time so he could hunt. The hare's word was *day*, because in the day-
light he could find grass to eat. The two argued with their magic words,
back and forth—*Darkness! Day! Darkness! Day!*—until eventually the
hare won, and day came. But, says the story, "The word of the fox was
powerful too," so when day was over, night arrived. And from then on
day and night took turns, "the nighttime of the fox following the daytime of the hare."[14]

Such stories express a profound belief in the power of words,
a belief still held by many native peoples. "Our language," says
contemporary indigenous American writer Simon Ortiz, "is the way
we create the world."[15]

Before you dismiss this view of language as primitive, consider this
scene: Suppose you are having dinner with a friend. You speak. "Pass
the bread, please," you say—and the bread is put into your waiting hand.
When you think about it, is that not a form of magic? All you did was
make some sounds, and your wish was granted! To see language as a kind
of magic is not silly or "primitive" at all; it's to recognize a basic truth:
Human language is powerful stuff.

Words can make things happen in other people and in the world. Words can make a tree bloom in someone's mind, or persuade someone to plant one. Words can bring us new thoughts and give us imaginative experiences we otherwise would not have had. Words can take us to places we'll never visit in real life. Words can bring a character to life—or kill one off. Words can inform, illuminate, explain, persuade, describe, and much more. Words can change the world: Think about the *Declaration of Independence*, or Martin Luther King's "I Have a Dream" speech. There is no end to the magic that words can make.

Powerful words *do* things to people: They transfer the writer's meaning precisely, they paint pictures in the reader's imagination, they move the reader intellectually or emotionally or physically, or in all of these ways at once. Skilled writers are like magicians, capturing our minds with the power of their spells.

Perhaps now some of you are saying to yourselves, "Yes, I understand the concept that words can make magic, but when I write I sure don't feel that *my* words do that!" Don't lose heart: Remember that you have an innate "language intelligence," which you've probably never had a chance to use in a conscious way. You don't have to be born with a special gift; you can develop the one you have. You don't have to "know already" how to use the power of words: You can learn.

To learn how to use that power requires immersing yourself in the world of words, so you can really get to *know* words, know everything you can about them, so you can choose the ones you need. No one is born with this intimate knowledge of words; that knowledge is something you acquire. You do that by waking up and exercising and training your word mind—the part of your brain that comes up with words, rather than thoughts or ideas or feelings.

The best way to get to know words is simply to play with them! So I invite you now to let go of your adult self, access the childlike part of yourself, and join me in some purposeful play with language. (If you need permission to play, I give it to you now!)

And if you would prefer to go immediately to sentence-construction techniques, and save learning about words for later, you'll want to begin with Chapter 8, on parts of speech.

CHAPTER 4

THE WORD HOARD

···

The oldest man, a leader of men
answered; he unlocked the wordhoard.

···

—KEVIN CROSSLEY-HOLLAND, *Wordhoard*

English is a very word-rich language, with more than half a million words in general use. While theoretically all these words are available to every writer at all times, in practice each writer has her own collection of words with which she writes; word choice is one of the main components of individual style or voice. The image I like to use for a writer's collection of words is the "word hoard."

This term comes from the earliest days of the English language, when Germanic peoples who became known as Anglo-Saxons were settling in England. The Anglo-Saxons lived originally in an oral culture; so for them, as for all other oral peoples, words were of fundamental importance: Only through words could the history, the laws, the customs, the stories of the people be passed on.

As a result, one of the most important people among the early Anglo-Saxons was the bard—in Anglo-Saxon he was called the *scop* (pronounced *shop*). Every king had to have one, for the bard kept in memory the brave deeds of ancestral heroes and composed long poems, such as *Beowulf,* which he would recite from memory on important occasions. Each bard was considered to have his own word hoard—like a treasure hoard of gold and jewels—from which he would pull out the exact words and phrases that would serve his purposes.

I love the image of a writer having his "hoard" of words to use in writing, and so I have adopted it. I invite you to use it, too, if it appeals to your imagination. What words lie in your treasure hoard, waiting for you to use them in a piece of writing? Let's find out, using a practice I call "Unpacking the Word Hoard."

Practice: Unpacking the Word Hoard

This practice builds on the basic practices you've already learned. It has two parts:

First, begin to freewrite (see Chapter 2). After a couple of minutes, let your attention shift from whatever you are saying to the words that are coming to you. And now begin to collect *only* words, one word at a time, keeping the pen moving as you do so. If your mind goes blank, keep writing the last word you wrote over and over, until you think of another one. Remember to breathe, to slow down.

You need not know a word's meaning to write it down. You are not trying to make sense, or to write complete sentences: You are just collecting words, letting one word lead you to the next. Try to stay in the moment with each word as it comes to you. Listen to it, savor it. (With this practice, as with all the exercises in this book, remember that you are in charge. If your words start taking you someplace you don't want to go, stop, take a deep breath, relax, and change direction.) Take five or ten minutes for this practice, then take a minute or two to reflect on how the practice went for you. What did you notice?

Now, for the second part of the practice, go through the words you collected, reading them out loud *slowly*, one word at a time, and mark the words you particularly like. Perhaps they have a certain energy, or you like the way they sound, or they remind you of something. The reason doesn't matter; just mark them. And, as you read, add to your list any new words you like that occur to you. Now take a moment to read your marked words out loud; listen to them. What do you notice?

THE BENEFITS OF UNPACKING YOUR WORD HOARD

I doubt you could find a simpler writing practice than "Unpacking the Word Hoard," but this simple practice, done with regularity, can teach you a lot. First, it wakes up your word mind, opening up and lubricating the mental channels through which words flow. With regular practice, this part of your mind will begin to participate actively in your writing: It will be engaged in giving you words to use, whereas, in the past, it might have dozed on automatic pilot through the time you spent writing. Second, the practice shows you the words you already have inside your hoard. Many beginning writers are delighted to discover words they didn't really know they knew—we tend to use, in ordinary conversation, far fewer words than we actually have in our word hoards. Third, this kind of writing practice wakes up your writer's ear by encouraging you to listen to words as they come to you. Fourth, it gives you practice in being fully present with your words, and it provides you with an opportunity to practice "letting words lead." Fifth, whenever you get stuck in your writing, you can use this practice as a way to get yourself going again. And—best of all—it's a lot of fun.

So I encourage you to do this practice frequently. Let yourself invent other ways of doing it, if you like. Keep it simple: Remember that while the English language has lots of "twenty-five cent" words like *perturb* or *effrontery*, *statuesque* or *decorous*, it also has lots of essential short, sturdy words like *of* or *but*, *say* or *stop* or *glow*. This practice may seem silly, but you will probably be surprised by the rewards it brings. Even though I have been writing for many years, it was only when I started to practice in this way—to let myself play with words—that I began to feel like a real writer.

Make Words Your Own

As you may have discovered during this practice, you can have a lot of words in your word hoard that you never use. This means that, like those hats or shoes you purchased that you never wear, these words are things you have, but don't really utilize. To make words our own, we have to *use* them. Some people do this by trying out words in conversation. We can also make words our own by using them in writing, by taking them as our materials to make sentences, or lines in a poem, or lines of dialogue. Let's give that a try now.

Practice: Make Words Your Own

From the list of words you marked, pick a few. Now use those words, and any others you might need (not necessarily from your list) to make a sentence, a line of a poem, or a line of dialogue. Let yourself just fool around with these words, play with them as if they were bits of clay, and see what you can make. You can make sense, if you like, or you can make nonsense. For instance, I could choose the words *blue* and *ceiling* and *elephant* from my list, and make this sentence: *The blue elephant is on the ceiling.* Don't obsess about the sentences you construct; they don't have to be perfect. (Remember, no one will ever see this material unless you choose to show it.) You might want to see how many different sentences you can make using the same chosen words. Or you might want to pick three or four new words from your list and see what you can make from them (again, adding any words you need to make a complete sentence).

When you have had enough of this little game, for now, take a few moments to read your sentences out loud. Try to listen to them without judgment. What do you notice? If you get any ideas for new sentences, or new ways to write the ones you created, by all means jot them down.

You may also want to take some time to reflect in your notebook about what you learned during these practices.

BUILD YOUR WORD HOARD

Many of us feel that we are held back from writing the way we want to because we just don't have the words we need. But our word hoards are not fixed for life! We can add words to them anytime we want. We can add to our word hoards the words we *want* to have for our own, or words that we need for a particular purpose. To add words to our hoards, all we need are the two complementary practices of collecting words and making them our own by putting them into sentences.

We can collect words in two ways: from inside ourselves (I call this "internal collecting") and from outside ourselves ("external collecting"). Let's now revisit the activity of internal collecting, which we used in unpacking the word hoard; then we'll turn to external collecting.

Build Your Word Hoard Part 1: Internal Collecting

You can use the basic practice of unpacking your word hoard anytime; and I recommend that, if you enjoy it, you do it often. Our word hoards are deeper than we suspect, and the more often you collect words from inside yourself, the more you will become consciously aware of the words available to you. You can also direct your creative faculty in its searching of your word hoard by asking it to play with one or more of the following practices.

The Vocabulary of a Subject

Are you a baseball fan? If you are, then the following sentences (which I took down while listening to a radio broadcast of a Red Sox game some years ago) will probably make sense to you:

> "He hits the ball on the infield: a room-service hop to Nomar, who fires it to Walker, on to first—double-play. And the twin killing ends the inning."

> "Here's the payoff pitch. Pedro comes to the set, he kicks and deals ... it's a cutter, over the inside corner."

> "They're knotted at one for Nomar. He swings ... there's a drive into center field. Nomar with a wall-ball ... here comes the throw ... and Nomar's into second with a pop-up slide. A wicked two-bagger for Nomar."

> "Now here comes Manny, with 17 homers and 60 ribbies. Boy, Carl Pavano is being tattooed here. He's done nothing but give up bombs since he arrived to the hill."

If you love baseball, you will know that a "room-service hop" is a movement a batted ball makes when it appears to have been summoned by an infielder to go right into his glove; that a "twin killing" is a double play, which enables the team on the field to put out two base runners; that a "two-bagger" is a double, a hit on which the batter reaches second base. If you are unfamiliar with the game, these sentences will probably sound like a foreign language.

Baseball has its own particular vocabulary, its own collection of words that writers on that subject need to know. In fact, *every* subject has its own vocabulary. If you want to write about trees, then you need to know the names of trees and the names of their parts and their processes of growth and decay. If you want to write about cooking, then you need to know the vocabulary of that subject. Even personal experiences have their own vocabularies: When you write about your grandmother, you will use words that are specific to her; when you write about a vacation at the ocean, you will want words that are specific to that experience. And if you are writing fiction, each of your characters will have her own words, as well as her own things to say. If a character is a doctor, she'll use one set of words; if she's a farmer, she'll use different words.

Build Your Word Hoard Practice: The Vocabulary of a Subject

Pick a subject you know something about. (If you can't think of one, start by making a list.) Then, without stopping, spend five to ten minutes collecting every word you can think of that has something to do with this subject. If you get stuck, just repeat a word. Don't worry about whether the words are "right" or whether they mean what you think they mean. Just play with them and see what happens. Say the words under your breath, so that they will have some voice to them instead of just appearing silently in your mind.

After you're done collecting, go back through your list and mark whichever words stand out for you, then play around with them to form sentences. Make sense, if you feel like it; be silly if you don't.

Give yourself at least ten minutes for this practice. Afterwards, if you like, take a moment or two to write down what happened as you did it. What did you notice?

You may discover that you don't have the vocabulary that you need to write about your chosen subject, especially if you are writing about a subject that is new to you. Don't assume that, because you don't have the vocabulary you need, you can't write about this subject. You can *learn* the vocabulary!

If your subject is one you already know a lot about, you may have found that, as you collected its vocabulary and then made sentences from some of the words you collected, you began to get ideas for things to say about your subject. You may want to take ten minutes to do what's called "focused freewriting" about this subject. Keep the pen moving, as with the basic "Be a Writer" practice (Chapter 2), but instead of letting your creative faculty go anywhere it wants to go, keep it focused on your subject. Use some of the words you collected, and let them serve as springboards for reflecting on the subject. Words can often be a "way in" to a piece of writing, so you may be pleasantly surprised by what your creative faculty comes up with in this exercise. You might even want to begin with just one of the words you selected and let it inspire this piece of focused freewriting.

Even if you don't plan to write specifically about the subject whose vocabulary you collected in the above practice, you may discover words that you can use in other contexts. You just never know when a word you've collected will be the perfect fit for a sentence or a line of poetry.

Build Your Word Hoard Practice: The Vocabulary of a Personal Experience

Choose a subject from personal experience (a place, a person, or an adventure, perhaps). Take five to ten minutes (or more, if you like) to collect, without stopping, every word that comes to you about this subject. Then, as before, select some words and make sentences (or lines of poetry or dialogue, if you prefer) with them. While your goal should be to just play with the words and see what happens, you may find yourself moving into freewriting about your subject.

If you find yourself stuck when you want to write about a subject, whether it be a personal experience or not, it can help to start by collecting the vocabulary of that subject. Sometimes just playing with those words can lead you to things you want to say.

Build Your Word Hoard Practice: The Vocabulary of a Character
Choose a character of your own invention, or use one from a book you love, and bring him firmly to mind. Then imagine that this character is speaking, and collect the words you hear him use. Just focus on words first, as you did in the above practices. Then, once you have collected a long list of this character's words, choose some of them to make sentences (or partial sentences, if you like) that this character would speak.

**Build Your Word Hoard Practice:
A Vocabulary That Fits Your Readers**
Have you ever noticed that you often speak differently to different people? *Hey, man, wazzup?* you might say to your buddy, while *Good morning, Mr. Jones* would probably be the way you'd address your boss. The same thing can happen when we write: We can choose to select words appropriate to our readers. You may want to experiment with this by picking a subject you know something about and imagining an audience. Now, just as in the previous exercises, unpack from your word hoard the words you need to use to write about your subject to this particular audience. After doing this for a while, pick a different audience and collect words again. For instance, you could pick your eight-year-old nephew the first time, and a professor or supervisor the second. What do you notice about the words you unpack? If you like, you might also want to select words from each list and write some sentences, first to one audience, then to the other. This will give you some good practice in what it feels like to write for different audiences.

Writing well is not just a matter of saying what we want to say; we also have to get that content into other people's minds, and often that means using language that they will be able to understand. Do we want to use ordinary language? Do we want to use a specialized vocabulary? Do we want our thoughts to be expressed in simple, down-to-earth words? Or do we want to use "fancy" words with lots of syllables in them? These are the kinds of questions we often have to ask ourselves when we write for others.

Build Your Word Hoard Part 2: External Collecting

When you unpack your word hoard using any of the above practices (or other similar ones that you may invent), you are collecting from inside yourself—what I call "internal collecting." You can also add to your hoard words that come to you from outside yourself—what I call "external collecting." You can collect words from anywhere: from books or newspapers, from overheard conversations, from signs or songs, from radio or television programs.

Build Your Word Hoard Practice: Collect from Conversation

Go to a place where you can overhear people talk without calling attention to yourself—a café, perhaps, or a park, or a sporting event. Now turn your attention to one person's voice and listen, not to the content of what she is saying, but to the words being used. Just pay attention to those words and notice them. Which ones grab your attention?

Now take this practice one step further and collect some of the words that appeal to you by jotting them down in your notebook.

When you've collected a number of words, see if you can make some sentences with them. If these are not words you would ordinarily use, perhaps they could be coming from a character you invent. Play with these words and see what you can discover.

Build Your Word Hoard Practice: Collect from Reading

When you read something you like, take time to read it again, not for content, but for language. Let your word mind engage with this piece; listen to it with your writer's ear. Write down in your notebook all the words that appeal to you. Read through your collected words, marking the ones that stand out for you right now. Look up the meanings of these marked words in a dictionary, if you need to, and then use some of them to compose sentences.

TRAINING YOUR WORD MIND

Although these practices of unpacking and building the word hoard are simple, they are important. Why? Because they give your writer's mind training in the two essential skills of writing craft: coming up with words, and putting those words into sentences. The exercises allow you to practice these skills without having to come up with content at the same time. As a result, the more you do the practices, the more you strengthen and develop your word mind. Soon you'll find that, when you sit down to work on a piece of writing, your word mind often gives you the words you need. With lots of practice, you'll move out of the frustrating position of being unable to find words for the things you want to say. You'll be on the way to developing your own writing style or voice.

The two basic practices of coming up with words and putting them into sentences underlie all the rest of the practices in this book. In the next chapter, you'll use these practices to learn more about how to use words to make meaning.

TAKE TIME TO REFLECT

Before you continue, take some time to reflect on what you've learned through the practices in this chapter. You may also want to make a list of the practices you want to repeat.

CHAPTER 5

MAKING MEANING

Have something to say, and say it as clearly as you can. That is the only secret of style.

—MATTHEW ARNOLD

A writer's style is formed in part by the words he chooses. But how does the writer make those choices? Does he just select the words he likes best? Or are there other considerations?

While it's certainly true that a writer's choice of words comes in part from personal preference, writers who want their words to have power need to select, from all the choices available, the words that best convey what they want to say. One of the things that gives words their power is *precision of meaning*. Skilled writers care about the accuracy of their words. They know, for instance, that even though a thesaurus may group certain words together, those words do not all mean exactly the same thing. They also know that words can be slippery creatures that may mean one thing to one person and another to someone else. And they are aware of the number of words we can collect into our word hoards, or even use in conversation, without knowing exactly what those words mean. Skilled writers are aware that they *must* know what the words they use mean, not just in a fuzzy I-sort-of-know-that way, but with exactness. Part of our responsibility as writers—our responsibility to ourselves, to our readers, and to the language we use—is to know words well enough to use them with such precision. For being able to use one's tools and materials carefully and precisely is one of the hallmarks of a good craftsman. A crucial part of the craft of writing is finding the right words for our purposes; and one of the things that makes a word "just right"—one of the things that gives it its power—is its meaning.

WHAT DO WE MEAN BY "MEANING"?

What are we talking about when we say a word "means" something? That question has occupied the mind of many a philosopher over the centuries. As writers, fortunately, we don't need to know the details of their arguments; we can take a practical approach. When we say a word "means" something, we are talking about the word's ability to refer to or represent a thing or an idea.

When we write, we *make* meaning out of words. We can have in mind something we want to say and search for the right words to communicate that "something" to others; or we can let words lead us to a discovery of what we want to say; or, as we write and revise, we can go back and forth between these two approaches. (We also make meaning by ordering our words; we'll cover that skill in the section on syntax.)

To make meaning with words is an activity, a doing of a certain kind of work. We can do this work sloppily, without taking the time and care to do a good job. Or we can do it with attention and passion, with relentless desire to make accurate use of all the power words possess.

Finding the exact word, the right word, in every sentence takes time and patience. We may need to spend time mulling over alternative ways of saying something; we may need to consult a dictionary and a thesaurus. We may need to rewrite a sentence many times until we've discovered the words that convey our meaning with precision.

But to do this work is to get a chance to play with words—for a writer, the most enjoyable kind of play. And even though, as they play, writers often experience frustration—the perfect word eludes them—they also experience those moments of intense pleasure and satisfaction when that just-right word suddenly appears and slides exquisitely into a sentence, perfectly communicating the writer's meaning. A writer's feelings at such moments echo those of a builder who watches a wall lift just as he envisioned it, or those of a batter who *knows* when his bat connects with a fastball that he's hit a home run.

There are two aspects of the meaning of words we need to be familiar with: denotation and connotation.

Making Meaning 1: Denotation

To command the *denotations* of words is to know their definitions as explained in a good dictionary. The denotation of a word is one of the main sources of its power. That's why skilled writers take such care to make sure they know the dictionary definitions of the words they use: To misuse a word, or to try to make it mean one thing when your readers know it means something else, is to lose all the power that word can give to your writing. A dictionary—an immense word hoard—provides us with the meanings of words that are public, explicit meanings, the meanings available to everyone.

A dictionary, then, is an indispensable tool for a writer; and most writers own and use more than one. Skilled writers consult a dictionary when they are unsure of the exact definition of a word; just as important, they spend time browsing through their dictionaries, at play in the land of language.

Practice: Explore Denotation

Take a few minutes to unpack your word hoard, then read the words slowly, out loud. Listen as if you were encountering these words for the first time. Mark any words that you feel curious about, that spark the question *What* does *that word mean?*

The words you mark don't have to be words you've never used. Sometimes it's fun to pick a familiar word and look it up. Now select one or more of the words you marked. Look up their meanings in the dictionary. What do you notice? Is this what you thought these words meant? If you own a second dictionary, look up some of your words in that one, too. Are there any differences in the definitions? If you like, write down the definitions in your notebook. Now, with the dictionary meanings of your words in mind, experiment with using some of these words in sentences. What do you notice? Try reading your sentences out loud. You can also make words your own by using them in conversation.

Practice: At Play in the Dictionary

Take some time to browse the pages of your dictionary. When a word catches your attention, write it down in your notebook, along with its definition(s). Now use the word in a sentence. What do you notice in doing this practice?

Practice: Verify the Meanings of Words

As you read, take note of words you like whose meanings elude you. Look up those words in a dictionary, then make sentences with them.

Practice: At Play in a Thesaurus

English, someone once wrote, is the only language that needs a thesaurus. That's because English has so many synonyms. To spend some time browsing in a thesaurus is to be amazed by the wealth of words in English—more words than any writer, no matter how prolific, could ever use in a lifetime. Like a dictionary, a thesaurus is a wonderful playground for writers who want to exercise their word minds and build their word hoards.

Give yourself some time, when you can, to simply flip the pages of a thesaurus and browse its entries. Take note of the words you like; collect them into your notebook, if you wish. Try using them in sentences.

How to Use a Thesaurus

As you browse in your thesaurus, you may find yourself occasionally feeling overwhelmed by the number of choices available for a particular word. Here, for instance, are the words collected by the editors of *Roget's Thesaurus* as synonyms for the word *hill:*

> down, brae, fell, hillock, knob, butte, kopje, kame, monticle, monticule, modadnock, knoll, hummock, hammock, eminence, rise, mound, swell, barrow, tumulus, kop, tel, jebel, dune, sand dune

Suppose that, as you are writing, you want a synonym for the word *hill*. Faced with these alternatives, how would you make a choice?

The most important thing to know about collections of synonyms for a given word is that their meanings are not identical. So when you are considering making use of a word from a list of synonyms, you will often need to look up all your possible choices in the dictionary to be sure you know their denotations. A *hillock,* for instance, is a small hill (according to my dictionary), and a *hammock* is a *hillock:* So *hillock* and *hammock* could substitute for each other, as well as for the word *hill*—as long as the hill you have in mind is a small one. But a *butte* is an isolated abrupt flat-topped hill in western U.S.—not an appropriate choice if the hill you're writing about is located in Maine and is covered with pines and spruce!

So you can't make effective use of a thesaurus without also having a dictionary nearby. Here's a way to practice the process of making considered choices from a list of synonyms:

Practice: Use a Thesaurus

Write a few sentences about a subject or take a paragraph from one of your existing pieces. Look through what you have written using your word mind: Are there any words in this passage about which you wonder, *Could I find a better word than this one?* Look up one of these words in your thesaurus and consider your choices. Don't forget to find the denotations of these words in your dictionary. Rewrite your sentences using the new word or words you have chosen, then read the sentences out loud. How do they sound to you now?

While this practice may seem time-consuming, it's worthwhile for a number of reasons. First, it will give you practice in the essential writing skill of making choices about words. It will also help you build your word hoard. Most of all, it will exercise your word mind so that, like well-trained muscles, it becomes stronger and more flexible. Writing, like hitting a baseball or playing a musical instrument, is an activity that involves making many decisions at once: The more "in shape" your brain is to make choices among words, the more skilled you will become as a writer. So the more you practice, with attention and care, the more easily words will come to you as you write and revise.

Making Meaning 2: Connotations

While a word's denotations are its explicit meaning, its connotations are its associations, the ideas or qualities it brings to mind through suggestion. If you imagine that putting a word into the mind of your reader is like casting a stone into a pond, then the denotation of the word is like the splash the stone makes as it hits the water, while the connotations of the word are like the ripples that follow the splash. For instance, if you write that a woman is wearing a "fire engine-red dress," the term *fire engine* suggests qualities like urgency and danger. If you write *Clouds were sailing across the sky*, the word *sailing* suggests ships and water. Skilled writers have learned to exploit these "ripples" of meaning that words can create in the minds of their readers. Let's take a look at how connotations work.

Some words have no connotations. These are usually words from science and technology that have very specific single meanings, such as *deuteron*, which means "a positively charged particle consisting of a proton and a neutron,"[16] or *nitinol*, an alloy of nickel and titanium.

But most of our words do have connotations. It's as if, having been used over and over, they have picked up familiar associations that accompany their dictionary meanings. So, for instance, the words *thin, slender, stringy,* and *svelte* are synonyms, having approximately the same denotative meaning. However, their associations are very different. You would not compliment a friend by saying, "How stringy you look today!" Replace the word *stringy* with the word *svelte*, and you'd put a smile on her face. Your neighbor's child might be "the kid next door" when he's behaving or "that brat" when he's not. British novelist Emma Darwin explains the importance of connotations: "When you're talking about effective language, you're usually talking about connotation: what else (beyond dictionary meaning) that particular word brings to the sentence."[17]

Practice: Explore Connotations

Pick a word from your thesaurus and write down some of its synonyms, looking them up in a dictionary if you need to. Pick one synonym that has positive connotations (such as *svelte*) and one that has negative connotations (such as *stringy*) and write a sentence using each one.

Do this exercise again with a different word. Read your sentences out loud, noticing the different effects of the words you've chosen. Do the particular connotations of your chosen word influence how you write the rest of the sentence?

Practice: Explore Connotations

Read your favorite writer, keeping an ear open for words chosen for positive or negative connotations. Collect these words in your notebook and experiment with making your own sentences with them.

Practice: Explore Connotations

Read over a passage from your own work, keeping your ear tuned to the connotations of your words. Are there any places where you might choose a different word, exploiting its connotations to enhance the effect of your sentence?

Practice: Explore Connotations

Some words have both positive and negative connotations. We can work with the connotations of this kind of word in another way as well—by placing it in a context that highlights one particular connotation. Take the word *fire* (as a noun) for instance; its most familiar denotations are "things that are burning" and "flames produced by things that are burning." But the noun *fire* also has connotations.

Take a few minutes now, if you like, to bring the denotations of the noun *fire* to your mind, and then listen for the words or phrases, the ideas or things, that this word suggests to you; write them all down. You may find yourself collecting synonyms for the word. If this happens, try to let your mind move beyond close synonyms and see what other ideas or things the word brings to your mind. You have now collected some of the word's connotations.

Now look through these connotations. What do you notice?

One thing you might notice is that this single word "fire" has some connotations that are positive (*heat, light, warmth, hearth, comfort, cookout*) and some that are negative (*fear, destruction, ruin*) and some that could be positive or negative depending on the context (*char, ember, smolder*).

Now select some of the positive connotations and write a sentence or two that highlight those connotations. A sentence suggesting positive connotations of the noun *fire* might read: *The cat crept closer to the heat of the fire and curled up contentedly on the hearth.* One that highlights the word's negative connotations might read: *The sirens of the fire trucks sounded closer and closer as we stood across the street from the looted store where the fire raged.*

One way to "charge" a word with meaning is to exploit its connotations. Training your mind, through practice, to be aware of the connotations of words, will help you write sentences in which your words are full of meaning. So repeat this practice as often as you can: Pick a word and write down all the connotations you can think of for it. Now pick one or two of those connotations, and write a few sentences that highlight those particular choices.

Public and Private Connotations

Think of the word *summer,* and write down all the words and phrases that it brings to your mind. Chances are good that your list will contain words like *heat, hot, swimming, sailing, lemonade,* and *vacation.* We can call these *public connotations,* meaning the associations a word will have in most readers' minds.

Now imagine that a person making that same list had, one July, a serious illness. Then the word *summer,* in that person's mind, might lead to an association with the word *illness* or *measles.* Try rereading the list of public connotations and inserting in it the word *measles.* Most likely your mind will reject the word, as if it's saying, *That word doesn't belong here!* That's because *measles* is not a public connotation for the word *summer*; it's a *private connotation.* It's a connotation that will mean something only to one person—the writer in whose mind the two words are associated.

Understanding the difference between public and private connotations is crucial to good writing. Private connotations have to be explained; public connotations usually need not be.

One of the key differences between unskilled and skilled writers is that an unskilled writer tends to assume that his readers are inside his head, able to read his mind. Skilled writers know this is not so. Many unskilled writers also believe that readers will be impressed by writing that is vague and difficult to understand. Skilled writers know that readers faced with such writing will be impatient, not impressed; most of the time, they will simply stop reading. To use private connotations without explaining them makes it difficult for people to understand what you mean. So, as you write and revise, take the time to ask yourself, when you have "charged" your words with connotations, *Will my readers understand the connotations of this word, or do I need to make myself clearer?*

The Value of Connotations

Aside from the danger of confusing (or losing) your readers through unexplained private connotations, the use of connotations in writing is one of its great pleasures, both for writers and for readers; it's one of our most useful writing tools.

One thing exploring the connotations of words will do for us is to build our word hoards. Even more important, practice with connotations will remind us that humans make meaning through language not only— as we are taught in school—through logic, but also through association. When we take time to practice the deliberate collecting of the connotations of words, we discover that one word can lead us to a whole world of associated words; we may also discover that exploring this particular world of words leads us to things to say about our subject we didn't know we wanted to say. Most important of all, an understanding of how connotations work gives us a valuable tool for transferring our meaning into the minds of our readers.

Some writers (and writing teachers) believe that writers need be concerned only with "expressing themselves"; that is, they need only cast some words on paper, practically at random, and let their readers make of these words whatever sense they will. I strenuously disagree with this approach, which seems to me akin to a house builder collecting some lumber and nails, and dumping them on his customer's lawn with a note: *Put your house together yourself.* It's the job of the writer, not the reader, to build structures of meaning. To do that job well, she needs to have something to say, and she needs to have the skills to transfer that "something"—her meaning—into the minds of her readers, so that they understand what she is saying and are moved by it as she intends.

Skilled writers have a profound appreciation for the ability of the human mind to associate one word with another. They know that, given the slightest opportunity, their readers' minds will slip away from what the words on the page are communicating into their own private associations. Skilled writers make use of all the tools of their craft to prevent that from happening. If they are communicating information or ideas, they want their readers to understand them exactly; if they are making verbal pictures, they want their readers to experience the reality those pictures communicate.

While the connotations of words are certainly not the only tool writers use to communicate, they are an essential element of the power of language. When we make careful use of the connotations of our words as we write and revise, we can keep the minds of our readers focused on exactly the meaning we are trying to get across. And so, as we work, we will avoid words with connotations that will send a reader's mind off on tangents; we will choose words that keep her mind on the track of thought or information or experience that we want it to be on.

 ## TAKE TIME TO REFLECT

What have you noticed in doing the practices in this chapter? What do you need to work on next?

CHAPTER 6

THE QUALITIES OF WORDS

She loved expressive words, and treasured them as some girls might have treasured jewels. To her, they were as lustrous pearls, threaded on the crimson cord of a vivid fancy. When she met with a new one she uttered it over and over to herself in solitude, weighing it, caressing it, infusing it with the radiance of her voice, making it her own in all its possibilities forever.

—LUCY MAUD MONTGOMERY, *The Story Girl*

In a way, every word is like a precious stone, with its own particular qualities: Some words feel heavy, others light; some seem to glitter, others are dull. As writers, we need to know all we can about the words we use; in addition to getting familiar with a word's denotations and connotations—its meanings—we also need to be able to recognize its *qualities*, so we can find the right word for our purpose. Just as a cook needs to know, not just intellectually, but *practically*, the difference between, say, margarine and butter—the differences in taste and texture and melting temperature—so a writer needs to know the difference in quality between, for instance, the word *domicile* and the word *home*, the word *food* and the word *egg,* the word *surrender* and the phrase *wave the white flag*. When we add to our knowledge of denotation and connotation a practical understanding of the qualities of words, we can make even more skillful use of their power. Knowing the qualities of words gives us an essential tool for choosing the words we want to use.

What are some of these qualities of words?

THE QUALITIES OF WORDS 1: FORMAL/INFORMAL

If we are writing for ourselves alone, as in a journal, it doesn't matter which words we choose. But if we have an audience in mind for our writing, then we need to consider the degree of formality our words should have. To understand the quality of formality in writing, think about how we dress. Writing for an audience is a bit like dressing to go out in public: We have to consider whether the clothes we choose will be appropriate to the occasion. If we're going to a job at a conservative law firm, we'll probably have to put on some kind of reasonably formal clothes, like a suit. We wouldn't show up for work in ripped jeans and sneakers; such attire, though, would be perfectly appropriate for a more informal occasion, like a backyard barbecue after a neighborhood basketball game.

When we write, we often need to consider the degree of formality our words should have, depending on the circumstances in which they will be read. Formal language tends to be language that is rather stiff and mannered, like a butler in a novel about the English upper classes. Words that feel and sound formal are usually Latinate words, made up of several syllables: *tendentious, prepossessing, rubicund*. Informal words are typically of Anglo-Saxon origin (or Norman words that have been Anglicized) and usually contain only one or two syllables. (For an introduction to the history [etymology] of English words, with practices that will show you how a knowledge of word history can improve your writing, visit my website: www.WhereWritersLearn. com.) Informal words are the ones that come to mind readily during ordinary conversation: *fat, meat, walk, grab, wink*, and so on. Informal language also includes slang expressions, such as: *get a grip; what's happenin'?; he's chillin'; let's rock.* You can check whether a particular word or phrase is formal or informal by looking it up in a good dictionary. The dictionary will tell you if the word is informal, or informal in some situations.

Practice: Formal and Informal Words
Collect some words that you consider formal, then see if you can come up with their informal equivalents. Then try this exercise starting with informal words. Which quality—formal or informal—do you like better?

Formality, Tone, and Voice
The degree of formality in the language you use in your writing helps create your voice on the page, just as it does when you speak. It also creates what's called the *tone* of your work. This tone has to be appropriate, not to an occasion, but to the purpose of your writing.

Listen to the difference in the voices of these two novelists:

> Nell could not help smiling at the naiveté with which Letty classed these trivialities with her marriage, but before she could make any attempt to show her sister-in-law how the very fondness which led Cardross to indulge her in small matters would stiffen his resolve not to permit her (as he thought) to throw herself away in a marriage doomed to failure, Farley, her butler, had entered the room, bearing on a salver a sealed billet, and on his countenance the expression of one who not only brought evil tidings but had foreseen from the outset that this was precisely how it would be.
>
> —Georgette Heyer, *April Lady*

> But by the time they reached the morgue it was too late. The ID had been completed and everyone had gone home. Rebus stood on the Cowgate and looked longingly back toward the Grassmarket. Some of the pubs there would still be open, the Merchant's Bar, for one. But he got back into the car instead

and asked Davidson to take him home. He felt tired all of a
sudden. God, he felt tired.

—Ian Rankin, *Let It Bleed*

The differences in the two voices come in part from the way each writer
puts sentences together (a subject we'll explore in Section 4); but word
choice is also key. Heyer, who is re-creating for her readers the world
of upper-class Londoners in Regency England, makes use of relatively formal words like *naiveté, trivialities, indulge, resolve, countenance.*
Rankin, who is bringing to his reader's mind the world of an alcohol-
ic police detective in contemporary Edinburgh, uses very ordinary
words like *late* and *looked* and *tired.* In each case, the author has chosen words appropriate to his or her purpose—in this case, the creation
of a particular fictional world and the people who inhabit that world.

The formality or informality of the words we choose also helps us
create the voices of people, other than the author, on the page. If we
have people talking in our writing, whether they are real people or
invented characters, the words we provide them with will help make
real their individual voices. For, just as our choice of clothing creates a
particular style and helps other people recognize us, so do our spoken
words show who we are. Skilled writers know this, and choose words
for their characters that will make sense for those particular people
and will help reveal what kind of people they are.

And so, Heyer's characters, London aristocrats of the early nine-
teenth century, talk like this:

"Yes, I dashed well do call it that!" replied his lordship, his
eye kindling. "Besides, it's all slum! I may have to listen to
that sort of flummery from Mama, but I'll be damned if I
will from you! What's more, it's coming it a trifle too strong!"

Rankin's detective, John Rebus, talks quite differently (and with con-
siderably fewer words):

"Flower's got a point though, sir," said Rebus, covering his
boss's embarrassment. "It's just that he's got the tact of a
tomcat. I mean, somebody'll have to fill in. How long's Frank
going to be out of the game?"

Practice: Formal and Informal Words

Imagine a person—someone you know, or a character you invent. Collect words for this character to speak, paying attention to the formality or informality of her language. Then have her talk on the page. If you like, invent more than one character and let them have a conversation.

What do you notice in doing this?

One of the things you may notice is that you don't have the words you need; your characters don't have their own individual voices: They all sound alike, or they all talk the way you do. Experienced writers spend time sitting in cafés or riding buses to listen to people talk. They often collect words and phrases, or even entire conversations, in their notebooks. If you want to build your word hoard for conversation, you can follow their example.

You can also study writers whose work you admire and pay attention to how their characters speak. Collect their vocabulary and practice using it yourself for your own characters. Eventually your characters will find their own individual voices.

THE QUALITIES OF WORDS 2: GENERAL/SPECIFIC

What is the difference between the word *food* and the word *butter,* or between the word *food* and the word *toast?* What's the difference between the word *sport* and the word *baseball,* or the word *football?* When I ask these questions in a writing workshop, it doesn't take long for someone to say, "*Food* is a general word; *butter* and *toast* are more specific." You can hear, and even feel, the difference in quality between general and specific words in even the most basic of sentences. Just listen to the difference between *I love sports,* and *I love baseball,* or between *We were served good food,* and *We were served lobster salad with fresh-baked rolls.* The meaning that is transferred through general words is less vivid, less powerful than that transferred through specific words. That's because the language of specific words is the language of detail; skilled writers—like skilled craftsmen in any medium—are masters of detail.

It's this attention to detail that usually separates spoken from written language. When we talk, we typically rely on generalities: *We had a good time* or *The food was delicious*. Perhaps we talk this way because we're in a hurry, we're not sure our listeners even want details, we've been taught that we can't talk too much or we'll bore people. Whatever the reasons, most adults in this culture tend to have only general words in their word hoards. While this may not be a problem in ordinary conversation, in writing we'll be at a serious disadvantage if we have nothing but general words to use.

That's because general words can communicate in only vague ways: *Have a nice day*. General statements are often called "empty" because they contain little or no content: *It was a great film. Jane is a nice person*. While we can get away with such statements in conversation—though no one who speaks only in generalities could be called a masterful conversationalist—when we write, if we want to communicate well, we *must* use specifics. That's because specifics are not vague; they are precise and exact. Specifics give readers sensory details, statistics, examples, particulars. They provide the substance of all good writing.

In the realm of the specific we are dealing with both content and craft. You can't just heave specific words into your writing at random; you have to use specifics to convey some particular piece of information or some exact details. But if you haven't done enough content research for your piece of writing, you simply won't have available to you the information and details you need. Suppose, for instance, that you want to write a few sentences describing a lake you visited recently. You don't want to settle for generalizations like *beautiful* or *lovely*. But as you try to come up with your sentences, you find yourself struggling. Why is this happening?

There are two possibilities. Either your word hoard is poor in words specific enough to help you make your description, or—just as important—while you were at the lake, you didn't pay enough attention to what was around you. You didn't collect enough sensory information— colors, quality of light, feel of the water, and so on—to be able to call the place vividly to mind now as you write about it.

You might find yourself in the same kind of struggle with other subjects as well. Suppose you want to write about why Ted Williams was a better baseball player than Willie Mays. Suppose you just *know* that's the case—but you have a hard time explaining your view to other people. The problem may be that you lack the words you need. Or it may be that you lack information: the statistics and specific anecdotes to provide content for your argument.

For while you surely can't communicate well without specific language, you also can't communicate without specific *information,* whether that information is sensory details, statistics, anecdotes, or examples. Many people struggle to write because they simply haven't collected enough material to work with. If this is the case for you, then, in addition to exercising and developing your ability to use words, you also need to get into the habit of collecting content material for your pieces of writing. (*How to Be a Writer* contains many practices that teach you how to collect and develop your material.)

Practice: General and Specific Words

Invent (or collect from conversation, newspapers, television broadcasts, etc.) some very general statements; write down as many as you can. Try to use as much general language as possible: *That was a good dinner. She's a nice person.* Read some of these aloud and pay attention to what happens in your mind as you hear them. What do you notice?

Now go back through your list and pick one of your general statements. Rewrite it to make it more specific. Invent details if you have to. Then take each remaining general statement and rewrite it, using specifics.

Now read each general statement out loud again, and then read the revised version out loud. What do you notice? What's the difference in the effect the general statement has on you and the effect the specific statement has?

The specific statement will make something happen inside your mind; the general statement will not. When we use specifics, whether the details of sensory experience or the details of statistics, we can make *pictures* for our readers. We can *show* them our meaning, not merely tell them what it is.

The Value of Specific Words

This technique of *showing* our readers what we mean is one of the most powerful ones available to writers.

The human brain is constructed to understand verbal communication most easily, to process and retain what is said most effectively, when that communication is done through pictures made out of words. In the next chapter, "The Language of the Imagination," we'll explore in more detail how skilled writers make verbal pictures. Professionals have a solid understanding of the qualities of words; they know that only certain kinds of words can be used to make verbal pictures. Most of the time, our "picture words" need to be specific. If we want to write like the pros, we need to become fluent in the language of specifics.

To say that the language of specifics is an essential writer's tool is not to deny our need for general words. We would find it difficult to write without general words like *sports* or *art* or *literature.* What's most important is to be aware that we have choices, and that we have the ability to decide, in any particular place in a sentence, whether a general word or a specific word will best serve our purpose. The question is not "good words versus bad words"; the question is "What do you want to *do* with your words?" And if what you want to do is to *show,* not just tell, your reader what you mean, then you will need to make primary use of the language of specifics. Here are a few ways to do that:

Techniques for Using Specifics

1. Use specifics instead of making a general statement. For example:

> [Cooper] was a tall, thin fellow, with a sallow face in which
> there was not a spot of colour. It was a face all in one tone. He
> had a large, hooked nose and blue eyes. … [His] large skull,
> covered with short, brown hair, contrasted somewhat oddly
> with a weak, small chin. He was dressed in khaki shorts and

a khaki shirt, but they were shabby and soiled; and his battered topee had not been cleaned for days.

—W. Somerset Maugham, "The Outstation"

2. Make a general statement, then follow it with specifics. For example:

Fog everywhere. Fog up the river, where it flows among green aits [small islands] and meadows; fog down the river, where it rolls defiled among the tiers of shipping and the waterside pollutions of a great (and dirty) city. Fog on the Essex marshes, fog on the Kentish heights. Fog creeping into the cabooses of collier-brigs; fog lying out on the yards and hovering in the rigging of great ships; fog drooping on the gunwales of barges and small boats. Fog in the eyes and throats of ancient Greenwich pensioners, wheezing by the firesides of their wards; fog in the stem and bowl of the afternoon pipe of the wrathful skipper, down in his close cabin ...

—Charles Dickens, *Bleak House*

In fact, [Rip] declared it was of no use to work on his farm; it was the most pestilent little piece of ground in the whole country; everything about it went wrong, and would go wrong, in spite of him. His fences were continually falling to pieces; his cow would either go astray, or get among the cabbages; weeds were sure to grow quicker in his fields than anywhere else; the rain always made a point of setting in just as he had some outdoor work to do ...

—Washington Irving, "Rip Van Winkle"

Then, while the pedlar ate his fill of meat and curds, Cateryne put more food into his pack—cheese, and two loaves made of beans and bran, and a gourd full of ale.

—Kevin Crossley-Holland, "The Pedlar of Swaffham"

3. Give specifics, then follow them with a general statement. For example:

Defenceless villages are bombarded from the air, the inhabitants driven out into the countryside, the cattle machine

gunned, the huts set on fire with incendiary bullets: this is
called pacification.

—George Orwell, *Politics and the English Language*

Practice: Use Specifics

Taking the passages above as examples, try out each of the following
techniques for using specifics:

1. Write a few sentences on a subject of your choice, using specifics.
2. Follow a general statement with examples or specifics.
3. Give specifics, then follow with a general statement.

What did you notice in doing these practices?

Specifics and Style

Perhaps you noticed that having to make your language more specific forced you to come up with more things to say, with more details
about your subject. Most of the time, this is a good thing—most inexperienced writers rely too heavily on generalizations. But some of you
may feel that you don't want so much detail in your writing. Making
choices about how many specific details to use is one more way that a
writer's style is created.

Some writers love detail. We could call their style elaborate or
highly ornamented. The paragraph from Dickens is a good example.

Other writers prefer a more plain style, using the minimum
amount of detail necessary to communicate and to create the effect
they intend. For instance:

It was late and everyone had left the café except an old man
who sat in the shadow the leaves of the tree made against
the electric light.

—Ernest Hemingway, "A Clean, Well-Lighted Place"

Do you want to develop a plain style, an ornamented style, or a style
somewhere in between? The choice is up to you.

Skilled writers don't make their choices about how much specific
detail to use simply at random. Their choices depend on their particular purpose, on what they are trying to *do* with their writing. If you

give a lot of detail about something, you are inviting your reader to spend time with that "something," to dwell there for a while. For instance, that paragraph from *Bleak House* comes on the first page of a thousand-page novel. Dickens wanted to make sure his readers were *shown* that fog, so that they would experience the fog-like atmosphere that envelops all the events in the story.

Practice: Read for Specifics
One of the best ways to get a feel for the power of specific language is to read the work of writers who use this language with skill. You can find such writers exercising their skill on virtually any subject and in many genres. (You won't find them—or only rarely—in academia or politics or government, where empty generalizations rule.) So take some time to read writers who can use language to show you something, and pay careful attention to the effect their words have upon you. If you like, mark passages you find especially effective, then go back later and see if you can discover which words or phrases created that effect. Write those words and phrases in your notebook, look up the meanings of any words you don't know, and practice using them.

Practice: Freewrite with Specifics
Do ten minutes of freewriting on whatever subject you like (or move from one subject to another). As you write, be aware of the words you're putting on the page. Don't judge them; simply notice whether they are general or specific. If you notice general words, see if you can make the following words or groups of words—which perhaps amplify the meaning of the general words—more specific. Keep your attention on being more specific, without trying too hard. Keep the pen moving. See what happens!

What did you notice?

Perhaps you noticed that this is hard for you to do. That would not be surprising, as the language of generalities is the language we are most familiar with. The language of generalities is easy to use; our brains don't have to work very hard to come up with words and phrases like *She's so beautiful* or *That's awesome!* To practice using specifics, though, means exercising the language "muscles" of our brains. As with any other form of exercise, we may at first have to overcome inertia. A few minutes of freewriting, with the conscious use of specific language, is a good place to begin.

The rewards of developing our ability to use specific language are twofold. First, we will exercise and strengthen the parts of our brains that deal with language. Second, we will provide ourselves with words that have great power. When we can recognize and make use of words that have the quality of being *specific*—as well as words that have the quality of being *concrete* (the subject of the next section)—then we will be much more effective communicators, and we will be able to make a very powerful kind of magic with words.

THE QUALITIES OF WORDS 3: ABSTRACT/CONCRETE

Our words have yet a third quality that's important for us to know about and be able to recognize: They can be what we call "concrete" words or "abstract" words. A concrete word is one that conveys to our minds something we can know through the senses, like *tree* or *birdsong*. An abstract word gives us something we can know only through the intellect, like *justice* or *hope*.

Practice: Abstract and Concrete Nouns

It's easiest to distinguish abstract from concrete by looking at nouns. (A noun is the *name* of a person, place, thing, idea, emotion, etc.)

Start by collecting nouns. Then look back through your list, and mark all the concrete ones (naming people or places or things we can know through our senses) and all the abstract ones (naming things or ideas we can know only through the intellect). If you find you have collected more of one kind of noun than the other, add words to make your list more balanced. Now read your list of words aloud slowly, paying attention to what happens inside your mind as you read each word.

What did you notice as you did this practice? What's the difference in effect between nouns that are concrete and nouns that are abstract? What happened in your mind and body when you heard each word?

The Difference Between Abstract and Concrete Words

When we read or hear a concrete word, what happens in our minds is this: A picture appears. Say, or read, the word *dog,* and you will picture a dog. Say, or read, the word *woman,* and you will picture a woman. Concrete words speak to our sensory intelligence, by way of our imaginations; they evoke in our minds something real, something we can see or hear, taste or touch. But when we read or hear an abstract word, no pictures will appear in our mind, except by association with the word. Say, or read, the word *justice* or the word *belief,* and the "picture-screen" in your mind will remain blank. Abstract words do not conjure up physical reality; they merely convey concepts and ideas.

To understand the difference between abstract and concrete words is to provide oneself with one of a writer's most powerful tools.

You may already be familiar with the difference in power between concrete and abstract words. But the overuse of abstract words is such a prevailing characteristic of professional, academic, and bureaucratic writing that I want to call attention to it for a moment.

Anyone who's ever taken a college course, or read a book by a professor, has most likely encountered writing like this:

> Though an increasing interest on the part of the educational community is being shown in transpersonal teaching, the literature reflects a lack of empirically based studies concerning the teacher characteristics associated with its adoption. The purpose of this study, therefore, was to attempt to identify characteristics (values, attitudes, and teaching philosophy) pertinent to transpersonal oriented non-public school teachers and to compare and contrast those characteristics to those of public school oriented teachers.
> —quoted by Richard Mitchell, *The Graves of Academe*

What happens in your mind when you read these words? Take a closer look at this passage: How many concrete words has the author used?

Now read this passage:

> Meanwhile, at home, we should try to keep out of reach, and even out of sight, valuable or dangerous objects that we don't

want children to touch. At the same time, we should keep on hand a good many objects cheap and durable enough so that a child can touch them and use them; we shouldn't have to worry if they get broken. Many ordinary household objects would be good presents for small children; an eggbeater, a saucepan, a flashlight. After all, it doesn't make much sense, in a family that will later spend tens of thousands of dollars on the child's education, to get upset, and to upset him, because he may ruin something worth twenty-five cents.

—John Holt, *How Children Learn*

What happens in your mind when you read these words? How many concrete words has the author used?

The differences in style between these two passages (both written by educators) are not created by word choice alone, but it's worth taking careful note of the difference in effect between the first author's obsession with abstractions and Holt's more judicious use of them. Can you understand what the first writer is saying? What about the passage from Holt's book? If you're like me, you found Holt's writing clear and comprehensible and the other passage impossible to understand. Holt has successfully communicated, transferred what he had to say from his mind to ours; the other writer has communicated nothing.

Does this mean that we should never use an abstraction? Of course not! Where would we be without words like *love* or *justice* or *peace*? But we need to devote special care to using these words. Abstractions are not precise; they are not specific. They are what I like to call "suitcase words"—words that contain many possible meanings and ideas. (This is why they are such useful tools for writers who want to disguise or hide the truth.) If you want to use abstractions well, you have to know not just their dictionary meanings, but what *you* mean when you use them. If you write *In this situation, we all want justice to be done,* or *Everybody needs love,* you need, first of all, to be sure of your own meaning: What are you trying to say through the abstractions *justice* or *love*? Then you need to make your meaning clear to your readers.

Since abstract words, like general words, are vague, the best way to make your meaning clear is to get more specific. *Show* your reader what you mean by those abstractions by giving specific examples, details, or statistics.

Practice: Use Abstract Language

Pick out an abstraction or two from the list you made earlier and write a sentence using it. Start with a short, simple sentence; then rewrite this sentence as many times as you need to, adding more sentences, if you like, and making clear to your readers how you want them to understand the abstraction in this particular situation.

What did you notice in doing this?

Here's something else to try: Bring an abstraction to mind, then try to write some sentences that will convey that abstraction to the mind of your reader without including the abstraction itself in your sentences.

To do these practices, you had to dig into your word hoard for concrete words. Let's play a little more with these.

Practice: Use Concrete Language

Collect some concrete words (via internal collecting or from your reading), and make sure you know what they mean. Then play with using some of these words to make sentences.

What do you notice in doing this?

One of the things you will notice, I suspect, is that using concrete language unencumbered by abstractions makes you feel more connected to the real world. Concrete language is the language of sensory reality, and to write about *the little brown dog* or *the red and orange sunset* puts us directly in touch with that reality in a way that abstract language—*the cute dog, the gorgeous sunset*—does not.

To use concrete language well is to make a very powerful kind of verbal magic, one we'll explore further in the next chapter.

Practice: Read for Abstract and Concrete Language

Select a passage from a favorite writer, and examine it for abstract and concrete language. What do you notice?

Practice: Freewrite with Abstract and Concrete Language

Do some freewriting and be aware of whether your words are abstract or concrete; try to concentrate on one or the other. What do you notice in each case?

As you do the practices in this section, you may notice that abstract words are often general, while concrete words are often specific. This is not always the case, though. A word can be general and abstract, like *humanity;* or general and concrete, like *food.* A word or phrase can even be specific though abstract, like *an on-base percentage of .400.*

The Value of the Qualities of Words

A word's particular qualities, be they abstract or concrete, general or specific, give that word a particular power. To make good use of this power, we need to think, not only about what we want to say with our words, but also about what we are trying to *do* with them. Simply putting our thoughts and feelings into words, though it may satisfy us and teach us something, is not enough when we are writing to others. When we write for readers, we have to think about what we want our words to do to *them.*

Although it's essential that readers understand what we're trying to say—confused readers stop turning the pages—it's equally important that our words *move* them in some way. Do we want them to laugh? Cry? Hold their breath? Then we need to know how to make use of the different qualities of words. When we can move easily between formal and informal language, general and specific, abstract and concrete, we have the foundation for mastering "the language of the imagination," the subject of the next chapter.

 ## TAKE TIME TO REFLECT

Take some time to reflect on paper about your experiences doing these practices. What have you learned? What do you still want to learn?

CHAPTER 7

THE LANGUAGE OF THE IMAGINATION

···

The artist seeks out the luminous detail and presents it.

···

—EZRA POUND

What do you think the imagination is? Many people think it's merely the ability to make things up, or to create fantasy. The imagination can do those things, but its real power is more fundamental. At its most basic, the imagination is the mental faculty that lets us create in our minds pictures of things—real or invented—that are not actually present to our senses. In our imagination, we can see the face of a friend who is far away; we can taste the hamburger we plan to eat for dinner; we can smell the perfume one of our characters is wearing.

Many people believe that it's only the gifted few who have "imagination"—but that's not so. The imagination is a natural human faculty, one we are born with, and *everyone* has one. Without the imagination, we couldn't function. From birth, we are constantly absorbing information about the world around us through our senses and turning that information into mental images. We all use that ability to make images quite unconsciously when we dream.

Then, you might ask, *why can some writers use their imaginations more easily than others?* They've just had more practice. They've practiced exercising their imaginations, and—even more important—they've developed their powers of observation, on which the faculty of imagination depends.

To work well, the imagination depends entirely on our senses. Our brains are designed to pay attention to and take in sensory information: the particular smell of burning cereal, for instance, or the sound of a snake hissing in the shadows. This "data" provided to the brain by the senses takes the form of mental "pictures," which we call *sensory images* or *perceptual images*. Many people go through life without paying much attention to the information their senses give them: They're wrapped up in their thoughts. But skilled writers have trained themselves in the activities of observation; they have learned to pay close attention to what their senses are collecting. In this way, their imaginations become a storehouse of raw material; when they write, they draw from this storehouse various details of color and light, of weather and landscape, of people's facial expressions and clothing and speech, and much more. If we want to have well-stocked imaginations, then we, too, need to train our powers of observation. From such a storehouse, the imagination of a skilled writer selects and combines sensory details to create people and places and events that may be real or may never have existed.

Some of you will know that you have such a storehouse; others may not be sure. For those in the second group, I suggest that you try the following exercises. (And if you want more, you can find them in my book *How to Be a Writer*.)

Practice: Wake Up Your Imagination

Put yourself, in your imagination, in a place you like. Using all your senses, notice what is around you. What do you see, hear, taste, smell, and touch? Try to notice as much detail as you can. Then, without worrying about your words, jot down all the details in your notebook.

Practice: Wake Up Your Imagination
If you find this exercise easy, then try inventing a place and putting yourself there. Once again, use your senses to notice all the details; write them down.

Practice: Wake Up Your Imagination
Read a passage from one of your favorite writers, paying particular attention to the pictures being made in your imagination. Now read the passage again. Can you identify the words or sentences that put those pictures into your mind?

IMAGES: THE LANGUAGE OF THE IMAGINATION

The imagination speaks in sensory images. Those pictures come to us naturally in dreams at night, or in daydreams. We can make more deliberate use of them when we write. Not all the images our imagination provides us with are vivid and detailed; some are vague and rather general, mere "sense impressions." But whether our mental images are vivid or vague, when we want to communicate those images, when we want to make them come alive in the imaginations of our readers, we need a particular writing skill: We need to be able to use words to *transfer* the pictures in our minds into the minds of our readers.

Here's a way to picture the process of image-transfer that happens in successful imaginative writing:

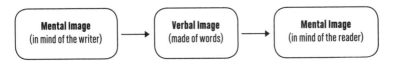

The process starts with an image in the mind of the writer, either an image of something real (say, a picture of a childhood toy) or an image of something the writer invents. The writer then must use language to transfer the picture in her mind as effectively as possible into the imagination of her reader, so that the reader can make his own mental picture. To effect this transfer, writers need to be able to construct images made out of words; these are known as *verbal images.* In order to make such images successfully, we have to train ourselves in the language of the imagination.

It may be that you find it easy to use your imagination: The pictures of people, places, things, or scenes are all there, and you can't wait to get them down on the page. But somehow when you try to do that, the words never transmit to others those pictures that are so vivid in your imagination. I suspect that most people who want to write "creatively" and get stuck (and then often give up) fall into this group.

Their problem is not, as they often assume, that they are not creative. Their problem is that they have never learned—or they have forgotten—how to use the language of the imagination, the language of pictures.

Francis Christensen, a scholar who spent his professional life trying to understand how language works, believed that there are two main things we can do with words: We can talk about something, or we can picture it. He called the two kinds of writing that result "discursive writing" or "representational writing." Discursive writing is the writing we do at work or in school. It's the writing we do to explain something or to give instructions, to persuade or to argue a point. Representational writing is different: When we do this kind of writing, we are trying to make pictures in our readers' minds, pictures of someone or something's appearance (description) or pictures of someone or something's behavior or actions (narration).

I want to emphasize the difference between these two kinds of writing, because understanding this difference is one of the keys to learning how to do what we call "creative writing." So let me repeat: In discursive writing, we are talking *about* something; in representational writing, we are *picturing* that thing (or person, place, or idea).

Skill in using the "picture-language" of the imagination allows writers to give us passages like this:

> He was dark, with the pale skin and black hair that a good
> many Highlanders possess, thin and rather scholarly
> looking in an angular and uncoordinated way. He wore
> a smooth tweed suit, worn slightly at elbows and knees

and buttonholes, a brown and white checked shirt, and a dark green tie, and he looked as though he might be a schoolmaster or a professor of some obscure science.

—Rosamunde Pilcher, *The End of Summer*

Or this:

The little shack, the rattling, rotten barn were grey-bitten with sea salt, beaten by the damp wind until they had taken on the color of the granite hills.

—John Steinbeck, "Flight"

What happened in your mind as you read these passages? When I ask my students this question, they all reply, *I got PICTURES!*

To make skillful use of the language of the imagination is to create a particularly powerful kind of verbal magic. Think about this for a moment, if you will: A few carefully chosen and arranged words, and we can *see* that Highlander and those buildings. We are, in a sense, under the spell of these words. Perhaps it's because they recognize the power of this kind of spell-making that so many professors and teachers and critics believe only certain special people can write this way.

The professors and teachers and critics are wrong. Absolutely, totally wrong.

Consider this: Humans have been using the language of representation—what I'm calling the language of the imagination—since the beginning of human speech. The language of the imagination comes *naturally* to all of us. But the language of school, especially higher education, is the language of discourse; there's no place in that world for the language of making pictures. So, sadly, many aspiring writers, having spent most of their lives in school, have lost touch with "picture-language."

But even if you haven't used the language of the imagination since you were a kid, you can still learn to make its power your own. All you need is some practice in making verbal images, starting with filling your word hoard with *the vocabulary of the senses.*

THE VOCABULARY OF THE SENSES

This type of vocabulary consists of specific, concrete words that communicate the information we receive through our senses. Each sense gives us different kinds of information. Our eyes perceive light and darkness, colors, texture, distance, movement, shape; our ears perceive the pitch and quality of sounds, their loudness or softness, their relative distance from us; our touch receptors give us temperature and texture; and so on. We also have body mechanisms, not strictly senses, that give us information about the qualities of motion and balance and body alignment.

Let's collect some of the vocabulary we can use to communicate the perceptions of our senses.

Practice: The Vocabulary of the Senses: Vision
Collect words that communicate perceptions given to us by our eyes. How many colors and shades can you name? What are some of the words you have for shapes, for sizes, for distances, for movement?

Now, in your imagination, put yourself in a place (real or invented), and look around carefully. Notice the kinds of perceptions your eyes can make. Collect all the words that name things you can see in this place.

Experiment with making sentences that convey visual perceptions.

Practice: The Vocabulary of the Senses: Hearing
Collect words that communicate the sounds things and people can make. (For example: hiss, murmur, growl, crash.) Also collect words that convey qualities of sounds (loud, soft, long, etc.).

Now, in your imagination, put yourself someplace and notice what you hear. Collect words for everything you can hear.

Experiment with making sentences that convey aural perceptions.

As you play with these practices for conveying sound sensations, you will probably notice that it's easy to collect words that seem to make sounds themselves. Words like *buzz, rasp,* and *smack* are composed of sounds that echo the sense the words make. When we choose such words, we are using the writing technique called *onomatopoeia*. Poets, in particular, love to make use of this technique, as when Tennyson proclaimed:

the buzzing of innumerable bees. There's no reason, though, for prose writers not to use the technique, too.

If you want to give it a try, experiment with this formula: *the* _____ (name the sound) of _____ (name whatever is making the sound).* For instance: *The buzzing of bees. The growl of the motor.*

Practice: The Vocabulary of the Senses: Touch

Collect the vocabulary of the fingers and the skin. What perceptions do these sense organs give us? (Softness, hardness, smoothness, roughness, temperature, and so on.)

Put yourself someplace in your imagination and touch everything that is safe to touch. Collect the words that name your perceptions. (You may find it helpful to close your eyes as you do this exercise.)

Experiment with making sentences that convey tactile perceptions.

As you do these practices for the sense of touch, you may find yourself stuck for words. That's because in English the greatest part of our vocabulary of the senses is devoted to words for sights and sounds. We have a much smaller vocabulary for the other senses.

Practice: The Vocabulary of the Senses: Taste and Smell

The nose and the taste buds often work together to give us sensory information; the vocabularies of smell and taste overlap. Collect words from these vocabularies: What kinds of information do our nose and taste buds give us? (For example: sour-sweet; bitter; salty; texture; temperature.)

Put yourself, in your imagination, someplace where there are lots of things you can safely smell and taste. Collect all the words that name your perceptions.

Experiment with making sentences that will communicate your perceptions to readers.

As you did these experiments in making sentences, you may have noticed that often you could use either a noun or a verb to convey sensory impressions. You can write either *I smelled the rose* or *the smell of the rose.* What else did you notice as you did these practices? You may want to take a few minutes to record your thoughts and questions.

Practice: The Vocabulary of the Senses: Body Language

In addition to the five senses, humans have what are called "proprioceptive mechanisms," which include our ability to sense what our muscles are doing, to maintain our balance, to notice our breathing, and so on. Most of the time we are unaware of these mechanisms; however, if we turn our attention to them, we can gather other kinds of perceptions that we can use in our writing.

To gather these perceptions we can do two things: observe other people's body language very closely, and pay attention to what is happening in our own bodies.

You can do the following practice in your imagination, if you like, but you may have more fun with it if you go to a place where there are people and pay attention to their body language. Watch someone for a while, and notice his gestures and other movements. Look at how relaxed or tense this person is; see if you can discover any movements that seem characteristic. Take notes on what you are observing, and also notice what the person is "saying" through his body. (We communicate as much through our body language as through our words!)

If you like, you can also explore body language by tuning in to your own body and collecting words that name or describe the things it does: balance, breathe, digest, clench and relax muscles, and so on. See how specific you can make your observations.

Practice: The Vocabulary of the Senses: Synesthesia

One of the ways that writers expand their vocabulary of the senses is to make use of a technique called *synesthesia*. (The word comes from Greek words that mean "blended feeling.") Though the word may sound advanced, the technique is one we use frequently in ordinary speech. We use a word that comes from the vocabulary of one sense to name something we perceive with a different sense. For instance, words like *sweet* and *sour* and *bitter* are taste words, but we use them to say things like "a sweet song," "a sour moment," or "a bitter cold."

Go back to the sensory words you collected in the above practices. Experiment with using some of them to picture something from a different sense.

Practice: The Vocabulary of the Senses: Combining Senses

In your imagination, go someplace (a real place or a made-up one) and use all your senses to notice what is around you. Collect onto the page as many details as you like. Now, using the vocabulary of the senses, make a picture that will communicate to readers what you have perceived in your imagination.

Practice: The Vocabulary of the Senses: Picturing Emotion

Write a short sentence that names an emotion or a mental or physical state. Use ordinary language. For example: *Joe is very happy.*

Now picture the person in the grip of that emotion (or in that condition): *Joe has a big smile on his face.* Do not use any word that names the emotion or condition; show it instead.

Try this a number of times, using different emotions or conditions, such as fear, fatigue, preoccupation, contempt, and so on.

What do you notice in doing this?

Practice: The Vocabulary of the Senses: Reading as a Writer

The best way to fill your word hoard with the vocabulary of the senses is to borrow words from skilled writers. As you read, make note of sensory words you like. Look them up in a dictionary to make sure you know what they mean. And then practice using them. Soon they will become a part of the vocabulary you can draw on easily when you write.

To use the vocabulary of the senses comes naturally to most people. Once you turn your attention to these particular words, you will probably find it very easy to make use of them. As you practice, you will find yourself avoiding abstractions and generalities and instead choosing sensory words to make verbal images.

Making Choices with Verbal Images

When we fill our sentences with the vocabulary of the senses, we are making verbal images. That is, we are making *word-pictures* that communicate to our readers the pictures in our own imaginations. Rather than talking about what it is we want to show our readers, we give them the sensory details and let those details act on their imaginations.

The writers we call "great" are masters in the craft of making verbal images. One of the things they know how to do is to choose, from all the details their imaginations give them, exactly the right ones to convey the specific sensory pictures they want to get across to their readers. In making verbal images, as with every other aspect of the writing craft, we need to learn how to make choices.

One thing we need to choose is the length of our images. Should the image we make *here,* in this place in our writing, be a short one— just a few words—or a long one—an entire paragraph, or even two or three? And what about the one we need *here?* The choices a writer makes about the length of verbal images is one thing that helps define his particular style.

Another thing to consider is how vivid we want a particular word picture to be. How many sensory details should we give? Which particular details do we want to use?

As you read, pay attention to how each author uses sensory details. One of the things that you may notice is that writers differ a great deal in the amount of specific detail they provide to their readers. Perhaps one way to think about this is that, as writers, we have to decide how much we want to insist on our readers seeing our mental pictures exactly the way we see them, and how much we want to allow our readers to use their own imaginations.

Whichever choice we make, though, we have to include enough detail so that we *activate* our readers' imaginations. Then we can consider how sharply we want to focus our images.

Creating Sharper Focus for Images

If you give the same amount of detail for everything you picture, your reader will quickly feel bored or overwhelmed. So you have to make choices—choices about where and when to sharpen the focus of your images.

Here are some techniques to play with that will help you create a sharper focus when you choose to:

1. Add Adjectives and Adverbs

Consider this image: *The girl walked down the street.*

What picture do those words make in your mind? If they make one at all, it will be vague and blurry, like an out-of-focus photograph. What about this version? *The small girl walked alone down the long, dark street, lined with unfamiliar houses.*

The adjectives and adverb make the picture more focused, more vivid.

Practice: Sharper Focus: Add Adjectives and Adverbs

In your imagination, make a picture of one person, animal, or object. Write a very general image (one short sentence is fine) for what you have pictured. Now rewrite your sentence, adding adjectives and adverbs to sharpen the focus.

2. Point to a Part of the Object or Action

Consider this image: *Joe drove slowly.* Now consider this revision, which sharpens the image by pointing to a part of it: *Joe drove slowly, hesitating at every corner.* (The "pointing" is from the general slowness of Joe's driving to the specific movement of hesitation.)

Here's another example: *Helen stopped talking and stared out the window.* Now here's a revised version, with pointing: *Helen stopped talking and stared out the window, her eyes grown suddenly cold.*

Practice: Sharper Focus: Pointing

Write a general image, then sharpen the focus using the "pointing technique."

3. Consider the Effect You Want Your Image to Have on Your Readers

The language of the imagination is a writer's most powerful tool to *make things happen* inside readers: to make them see, hear, and taste; to create sensations and emotions inside them. To do this effectively, we can't use every single detail our imagination has to offer. We have to make choices. Usually the choice we make depends on what we want our language pictures to *do* to our readers.

Practice: Sharper Focus: Choosing Details for Effect

Begin this practice by choosing an image to make in your mind: one from a previous practice, one you invent now, or one from a piece of writing you are working on. Keeping that image in mind, consider the effect you want it to have in your reader's mind when you transfer it there using words. Ask yourself, *What do I want to make happen inside my reader?*

Now spend some time with the image in your mind, noticing its various details, and thinking about which ones you might choose to put into words, so that the verbal image you make will have the effect you want it to have on your reader. Collect these details onto the page, using any words that will help you remember them; then, using the vocabulary of the senses, construct one or more verbal images to affect your reader the way you intend. (Remember that we have other senses in addition to sight and hearing.)

If you want to find out whether your verbal images work the way you want them to, ask a trusted friend to read them and to tell you what happened inside him as he took in your words. What pictures did he get? What did he feel or think?

Practice: Sharper Focus: Imitation

The best way to learn how verbal images work on readers is to pay attention to how you react when you read stories or poems that engage your own imagination.

Take a passage from a favorite author, and, as you read, make note of verbal images that affect you powerfully: images that make pictures in your imagination, images that make you feel sensations or emotions. Then go back to each one in turn and copy it into your notebook. Read it over slowly, noticing what happens inside you. Read it again and see if you notice anything else. Now go back through the passage and see if you can discover what, exactly, the writer did with words to make the passage affect you as it did. You may want to write some notes to yourself about what you have learned.

Then, in whatever way you like, imitate this passage.

4. Choose Between Static or Moving Images

As you practice imitating verbal images made by skilled writers, you will probably notice that some of them have no movement in them, while others have a great deal of movement. What you are noticing is the difference between *static images*—the ones that don't show movement—and *dynamic images*—the ones that do. When we create static images we are writing *description*. When we create dynamic images we are writing *narration*. While we can, if we like, write separate descriptive and narrative passages, we can also combine the two.

Here are some examples of description:

> It was a little after seven on a summer morning, and William Potticary was taking his accustomed way over the short down grass of the cliff-top. Beyond his elbow, two hundred feet below, lay the channel, very still and shining, like a milky opal. All around him hung the bright air, empty as yet of larks. In all the sunlit world no sound except for the screaming of some sea-gulls on the distant beach ...
>
> —Josephine Tey, *A Shilling for Candles*

> This room was very long and narrow, and all along one side were windows with white, ruffled curtains drawn back at the sides, and with small, shining panes of glass, through which the sun poured golden light on a long shelf of potted plants ...
>
> —Dorothy Canfield Fisher, *Understood Betsy*

Practice: Static Images

1. Bring an image to your mind. Make sure the picture is of something that doesn't move.
2. Collect sensory details from that image and write them down.
3. Select the details you want to use.
4. Compose the image in words.

What did you notice in doing this practice?

Practice: Static Images
Collect several examples of static images from your reading and copy them into your notebook. Choose one (or more, if you like) to imitate. What did you notice in doing this practice?

Practice: Moving Images
To create a picture in words of a moving image is to create *narration,* to tell a part of a happening. Here are some examples of moving images:

> Rainsford sprang up and moved quickly to the [ship's] rail, mystified. He strained his eyes in the direction from which the reports had come, but it was like trying to see through a blanket. He leaped onto the rail and balanced himself there, to get greater elevation; his pipe, striking a rope, was knocked from his mouth. He lunged for it ...
> —Richard Connell, "The Most Dangerous Game"

> [The boys] ran across the churchyard for the sport of leap-frogging over the most convenient tombstones, then shouted as they hurled themselves on the grass and rolled down the mound ... They pelted across the village street and scrambled to the top of the further mound.
> —Barbara Willard, *The Sprig of Broom*

Try this practice to create moving images:

1. Bring an image to your mind of something or someone, then let that person or thing move.
2. Collect sensory details from that moving image and write them down.
3. Select the details you want to use.
4. Compose the image in words.

What did you notice in doing this practice?

Practice: Combine Static and Moving Images
Though it's good practice to make static and moving images in isolation, much of the time, when we write, we combine them. For instance:

On the steps of the Great London Road police station in Edinburgh, John Rebus lit his last legitimate cigarette of the day before pushing open the imposing door and stepping inside.

The station was old, its floor dark and marbled. It had about it the fading grandeur of a dead aristocracy. It had character.

Rebus waved to the duty sergeant, who was tearing old pictures from the notice-board and pinning up new ones in their place. He climbed the great curving staircase to his office. Campbell was just leaving.

—Ian Rankin, *Knots and Crosses*

Two gentlemen who were in the lavatory at the time tried to lift him up: but he was quite helpless. He lay curled up at the foot of the stairs down which he had fallen. They succeeded in turning him over. His hat had rolled a few yards away and his clothes were smeared with the filth and ooze of the floor on which he had lain, face downwards. His eyes were closed and he breathed with a grunting noise. A thin stream of blood trickled from the corner of his mouth.

—James Joyce, "Grace"

Now practice this technique yourself:

1. Bring an image to your mind of something or someone. Let that person or thing be still first, and then move. You can go back and forth between stillness and movement, if you like.
2. Collect sensory details from both the static and the moving images, and write them down.
3. Select the details you want to use.
4. Compose the image in words.

What did you notice in doing this practice?

A Note on the Process of Making Images

These practices are designed to help you learn how to make verbal images that will transfer what's in your imagination to the imagination of your readers. They are also designed to help you understand the whole step-by-step process that goes on when we use the language of the imagination. The process that I've encouraged you to follow—making the image in your mind, collecting details, choosing details, finding the right words for your verbal images—may seem laborious and too slow. Remember that what you are doing here is practicing, the way you might practice the different skills involved in learning to ride a bicycle or to hit a baseball. Eventually, if you practice enough, the skills will become automatic and the whole process will happen very quickly.

Even professional writers falter occasionally, though. And if you understand the process of making verbal images—an understanding based on having actually followed the process many times—then when you do get stuck, you can return to the steps and follow them to get your mind moving again.

Please don't forget the first step of the process in your quest to find just the right words. Remember that to make powerful verbal images requires two complementary skills: the ability to make the images (or perhaps I should say, to let the images appear) in your own mind; and the ability to use language to communicate those images to others.

A well-stocked imagination is just as important to a writer as a well-stocked word hoard. And I've found, when I get stuck composing verbal images, that encouraging my imagination to give me more pictures works better than searching desperately for the perfect word.

5. Use Comparison

So far in our exploration of images we've been experimenting with using concrete, specific words to make verbal pictures of people or places or things or scenes given to us by the faculty of imagination. (These pictures can be based on observation or invention, or a combination of both.) We've considered how detailed to make our pictures, and what effect we want them to have on our readers. We've tried sharpening our images by adding more detail or choosing a specific detail to focus on. All these techniques help us transfer into words a close representation of the pictures in our mind.

The verbal images we create in these ways are called *literal images*. Literal images are attempts to reproduce in words an object or a person or an experience and to make that reproduction as realistic as possible.

But often, as we make images, we discover that literal images are not enough. Sometimes in order to communicate what something is, we need to write about what it is *like*. We need to compare it to something else. Listen to these examples and notice what happens in your mind as you hear them.

> When the veteran Menelaus saw [Paris] striding towards him in front of the crowd, he was as happy as a hungry lion when he finds the great carcass of an antlered stag or a wild goat and devours it greedily in spite of all the efforts of the sturdy huntsmen and the nimble hounds to drive him off …

> But when royal Paris saw that it was Menelaus who had taken up his challenge, his heart failed him completely, and he slipped back into the friendly ranks in terror for his life, like a man who comes on a snake in a wooded ravine, recoils, and with pale cheeks and trembling limbs goes back the way he came.
>
> —*The Iliad* (trans. E. V. Rieu)

You probably noticed, as you read these passages, that your mind was filled with *two* images at the same time. The writer presents one thing, and then in order to portray it vividly, he compares it to something else.

The human brain seems to be constituted to make sense of experience by perceiving and stating resemblances. To make comparisons is one of the ways we learn: We try to understand new things by comparing them to something we already know. We ask not *What is this?* but *What is this* like?

We make such comparisons all the time in ordinary conversation. A friend might ask us to describe a new acquaintance; we might respond with literal details of his height, hair color, eye color, and so on, to give her a picture. More likely, though, we'd make a comparison: *He's like Robert Redford with dark hair.* If our friend is a movie-goer, she will immediately "get the picture."

Our ordinary conversation is shot through with comparisons: *He's crazy like a fox. The cat is as dead as a doornail. The team came on like gangbusters. That girl is a peach.* The language parts of our brain make comparisons quite naturally. When we make comparisons in words, we are creating what are called *figurative images*.

Figurative images are a bit like pieces of chipped rock. As they are used, over and over, their rough edges become more and more smoothed down, and they lose their definition and their particular identity. After a while, the power that figurative images had when they were new disappears. The first person to compare a pretty girl to a peach, for instance, made a figurative image that might have startled his listeners; but after that image was passed on from one person to another, around and around among the same group of people, it would no longer have had any impact.

We call such worn-out figurative images *clichés*, and we usually need to avoid them in our writing because they no longer have the power to affect our readers. Instead, we need to make use of our natural ability to make comparisons to create fresh images that will help our readers see (or hear or taste or touch) whatever we are picturing. Let's take a look, then, at the process of creating figurative images.

Making Figurative Images

We make comparisons in language in two ways: by saying A is *like* B (or A is *as* _____ [some quality] as B); or by saying A *is* B. When we use *like* or *as* we are making a figurative image known as *simile*. (*Simile* is the Latin word for *like*.) When we leave out the *like* or *as,* we are making a figurative image called *metaphor*. (*Metaphor* comes from the Greek word for *transfer*.) With metaphor we use a word or phrase to "transfer" the qualities of one thing to something else that does not literally have those qualities: In other words, we describe one thing in terms of another. If we want to use these two techniques of simile and metaphor effectively, we need to understand and keep in mind both the similarities and the differences in the way they work.

Both simile and metaphor make a comparison, find a point of resemblance, between an A and a B. The purpose of the comparison is to say something about A. So B has to present a picture of something better known, more familiar, or more vivid than A. The more concrete and detailed the picture of B, the more the reader will be able to picture A. Often skilled writers make the picture of B an image of something very ordinary:

> The sound faded, solitude swept back like a huge wave …
> —Eva Figes, *Light*

Homer, in the examples given earlier, knew just how to picture Menelaus, the Greek leader, and Paris, the Trojan (who had abducted Menelaus's wife, Helen), to the imaginations of his audience of shepherds and sailors. He created down-to-earth images of things his listeners were familiar with—a hungry lion tearing the carcass of a goat, a man coming upon a snake in the woods.

Other writers like to make B something more surprising:

> He could hear Jonas' voice. It had an odd nasal twang to
> it. He seemed to be doing most of the talking. Christopher
> could hear an occasional mumble and grumble from [Jonas']
> client, like a double bass interrupting a long saxophone solo.
> —Michael Gilbert, *Flash Point*

Figurative language can create even more pointed effects. Listen, for instance, to the way Dickens gives us a picture of lawyers (whom he hated):

> Here, in a large house, formerly a house of state, lives Mr.
> Tulkinghorn [an eminent lawyer]. It is let off in sets of chambers now, and in those shrunken fragments of its greatness,
> lawyers lie like maggots in nuts.
> —Charles Dickens, *Bleak House*

Practice: Figurative Images: Similes

A simile is a direct comparison of two different things, using the words *like* or *as* (and sometimes *as if, seems,* or *appears*). Here's a practice in making similes:

Bring to your imagination a person or an object. This is the "A" of your comparison. Now make a list of everything you can think of that A is *like*. Give your imagination free rein; write down all the possibilities that occur to you, without judging them.

Now look back through your list and mark the items you like. Pick one item to begin with: This object or person is your "B." Write a sentence comparing A to B, using *like* or *as*. Remember to develop B into a clear and powerful verbal image, using concrete, specific language.

Make more similes using other items from your list.

Practice: Figurative Images: Metaphors

When we make a metaphor, as when we make a simile, we make a comparison between two unlike things; we apply a word or phrase to something to which it is not literally applicable. With a metaphor, though, we do not use *like* or *as*. Rather than saying, for instance, *Life is like a river,* we say, *Life is a river* (or *Life, a river…*). Without the *like* or *as*, the qualities of one thing or person (B) are transferred directly to the other (A). The result is usually a more powerful comparison than if we had made the same comparison using a simile. When Romeo speaks of Juliet, he says, "Juliet is the sun," not "Juliet is like the sun." When pop songwriters sing of love, they say, "You are my sunshine," not "You are like my sunshine."

Here are more examples:

> Love is a kind of warfare.
> —Ovid, *The Art of Love*

> So everything was ready. And just as the June sun rose behind a light cloud, a great coin of gold, John kissed his wife and his children goodbye.
> —Kevin Crossley-Holland, "The Pedlar of Swaffham"

Our minds work naturally in metaphor; our language is full of what are called "fossil metaphors," such as *the teeth of the wind,* or *the mouth of the river.* To play with making metaphors is to play with some of the most basic material of language. Here's one way to play:

Go back to your list of similes. Rewrite each one as a metaphor.

When you do this exercise, you will probably discover that some similes cannot be transformed into metaphor. They don't make sense as metaphors, or they sound silly.

It's important to remember, when making figurative images, that even though you want your comparison to grab your reader's attention, the comparison also has to make sense. Trying to create a comparison between two things that have nothing in common won't work. In the same way, if A or B has connotations that weaken the comparison, the figurative image will sound silly and make your readers laugh.

The most effective figurative images are often the simplest; grounded in concrete language, they make pictures that speak clearly to a reader's imagination. Figurative images like this are especially useful for picturing abstractions.

Practice: Figurative Images: Picturing Abstractions

Make a list of abstractions: beauty, truth, justice, faith, poverty, and so on. Then see if you can make figurative images to show some aspect of each abstraction. You may find it helpful to take one at a time and freewrite a list of everything you can think of that this abstraction is like, without censoring any possibility. Then choose the ones that seem most effective, and make similes or metaphors for each one.

Practice: Figurative Images: Making Choices

Now that you've added figurative images to your techniques of making verbal images, you have another set of choices to make as you write: In any particular passage, do you want to use literal or figurative images; and, if you choose figurative images, should they be similes or metaphors? Consider, for instance, the following three ways of communicating the same imagined picture:

> The man peered into the darkness and shook his head. (*literal image*)

> The man peered into the darkness, thick as a woolen blanket, and shook his head. (*simile*)

> The man peered into the darkness, a thick woolen blanket, and shook his head. (*metaphor*)

These three techniques are not always interchangeable (in the previous example, is simile better than metaphor?), and their effect can be very different. Skilled writers, their abilities honed by lots of practice, develop an instinct for making choices between literal and figurative images. You will probably need to do a lot of experimenting with the two kinds of images, as well as a lot of reading, to develop that instinct in yourself.

Here's one practice to try. Go back to some of your literal images and see what happens when you rewrite them as figurative images. Now take some figurative images and rewrite them as literal images. Which do you think work better? Why?

Practice: Figurative Images: Learning from the Pros
Read your favorite writers for figurative images (or use the examples above). Copy some of the images you like into your notebook. What makes them work? See if you can imitate these techniques.

The Value of the Language of the Imagination
The language of the imagination is one of a writer's most powerful tools for getting what we want to say into the minds of our readers. Why? Because it speaks to two mental faculties at once.

Discursive language, which talks *about* things, gives us plain meaning; it speaks only to the intellect.

But representational language (which I have been calling "the language of the imagination") speaks both to the intellect *and* to the imagination. In other words, when we read a verbal picture, our intellect takes in the ordinary meanings of the words, and, at the same time, our imagination (if it has been engaged) makes the picture. So we "get" what the writer is saying in two different ways at once.

Does this mean that we should never use discursive language? Of course not: If it's appropriate to our particular purpose, then we have to use it. (For instance, all these chapters are written in discursive prose.) Both discursive language and the language of the imagination are tools we can use; the more familiar we are with each of them, the better we can use them.

BALANCING SHOWING AND TELLING

I hope by now you are excited about developing skill in using your faculty of imagination and its particular language of verbal images. Once your skill with the language of imagination equals your skill with the language of discourse (whether that be the language of ordinary speech or academic/professional language), then you can choose, as you write and revise, which language you want to use in any given piece of writing, and in any given passage or sentence within a particular piece. How you choose will depend primarily on the effect you want your words to have on your readers: Do you need to engage only their intellects, or do you want to engage both intellect and imagination?

If you want to write fiction, poetry, or memoir, you may now be wondering whether you need discursive language at all. In those genres, you will need to make primary use of the language of the imagination—and you will also discover that you can't picture everything. There will be times when you need to get information across to readers as quickly as possible, times when you need to summarize happenings, times when you need to make an author's comment on events. At times like these, you will need the language of discourse.

Despite the mantra that seems to obsess some writing teachers to the exclusion of common sense—*Show, don't tell!*—there are times when telling is more effective than showing: Skilled writers know how to do both. Through experience, and by learning from professional writers, you can develop your instincts for making the choice whether, in any particular place in your work, you need to show or to tell.

 ## TAKE TIME TO REFLECT

Do some reflecting on what you have learned through the practices in this chapter. What do you need to work on next?

LOOKING AHEAD

In these first lessons we've explored the choices writers need to make about the words they use—the area of craft called diction. We've looked at the power words have based on their meanings, their qualities, and on whether they are chosen to talk about things or to picture them. We've played with one essential component of making magic with words: choosing the right ones. Now we turn to another essential element of word-magic: choosing the most effective ways to combine our chosen words into sentences. From now on, in this book, we'll be exploring the craft of "getting the spell right"—and to do that, we need to understand, first, the power words have because of the particular roles they play in sentences. So, in the next section, we explore parts of speech.

SECTION 3

The Power of Function: What Words Do

In every manual on virtually any discipline from meditation to golf, stress is laid on the necessity for regular practice. Writing is no exception.

—JOHN FAIRFAX AND JOHN MOAT, *The Way to Write*

So far we've been looking at how we can make magic with language by choosing individual words. But single words rarely function on their own; most of the time they work *together,* in groups—groups that grammarians call phrases and clauses and sentences. To make magic with language, we have to know the meanings and qualities of individual words—*and* we need to know how to put these words together. To accomplish this, we must understand how words function when they work together. If we want to take our chosen words and make effective spells with them—sentences and paragraphs that will grab and keep our readers' attention—then we have to learn, not just what words mean, but what they *do.*

WHAT WORDS DO

In every sentence, every word has a certain kind of work to do, a particular role to play. Grammarians use the term *parts of speech* to label and classify these different roles words play. If you imagine every sentence as a tiny drama, then you can also imagine every word as taking a particular kind of role—or actor's *part*—within that drama. Some of those roles are more important to a sentence than others, just as the leading role in a play is more important than a bit part. But every one of these roles, every part of speech, has its own particular importance. To put it another way, every part of speech has its own particular power; and anyone who wants to become a skilled writer needs to know how to make use of that power.

If you studied grammar in school, you may have found this material boring. That's because in grammar classes we're usually taught only to analyze sentences, not compose them. But the usefulness of analysis is limited: Would an aspiring professional pitcher, for instance, spend all his time analyzing game films without ever throwing a single pitch? Here we'll take a different approach: First we'll practice using parts of speech, then we'll turn to the practice of phrases, where we start to combine words into functional units.

A basic understanding of how parts of speech and phrases work is an essential tool for writers, one that will help you develop the skill you need to keep your readers spellbound. Remember, though, that intellectual understanding alone is not enough; you need to put your understanding into practice. So, I implore you, do not merely read through this section! Do the practices, or make up ones of your own. The time you spend doing this will reward you for the rest of your writing life.

CHAPTER 8

PARTS OF SPEECH

We're born to love grammar. We are taught to hate it.

—MAX MORENBERG, *Doing Grammar*

When talking about parts of speech, grammarians have traditionally placed words into nine categories: nouns, verbs, adjectives, adverbs, determiners, prepositions, conjunctions, pronouns, and interjections. (Some contemporary grammarians add other categories.[18]) The first four of these parts of speech—nouns, verbs, adjectives, and adverbs—are called *content* parts of speech, because they convey content (meaning) to the minds of readers. The next three—determiners, prepositions, and conjunctions—are known as *structural* parts of speech; instead of conveying content themselves, they help structure, or organize, the content words. Pronouns and interjections have their own particular work to do. Let's take a look at each of these in turn.

PARTS OF SPEECH 1: CONTENT PARTS OF SPEECH

Content Parts of Speech 1: Nouns

When grammarians call a word a noun, they mean that it does a certain kind of work: the work of *naming*. So a noun is a word that names something: a person, a place, a thing, a condition, a state of being, an idea, a quality, and so on. The words *summer* and *river* are nouns; so are the words *love* and *peace, Rebecca* and *Varitek*. English contains more nouns than any other part of speech.

Some people believe that, of all the parts of speech, nouns have the most power. That's because a noun can, all by itself, make something happen in a reader's mind: It can bring a concept to mind, or create a picture. Read the following words one at a time and notice what happens in your mind. *Lake. Doughnut. Dog. Love. Terror.*

So strong is this ability of nouns to evoke meaning that we can even take three or four of them, put them in order, and thereby suggest a complete sentence, without any other parts of speech. Consider this: *snow, car, shovel.* Or this: *dress, party, admiration.* Can you hear the idea inside each of these not-quite sentences?

The Power of Names

The power of nouns is the power to call things into being by naming them. As I noted earlier, you can see this power in creation myths from many cultures, where things come into being because someone names them. Nouns, more than any other part of speech, connect words to the richness of the world. "Naming," says author and writing teacher Frances Mayes, "is one of the great involvements of the writer, the bonding of words as close to the subject as possible."[19]

If we want to become skilled writers, we need to know how to make use of the power of names.

Practice with Nouns: Internal Collecting

Unpack your word hoard, putting all your attention into collecting only *nouns*—words that name people, places, or things (tangible or intangible). As you do this, you may want to try being aware of whether the words you are collecting are general or specific, abstract or concrete; you can, if you like, collect many different names for the same thing or idea. Keep your pen moving for five or ten minutes, and see what happens.

When you're done with this practice, take a moment to reflect on paper about what you noticed as you collected nouns. Then read through your list and mark the words you particularly like. Look up their meanings in the dictionary, if you need to. Then use some of those words to construct sentences. Read your sentences out loud. What do you notice?

Now try this: Pick a noun, then collect all the nouns you can think of that you associate with this noun. Select some of these nouns and use them to make sentences. What do you notice this time?

Perhaps in doing these practices you noticed that you don't know the names of many things in the world around you. Many people in my workshops have that experience. Most of us, these days, are sadly out of touch with the physical world that exists outside our own heads. Thanks to the mass media, we may know the name of every song recorded by our favorite pop singer, but we don't know the names of the streets we walk on, or the names of the materials used to build the houses lining those streets, or the names of the different kinds of clouds above them. If, then, we ever want to create a picture of a world for our readers, we will have a difficult time doing it.

Fortunately, we can easily add to our store of nouns, just by choosing to learn the names of things. For instance, I used to wander around being vaguely aware of trees, but I didn't know the names of any of them. Then I decided to learn their names, with the help of a friend and some guidebooks. In the process I acquired much more than some new nouns: Because I could name the trees around me—*That's a maple, that's an oak*—my experience of trees changed completely. To learn the name of a stranger makes her real to us in a new way. No longer is she a nameless face but *Jane O'Donnell* or *Martha Greene*, a particular individual. In the same way, trees became more real to me, more alive, because I learned their names. To name something precisely is a step towards knowing it.

Practice with Nouns: External Collecting

If you want to undertake a similar journey into learning the names of things, you can do so easily. Field guides to animals, birds, clouds, rocks, architecture, and many other subjects are readily available. Or perhaps you have a friend who shares your interest in a subject and can tell you the names of things in that field. As you converse with your friend, or browse in a field guide, every time you come across a noun you like, write it down in your notebook, along with its definition, and then use it in sentences to make it your own.

You can find lots of similar ways to add nouns to your word hoard via external collecting. As you read, collect the nouns you like. As you listen to people talk (in person, on the radio, on television), names will come to you that attract your attention. If you write them down and use them, they will become yours.

Understanding Nouns: Kinds of Nouns

Nouns can be classified into four categories: common nouns, proper nouns, compound nouns, and collective nouns. Exploring each category in turn can provide you with more naming words for your word hoard.

1. **COMMON NOUNS**—sometimes called "generic" nouns—name people, places, things, conditions, ideas, and so on. We can recognize common nouns because they are not capitalized (except when they come at the beginning of a sentence). *Dog, lake, earth, attitude, sensitivity* are all common nouns. Common nouns can be general or specific, abstract or concrete.

2. **PROPER NOUNS** name a *specific* person or place or thing: not just any man, but *Mr. Satterthwaite;* not just any lake, but *Lake Champlain;* not just any kind of soft drink, but *Coke.* We can recognize proper nouns easily because they are always capitalized, even when they don't begin a sentence.

3. **COMPOUND NOUNS** are made up of two or more nouns that together name one thing, person, or place. *Football game, rock star, book report* are examples of compound nouns. Some compound nouns are hyphenated: *movie-goer, attention-grabber.*

4. **COLLECTIVE NOUNS** name groups of things or people or places. When we talk about *a bunch of flowers, a herd of cows,* or *a crowd of people,* the words *bunch, herd,* and *crowd* are collective nouns.

Practice with Nouns: Kinds of Nouns

For each kind of noun in turn, first collect as many as you can, then go back through your list and read over your words. Notice the particular power each word has. Then mark the ones you like, and make them your own by putting them into sentences.

1. Collect Common Nouns

Don't try to be fancy here: Any old common nouns will do. If you're stuck at first, try looking around you and writing down the names of everything you can observe. Here are some more examples of common nouns:

> desk, foot, stitch, beauty, gathering, rain, loneliness, fate, grief, clown

2. Collect Proper Nouns

You can collect names you already know, or make some up. Think about places or people you know, or that you'd like to know: What are their names or their nicknames?

3. Collect Compound Nouns

First collect ones you know. Then make some up. Here are some more examples:

> bus stop, frat party, crash pad, ski resort, firefly, storm-bringer, baseball

Sometimes a compound noun is two nouns joined together, without space or punctuation (*rooftop*); sometimes a compound noun is two nouns, separated by a space, that function as one word (*garbage collector*); sometimes a compound noun is hyphenated (*six-pack*). And sometimes other parts of speech can find their way into a compound noun (*softball, breakfast, merry-go-round*).

4. Collect Collective Nouns

There's a wonderful book called *An Exaltation of Larks* by James Lipton, that describes the vogue for collective nouns in the Middle Ages and gives examples (with pictures). You may want to take a look at it if you like collective nouns.

If you want to play with collective nouns, try the following game. Collect nouns: some concrete, some abstract; some singular, some plural.

Then use them in the collective noun construction: *A (or an)* _____ *(singular) of* _____ *(plural).*

For example:

- an arrogance of academics
- an abstract of philosophers
- a comfort of chairs
- a monstrosity of modern paintings

Let your word mind play; don't censor what you come up with. This is a great practice for getting used to letting your word mind take over.

Here's an example of both compound and collective nouns from a professional writer, the beginning of Kevin Crossley-Holland's retelling of "The Pied Piper of Hamelin":

> Rats! There was a ruin of rats. A rat-attack! A plague of rats.

Practice with Nouns: Make Sentences with Nouns

Select some nouns from your lists and put them together into sentences. Experiment with using different kinds of nouns in one sentence. Afterwards, read your sentences out loud. How do those nouns sound to you?

Practice with Nouns: Freewriting with Nouns

Do some freewriting, making complete sentences, and keep your word mind focused on nouns. Afterwards read your sentences out loud. How do they sound to you?

Practice with Nouns: Read for Nouns

As you read, pay the most attention to nouns. Does your author use a lot of nouns? What kind? What is the effect of these nouns?

Understanding Nouns: The Noun-Based Style

Some writers choose to write sentences composed primarily of nouns; we can say that their writing style is a *noun-based style*. Here's an example from *The Crofter and the Laird*, a book by John McPhee about Colonsay, an island off the coast of Scotland. As you read, take mental note of the nouns he uses.

After our own voyage to Colonsay, over green and foaming waters in a wind that made tears run down our cheeks, the first person we saw was Donald Gibbie, standing there on his pier in the lee of Cnoc na Faire Mor (Big Lookout Hill), in his Wellington boots, his dungarees, his heavy gray pullover, and his brown-and-tan knitted cap, with his hands clasped behind his back, a frown on his face, and a look of felt responsibility in his eyes ...

Here are more examples of noun-based style:

But such wonderful things came tumbling out of the closets when they were opened—bits of mouldy pie, sour bottles, Mrs. Jellyby's caps, letters, tea, forks, odd shoes and boots of children, firewood, wafers, saucepan lids, damp sugar in odds and ends of paper bags, footstools, blacklead brushes, bread, Mrs. Jellyby's bonnets, books with butter sticking to the binding, guttered candle-ends put out by being turned upside-down in broken candle-sticks, nutshells, heads and tails of shrimps, dinner-mats, gloves, coffee-grounds, umbrellas—that [Mr. Jellyby] looked frightened and left off [looking interested] again.
— Charles Dickens, *Bleak House*

Coins, paper clips, ballpoint pens, and little girls' pocketbooks are found by workmen when they clean the sea lions' pool at the Bronx Zoo.
— Gay Talese, "New York Is a City of Things Unnoticed"

Do you like this kind of writing? Then try it for yourself, putting to work your newfound understanding of nouns. Pick a subject and compose some sentences on it, concentrating on using mostly nouns. Or take a passage from something you've already written, and revise it so that nouns predominate in most of the sentences. Read your sentences out loud. What do you notice?

Perhaps you will fall in love with the power of nouns, with their amazing ability to call things into being in our minds. You may discover that when you choose nouns that are concrete and specific—when you find the exact name you need—you can often eliminate unnecessary adjectives.

Content Parts of Speech 2: Verbs

A verb is a word that makes things happen. Nouns are the building blocks of sentences, but, used alone, they are static. They can evoke pictures or concepts in a reader's mind, and so they have lots of power, but those pictures can't move. Try saying these words out loud, one at a time, and see what happens: *snow, justice, crayon.*

Now try this exercise again, with verbs added. Notice the difference in the pictures or ideas that come to your mind.

> The snow fell.
>
> Justice failed.
>
> A crayon broke.

Now the pictures and ideas have some movement to them. The word taking the role of verb in each of these examples—*fell, failed, broke*—makes that movement happen.

Some writers believe nouns are more powerful than verbs; others believe the reverse. (F. Scott Fitzgerald, for instance, said, "All fine prose is based on the verbs carrying the sentences. They make sentences move.") As you experiment with these two parts of speech, you'll get to make your own decision. Just remember that these two parts of speech do very different things, and each has its own particular kind of power. When a word takes the role of a verb, its power is to *assert* something or to convey *action,* to make things *happen.*

Some of you may be thinking, *But what about verbs like* is *or* seemed? *They don't make much of anything happen.*

You're right. They don't. When it comes to conveying action, all verbs are not created equal. But before we explore the differences among verbs, let's play a bit with this particular part of speech.

Practice with Verbs: Internal Collecting

As you did with nouns, now collect any verbs that come to you as you keep your pen moving across the page. Use any form of the verb that comes most easily to you: *going, goes, go, to go,* and so on. (If you get stuck, repeat the same word over and over until your mind gives you another one.)

What did you notice as you did this?

Now make some of these verbs your own by using them to construct sentences. As a variation of this practice, select some nouns from your noun lists and some verbs from the list you just made. Now play with these by using them to make short sentences. (Add any other words you need to make complete sentences, but try to keep the sentences reasonably short.) Use any tense or form of the verb you like. Experiment with combining nouns and verbs that you have never before put together. You might, for instance, try putting abstract nouns with verbs that evoke physical action. (When I did this, I got sentences like, "Hope hypnotizes us," and "Solitude stills the heart.")

What happened as you did this exercise?

Read your sentences out loud. How do they sound to you?

Understanding Verbs: Kinds of Verbs

Now that you're getting a feel for verbs, let's look more closely at this part of speech. Verbs fall into four main categories, depending on the kind of action they convey.

1. THE BE VERBS: This includes all the forms of the verb *to be.* This verb conveys little action, and so some contemporary writers on style advise writers to do away with it altogether. But without this verb, our writing would be impoverished, for it enables us to express the *condition* of things: *Joe is sad. Mary is late.* In the hands of a skilled writer, the *be* verb directs our attention to nouns and adjectives. For instance:

> The Creative is heaven. It is round, it is the prince, the father, jade, metal, cold, ice; it is deep red, a good horse, an old horse, a lean horse, a wild horse, tree fruit.
>
> —*The I Ching (The Book of Changes)*

The fact is that the British have a totally private sense of distance. This is most visibly seen in the shared pretense that Britain is a lonely island in the middle of an empty green sea.
—Bill Bryson, *Notes from a Small Island*

2. THE LINKING VERBS: Verbs in this category—*become, seem, appear, look, grow, remain, feel,* and others—have more oomph, more energy to them than the *be* verb, though the degree of action they convey is still low. As their name implies, they serve to link one thing to another: *Joe seems sad. Mary appears happy.* Because these verbs don't have a lot of power themselves, sentences in which they appear must rely on other parts of speech for their energy. For example:

Suddenly the sea grew angry. The sky grew dark.
—Bob Barton, "The Honest Penny" in *The Bear Says North*

3. THE INTRANSITIVE VERBS: When we think of verbs, most likely the ones that come to our minds first will be the intransitives: *walk, run, skip, talk,* and so on. Verbs in this category do indeed possess energy—lots of it: *Joe yelled. Mary laughed. The bowl shattered.* Intransitive verbs can be recognized by their defining characteristic: The action they convey is complete in itself and requires no other words. When you want to add more verbs to your word hoard, simple intransitives are a good place to start. Here are a few examples:

Some of the world's foremost diplomats swear by [this barber's] scissors, marvel at his speed, and relax comfortably under his razor.
—Gay Talese, "New York Is a City of Characters"

Suddenly, foul weather came upon them. Thunder crashed, waves lashed, the rain came down in torrents. The ship drove and drove through heaving seas.
—Bob Barton, "The Honest Penny" in *The Bear Says North*

4. THE TRANSITIVE VERBS: Verbs in this category also convey action— so much so, in fact, that the action expressed by a transitive verb can only be completed by adding another word or group of words to the verb. When, in reading, we come to the end of a group of words like *John threw* or *Mary bought*, we feel a sense of incompleteness. We want to know *What* did John throw? *What* did Mary buy? The action of each verb must be carried over into another word or group of words (known as the *direct object*). For instance: *John threw the ball. Mary bought a new sweater.* Here are more examples:

> I met Symmington in the town later in the day.
> —Agatha Christie, *The Moving Finger*

> Young Frost rubbed his hands in anticipation of what was to follow … He nipped the man's cheeks, he tweaked his nose, he dove into his leather boots and froze his toes.
> —Bob Barton, "Frostbite," in *The Bear Says North*

Many verbs in English can be either transitive or intransitive; these verbs have both kinds of power, depending on how they are used. For example:

> Susan ate quickly. (*intransitive*)

> Susan ate the spaghetti. (*transitive*)

Your dictionary will tell you whether a given verb is transitive, intransitive, or both.

Practice with Verbs: The Kinds of Verbs

To know these four different kinds of verbs—not intellectually, but deep in your writer's bones—will give you the ability to make your writing move. Practice, with awareness, will help you develop this ability. Here are some practices to try:

1. Take the *be* verb and make sentences with it. What do you notice about these sentences?
2. Do the same thing with linking verbs.
3. Collect intransitive verbs. Choose some and make sentences with them.
4. Do the same thing with transitive verbs.
5. Take some time to read your sentences out loud and to notice how they sound to you.

6. Write a sentence using one kind of verb, then rewrite it using a different kind. Read the versions out loud and notice how they sound. Which do you prefer?

7. Take a passage from something you've written, and mark all the verbs. Label each verb with the name of the category it belongs to. Rewrite the passage using verbs that convey more action.

If you do these practices on a regular basis, you will quickly gain command of the four kinds of verbs. Then, as you write and revise, you'll be more aware of your available choices. With more possibilities to choose from, you will have an easier time writing sentences whose power comes from their verbs.

When you use a verb, it's helpful to know what category it belongs to. To make use of an *is* or a *seems* is not always bad, as some writers on style maintain. The question—the crucial question—is this: Which kind of verb will best serve your sentence?

Perhaps, though, you find yourself struggling to come up with intransitive and transitive verbs. Here are some games to play that will help add some of these powerful verbs to your word hoard.

Practice with Verbs: The Power of Verbs

Begin by collecting any verbs that occur to you. Now read through your list, listening for the verbs that seem to you to have the most power. Mark those verbs, and see if you can figure out what it is that gives them their power. Now see if you can collect more verbs that have that kind of power. If you get stuck, you may want to try some external collecting by browsing through a dictionary or thesaurus.

Practice with Verbs: "Body" Verbs

Bring your attention to your body, as you freewrite to collect verbs. Let your mind range over your body and collect verbs from different parts of it and from actions performed by those parts. Try to feel the action in your body. For example:

> arm, knee, kneel, bend, elbow, hand, face, smile, breathe, beat, crush, stamp

Now bring your attention to your senses. Collect verbs that express things the senses do.

Select some verbs from your lists and use them to make sentences.

Practice with Verbs: Verbs with Concrete Nouns

Pick a concrete noun—a thing or a person. What are some things it can *do?* Try to sense the action physically. Collect the verbs that express those actions. Keep bringing your attention back to your chosen object or person or animal. Keep picturing it. What does it *do?* For example:

> cat, howl, yowl, scream, scratch, pad, purr, complain, smile, sneer, snoop, sleep, sit, stare, smell, sniff, rip, nap, walk, run, climb, frighten, hunt, stalk, hover, wait

Now make sentences, not necessarily about your chosen noun, using these verbs.

Practice with Verbs: Verbs with Abstract Nouns

Bring your attention to your mind. Collect verbs that express things that the mind does, without going through the senses. For example:

> judge, question, admit, compare, analyze, compute, contrast, adjudicate, believe, indicate, infer, argue

What's the difference between verbs like these and the verbs you collected in the previous practices? Experiment with making sentences using some of these verbs.

Practice with Verbs: Verbs and Emotions

Bring your attention to your heart and emotions. List some emotions. Pick one. Collect the verbs that go with that emotion. For example:

> love, embrace, kiss, touch, caress, stroke, cuddle, hug

If you get stuck, try using a thesaurus or a dictionary. Then, once again, select some of these verbs and use them in sentences. How do these sound to you?

Practice with Verbs: Free Play

Make a list of nouns (or select nouns from previous lists). Make a list of verbs. Play with combining nouns and verbs into short sentences. Let your word mind experiment: *What would happen if I tried THIS?* No one will be grading your experiments, and if you don't let yourself make them, you'll never know whether a certain combination of noun and verb might in fact work.

All these games will build the flexibility and inventiveness of your word mind. Then, as you write and revise, you will be able to ask yourself, *What effect do I want to create in this sentence? What verb will help me do that?*

Understanding Verbs: Verbs and Time

In addition to conveying action, to one degree or another, the main verb in a sentence also tells readers *when* that action takes place: in the present, the past, or the future.

The way verbs indicate present, past, or future is with *tense*. Verbs reveal tense by the particular form they take. Any native speaker has already mastered these forms, and knows, without thinking about it, that *Joe laughs* indicates an action that is happening now, in the present; that *Joe laughed,* with the added *-ed,* indicates that Joe's burst of laughter happened in the past; and that *Joe will laugh* tells us that sometime in the future Joe will start laughing.

Many of the verbs we use in English follow this regular pattern of changed form. Some don't: They are called *irregular verbs.*

The three tenses—present, past, and future—are known as the *primary tenses.*

These primary tenses can often be replaced by *progressive tenses:*

Present progressive: *Joe is laughing.*

Past progressive: *Joe was laughing.*

Future progressive: *Joe will be laughing.*

There also exist in English what are called the *perfect tenses:*

Present perfect: *Joe has laughed.*

Past perfect: *Joe had laughed.*

Future perfect: *Joe will have laughed.*

We can, if we need to, combine the progressive and perfect forms of a verb to create the *progressive perfect tenses:*

Progressive present perfect: *Joe has been laughing.*

Progressive past perfect: *Joe had been laughing.*

Progressive future perfect: *Joe will have been laughing.*

Any good grammar book will help you review the tense of verbs, should you need to do that.

Understanding Verbs: Verbs and Pace

Since verbs convey action, they make a contribution to the pace of a sentence; that is, to the feeling of energy or activity it conveys to readers. One simple way to intensify the energy of a sentence is to repeat this part of speech; that is, to make use of more than one dynamic verb.

Understanding Verbs: Verb-Based Style

When a writer loads his sentences with verbs, the resulting passage can be said to exhibit a *verb-based style.* Here are some examples:

> Soon every field-mouse was sipping and coughing and choking, and wiping his eyes and laughing and forgetting he had ever been cold in all his life.
>
> —Kenneth Grahame, *The Wind in the Willows*

> How blessed that woman was. One girl pounded flour; another cut vegetables; another cooked; and another carried water from the well. One boy ploughed; one hunted; one fished; and one hauled some logs …
>
> —Kevin Crossley-Holland, "Children of the Tree"

Practice: Verb-Based Style

Do you like this kind of writing? Then try it for yourself, putting to work your newfound collection of verbs. Pick a subject and compose some sentences on it, concentrating on using mostly verbs. Or take a passage from something you've already written, and revise it so that verbs predominate in most of the sentences. Read your sentences out loud. What do you notice?

Content Parts of Speech 3: Adjectives

Grammarians tell us that when a word takes the role of an adjective, its function is to modify a noun. In other words, an adjective tells us more about the noun it modifies. It makes the noun more specific by giving to it particular qualities. That's the power of adjectives.

Adjectives help "dress" nouns. If you like, you can imagine an adjective as similar to an actor's props or costume, which help him play his role better. A villain, for instance, might be wearing a black coat and hat and carrying a cane that hides a knife. Adjectives can add to the power of a noun by making it more specific.

Listen to the difference in these sentences:

> The dog barked.
>
> The little brown dog barked.
>
> The man cried.
>
> The old man cried.

Adjectives add information to nouns, but they can be removed from a sentence, and the sentence will still make sense. If we remove the adjectives from the second versions of the sentence examples above, we still have complete sentences.

Practice with Adjectives: Internal Collecting

Let's begin our exploration of adjectives by collecting some, as we did with nouns and verbs. Keeping your pen moving across the page, bring adjectives out of your word hoard, ignoring other parts of speech. If you're not sure whether a word is an adjective or not, put it down anyway. (Then, later, look up the word in your dictionary.)

At the end of five or ten minutes, take a moment to reflect on what you noticed as you did this. Then read over your words, preferably out loud, and mark the ones you like. What do you notice about this group of words?

Probably you will find that when you say an adjective out loud and notice what happens in your mind, what you notice is that the adjective brings a noun along with it. The adjective *bright* might bring a picture of the sun; the adjective *happy* might bring a picture of a child at play. You are getting a demonstration of the linguistic reality that, to do their work, adjectives need nouns.

Practice with Adjectives: Adjectives and Nouns
Take some of the adjectives you marked in the last exercise, and put each one into a sentence. Notice what happens as you do this. Read your sentences out loud, and, if you like, reflect on what you are learning so far.

The Power of Adjectives
An adjective doesn't have the same power as a noun. It doesn't bring some person, place, or thing into existence in our minds in the same way a noun does. Nonetheless, adjectives have their own particular power, which skilled writers know how to use.

The power of adjectives is that they add something to nouns, making those nouns clearer or more specific or more precise. The writer Shirley Jackson has called adjectives (along with adverbs) "coloring words." Jackson tells apprentice writers that coloring words "must be used where they will do the most good." She reminds us that "not every action needs a qualifying adverb, not every object needs a qualifying adjective." Remember, she warns us:

> "Your reader probably has a perfectly serviceable mental picture of a lion; when a lion comes into your story you need not burden him with adjectives unless it is necessary, for instance, to point out that he is a green lion, some-

thing of which your reader might not have a very vivid mental picture."[20]

Jackson's advice reminds us that adjectives have to *add* something to the nouns they modify; they have to make the noun more vivid, more precise, more powerful. To tell your readers, for instance, that flowers in a garden were "pretty" is unnecessary; the word *pretty* adds nothing to the noun *flowers* because flowers are almost always pretty. Then, too, the adjective *pretty* is a general one, which won't add more detail to your readers' picture of the flowers.

To be effective, adjectives need to be carefully chosen. This doesn't mean that we must rack our brains (or our thesauruses) for polysyllables; it means that we need to understand the effect we want our adjectives to have and choose them accordingly.

Even one well-chosen adjective can "color" a noun. Take a simple sentence like *The hitter took a swing at the ball.* Now read the following sentences and notice the effect each one has:

> The young hitter took a swing at the ball.
>
> The old hitter took a swing at the ball.
>
> The tired hitter took a swing at the ball.
>
> The eager hitter took a swing at the ball.

What do you notice? The effect of each sentence is slightly different because the adjective before *hitter* is different. Each adjective adds a slightly different quality or "color" to the noun. It doesn't change the noun's basic meaning; it adds to it. (Sometimes adjectives also limit.)

Many people have been taught that using adjectives in writing is "wrong"; often writing teachers declare that good prose relies entirely on nouns and verbs. Such advice ignores the very real power that adjectives possess. While nouns and verbs provide the skeleton of sentences, it is often the adjective or adverb that "carries the news of the sentence," that moves the prose forward. One writer on style even says, "The modifier is the essential part of any sentence."[21] If you've never thought about adjectives in this way, you may want to do more practices using them.

Practice with Adjectives: Coloring

Write a few short sentences without any adjectives. Pick one that you like. Now write it over several times, adding different adjectives to the same noun. Make sure that each adjective you use adds some "news" to the sentence. Read your sentences over, out loud. What do you notice?

If you find this practice difficult, that may be because, like so many of us, you tend to make use only of adjectives that express a judgment: *great, awful, fabulous,* and so on—adjectives that are general and abstract. To use adjectives to add color to nouns, we need instead to choose adjectives that are specific and concrete.

Try collecting specific and concrete adjectives, and then do the "coloring" practice again.

Practice with Adjectives: External Collecting

As you read, notice adjectives and adjective-noun combinations that appeal to you. Collect them in your notebook and try them out in sentences of your own.

Pay special attention to those sentences where the writer has chosen an adjective that is exactly right for its purpose. For instance:

> The *quick dark* eyes in the *half-dead* face widened for a *shocked* moment.
>
> —Helen MacInnes, *The Venetian Affair*

> "Well, Mr. Bredon," said Mr. Pym, switching on an *automatic* smile and switching it off again with *nervous* abruptness, "and how are you getting on?"
>
> —Dorothy Sayers, *Murder Must Advertise*

Practice with Adjectives: Adjective-Noun Combinations

Another way to increase the power of your adjectives is to recognize, and avoid, generic adjective-noun combinations. *Beautiful flowers, restful sleep, delicious food:* such combinations are so familiar that they barely register in our minds. Here's a practice that will train you to look beyond the predictable when you add adjectives to nouns.

Make a list of nouns. Make a list of adjectives. Go back through each list and mark the words you like. Then pair adjectives and nouns in sentences, letting yourself experiment with different combinations of these parts of speech. Try making combinations of abstract and concrete nouns, abstract and concrete adjectives. Later, read your sentences out loud. What do you notice? What does your ear tell you?

Adjectives and adverbs are like seasonings in cooking. Herbs and spices can bring out the flavor of particular ingredients and add certain qualities to a dish. But you have to know how to use them. A pinch of cinnamon, a quarter-teaspoon of cardamom, and you have something delicious. But add too much, or too many spices, and you'll end up with a tasteless muddle. As Mark Twain once wrote, "When you catch an adjective, kill it. No, I don't mean utterly, but kill most of them—then the rest will be valuable."

So, how many adjectives can we use in a single sentence? The best way to find out is to read skilled writers, and then to experiment on your own.

Some writers rely only on the one-adjective-per-noun formula. But others know how to use more than one adjective with a single noun, thereby gaining more of the power this part of speech has to offer. Here are some examples:

> [The church] was an *old* one with two *grim* iron gates and a *long, low, shapeless stone* front.
> —Frank O'Connor, "First Confession"

> Miss Climpson felt *braced* and *ready*.
> —Dorothy Sayers, *Strong Poison*

> "That Sengupta, I swear," Sorava went on. "What a *skinny, scrawny, sniveling, driveling, mingy, stingy, measly, weasely* clerk!"
> —Salman Rushdie, *Haroun and the Sea of Stories*

Understanding Adjectives: Adjective-Based Style

When a writer understands the power of adjectives and is accomplished in their use, he or she may write sentences that display an *adjective-based style*. For example:

> The catcher (in baseball) has more equipment and more attributes than players at the other positions. He must be large,

brave, intelligent, alert, stolid, foresighted, resilient, fatherly, quick, efficient, intuitive, and impregnable.

—Roger Angell, *The New Yorker*

He was a big muscular young man with strong burning brown eyes, a big square jaw and massive cheekbones that might have been sculptured out of reddish rock.

—H.E. Bates "The Fabulous Mrs. V"

Practice: Adjective-Based Style

Play with writing sentences in which adjectives predominate. Read your sentences aloud. How do they sound to you?

Content Parts of Speech 4: Adverbs

Adverbs do the same work for verbs that adjectives do for nouns: They act as modifiers or "coloring words." For instance:

He ate *greedily.*

The cat leapt *gracefully* onto the chair.

The verbs in a sentence present action; the adverbs give additional information about that action: how it was done, or when, or where. Sometimes adverbs can do some additional work, by serving as modifiers for adjectives and other adverbs. Adverbs can't modify nouns.

Practice with Adverbs: Internal Collecting

Collect some adverbs. (If you're not sure whether some of your words are actually adverbs, put them down anyway.) Then choose a few from this list, and put them into short sentences. Try words you weren't sure about. Can you use them in a way that "colors" a verb? (Or another adverb? Or an adjective?) If not, they aren't adverbs. If you're still not sure, look up the words in a dictionary.

What do you notice in doing this practice?

Perhaps you notice that many of your adverbs are adjectives with the suffix -*ly* attached. To build your collection of adverbs, you may want to collect adjectives and see how many of them can become adverbs through the addition of this suffix.

Practice with Adverbs: External Collecting

As with the other parts of speech, you can add more adverbs to your word hoard simply by being on the lookout for them as you read, and as you listen to conversations. When you find adverbs, or adverb-verb combinations you like, write them in your notebook and make them your own by using them in practice sentences.

Practice with Adverbs: Verbs and Adverbs

Skilled writers don't rely exclusively on well-worn combinations of adverbs and verbs, or adverbs and adjectives. Their well-trained word minds enable them to come up with unusual and telling combinations. For instance:

> Louisa Mebbin adopted a protective elder-sister attitude towards money ... francs and centimes clung to her *instinctively* under circumstances which would have driven them *headlong* from less sympathetic hands.
>
> —Saki, "Mrs. Packletide's Tiger"

To get your own word mind out of adverb-verb ruts, try collecting verbs, then collecting adverbs, and then play with putting them together in various ways. See what you can come up with. Then create sentences in which you use some of these combinations.

Understanding Adverbs: Adverb-Based Style

When a passage relies heavily on adverbs for its meaning and effect, we can say that it exhibits an adverb-based style:

> But, for once, Nigel was wildly, abysmally wrong.
>
> —Nicholas Blake, *The Smiler with the Knife*

> But they were, undoubtedly, there.
>
> —Rosamunde Pilcher, "An Evening to Remember"

Content Parts of Speech 5: When Is a Noun Not a Noun?

Nouns as Adjectives and Adverbs

As you experiment with content parts of speech, collecting nouns and verbs, adjectives and adverbs, you will soon notice that many English words can play more than one role. Nouns, for instance, can sometimes take on the role of adjectives:

> The chill of the *night* made him shiver.
>
> The *night* chill made him shiver. (*Night* used as an adjective, modifying *chill*.)
>
> The long days of *summer* were never long enough.
>
> The long *summer* days were never long enough. (*Summer* used as an adjective, modifying *days*.)

Some nouns (certainly not all) can also play the role of adverb. For example:

> After dinner Simone went *home*.

Practice: Nouns as Adjectives and Adverbs

Collect some concrete nouns. Select some, and use them, as nouns, in sentences. Then see whether you can rewrite the sentences using some of the nouns as adjectives. Read the two versions of each sentence out loud. What do you notice?

If you like this technique, collect examples of its use by skilled writers, and then imitate their sentences. Look, too, for examples of nouns used as adverbs, and practice using them.

Nouns as Verbs

Nouns can also take on the role of verb in sentences. The word *moan*, for instance, can be a noun; it can also be a verb. The words *catch, throw, snow, move, dog, table, egg*—and hundreds of other nouns—can also take on the role of verb in sentences. We can write *The snow fell all day*, or *It snowed all day*. Such uses of nouns as verbs are so common that words that can play both roles are noted as both nouns and verbs in our dictionaries. Skilled writers know how to make good use of the versatility of such words.

Practice: Nouns as Verbs

Collect some nouns that can also be used as verbs. (Check your dictionary to be sure.) Write pairs of sentences for each word, using it first as a noun, then as a verb.

Try the same practice starting with collecting verbs.

What do you notice?

Practice: Nouns as Verbs

As you read, notice when a writer uses a noun as a verb. What is the effect of concrete nouns used as verbs? Abstract nouns? Collect examples of sentences where nouns are used effectively as verbs.

Many words in English can also take on new roles with the simple addition of a suffix (ending). We've already seen that many adverbs are adjectives with an *-ly* added. (We could also say that many adjectives are adverbs with the *-ly* ending removed!) We can also create adjectives by adding prefixes or suffixes to nouns and verbs. Many of our common adjectives were formed in this way: *beautiful (beauty+ful); happy (happ+y); contemptible (contempt+ible)*. In the next section we'll take a look at some other ways we can make use of this ability of English words to play multiple roles.

Before you move to that section, though, I recommend that you make sure you have a solid grasp of the basics of content parts of speech. The material in the next section is more advanced, and if you haven't acquired, through practice, a good understanding of the basics, you may be confused by what follows.

Content Parts of Speech 6: When Is a Verb Not a Verb?

Like actors in their plays, some words can take on more than one role in sentences; that is, they can "play" more than one part of speech. Verbs are particularly versatile in this respect: When they take certain specified forms, verbs can play the roles of noun, adjective, or adverb. To understand how this happens, we need to revisit the main functions of a verb—to convey the action of a sentence and to indicate tense. When a verb is doing this work—as the word *laughed* does in the sentence *Joe laughed loudly*—it is said to be in *finite* form. (Sometimes a verb doing this work is called a *predicate verb*.)

Verbs, though, can also find their ways into what grammarians call *nonfinite* forms; and it is in these forms that they serve, not as the main verb of a sentence, but as nouns or adjectives or adverbs. Verbs in these nonfinite forms are known as *verbals*—constructions that will quickly expand your options for making sentences.

When is a verb, then, not a verb? When it's a verbal. And when it's a verbal, it's one of four kinds: *a present participle; a past participle; a gerund; an infinitive.*

Verbals 1: The Present Participle

The present participle is the *-ing* form of a verb: *swimming, walking, giggling* are all present participles. We most frequently use the present participle as part of the main verb of a sentence, as in *The dog is barking.* (When we use a form of *be* with a present participle we are creating the *present progressive* tense of the verb.)

That present participle—the word ending in *-ing*—can also be used as an adjective: *The barking dog kept him up all night.*

Our vocabulary is filled with present participles acting as adjectives: *the flowing water; the driving rain; the shimmering light.*

Practice with Verbals: Present Participles

To get familiar with how present participles can be used as adjectives, first collect some verbs in their *-ing* form. And to make sure you know how to use these participles as part of the main verb of a sentence, try making sentences with the participles in that role. Then try using the participles as adjectives. In some cases you will need to add another word or two so that the participle can take this role. For instance:

> Mary is teasing the cat. (*teasing* as part of the main verb of the sentence; *is teasing*, the present progressive tense of the verb, *to tease*)
>
> A little teasing wind blew up. (*teasing* as an adjective)

Verbals 2: The Past Participle

The past participle is the form of a verb that we use to create past tense for the main verb in a sentence: *Joe baked the bread for two hours. The right fielder dropped the ball.* Often that past participle ends in *-ed;* many times, though, it does not. *Frozen, gave, spent, wrote* are examples of past participles that do not end in *-ed.* Like its sister, the present participle, the past participle can also take on the role of adjective: the *baked* bread; a *dropped* football; *boiled* eggs; *frozen* food.

> Joe's *baked* bread sat on the counter, giving off an enticing smell.
>
> The *painted* fence shone in the sunlight.

Practice with Verbals: Past Participles

Collect some past participles. (You may find it easier to do this by writing some short sentences in the past tense, and then extracting the past participles.) See how many of them can serve as adjectives, and write sentences using them in this way. (Note that not all past and present participles can be used as modifiers.)

What did you notice doing these practices? Were you surprised at how many familiar adjectives are actually present and past participles taking on the role of adjectives? Perhaps you also noticed that using participles in this way lets you get more information into a sentence. Even more important, when we make use of participles and other verbals, we can get the energy of a verb—that feeling of action—into a sentence without having to add extra main verbs. The ability to do this is one of the marks of a highly skilled writer. For example:

> *Peeping* through another glass-*panelled* door, [Miss Rossiter] observed Mr. Ingleby *seated* on a *revolving* chair with his feet on the cold radiator, and *talking* with great animation to a young woman in green, *perched* on the corner of the writing-table.
>
> —Dorothy Sayers, *Murder Must Advertise*

> Jonathan Argyll lay contentedly on a large slab of Carrara marble, soaking up the mid-morning sun, smoking a cigarette and considering the infinite variety of life.
>
> —Iain Pears, *The Bernini Bust*

Verbals 3: Gerunds

As present participles, in their -*ing* form, verbs can also play the role of nouns. When they take on this role, they are known as *gerunds*.

> *Swimming* is my favorite sport.
>
> I love *reading*.

Practice with Verbals: Gerunds

Go back to your list of present participles and select some that can serve as nouns. Try them out in sentences in this role, adding any other words you need.

Verbals 4: Infinitives

When a verb is in its "infinitive" form, it starts with "to." In this case, the word *to* is not considered a preposition, but a part of the verb. When a verb is in this form, it can take other roles:

1. AS A NOUN:

> *To see* is *to know*.

2. AS AN ADJECTIVE:

> The dog *to watch* in the competition is the brown-and-black one.

3. AS AN ADVERB:

> We went out *to buy* food for dinner.

Practice with Verbals: Infinitives

Collect some infinitives. Try them out in the role of noun, adjective, and adverb.

Practice with Verbals: Reading for Verbals

The best way to learn how to use verbals is to see how the pros do it. As you read your favorite writers, notice the verbals they use. Write down some of their sentences containing verbals, and then imitate their use of past and present participles, gerunds, and infinitives.

Practice with Verbals: Writing with Verbals

Do some freewriting and, as you come up with things to say, try at the same time to concentrate your word mind on using verbals. You may feel, at first, very awkward. Just remember how you felt when you first tried to swing a tennis racket or a baseball bat to hit a ball, or how you felt when you got on a bicycle for the first time. Keep doing this practice, and the ones above, and eventually verbals will be yours to use whenever you wish.

You may also want to revise passages of your writing, seeing where you can use verbals to make your sentences stronger. Don't forget to test the results by reading your work out loud and listening to how it sounds.

The ability to use verbals well, you'll find, will vastly expand your options for constructing sentences. Though it may take you a while to feel comfortable with them, once you have added this particular tool to your repertoire, I suspect you'll be delighted with what it can do for your writing.

A Word About Pronouns

A pronoun is a word that substitutes—or "stands in"—for a noun, like an understudy substituting for a principal actor. Which pronoun would you use to substitute for *The boy? The girl? The dogs?* Pronouns allow us, among other things, to avoid having to repeat a noun over and over. In so doing, they give us the opportunity to direct our reader's attention to other information in a sentence.

Most likely, if you are a native English speaker, you have absorbed all you need to know about using pronouns from listening to other people talk and from your reading. If, however, you get confused about whether you should write *me* or *I,* or *she* or *her,* in a given sentence, I recommend that you spend some time reviewing how pronouns work with the help of a good grammar book.

A Word About Interjections

Wow! Far out! Awesome! No way!

Grammarians call words like these *interjections.* My grammar book says *interjection* is the name for words that "appear intrusively in a sentence and carry some force or charge of feeling." We use interjections all the time when we speak informally, and they can also be used in writing, especially when we are putting words into the mouths of our characters.

Content Parts of Speech 7: Developing Your Own Style

Some writers on style deplore adjectives and adverbs: *Avoid them!* they proclaim. Others tell us never to use forms of the verb *to be.* There are even a few who condemn nouns. Rather than listening to any of these voices, consider this alternative way of using parts of speech: Remember that every content part of speech has its own particular power, and that, if you practice, you can learn to use that power for your own purposes. You can train your word mind to be aware of the possibilities of nouns and verbs, adjectives and adverbs. And you can train it to make choices among these content parts of speech. The choices you make will help create your own individual voice on the page, your own writing style.

For style is not a matter of diction alone. While the particular words we choose are, naturally, essential to the making of our sentences, the choices we make about how to put those words together is equally important. Do we want, for instance, to write: *He walked quickly?* Or *He walked with a quick step?* Or *His step quickened?* Or even *He walked with a quickness that amazed her?*

Skilled writers know how to listen not only to the meaning of their words, but also to what those words are *doing* in sentences. In the moment of composition, the mind of a skilled writer considers possibilities and makes choices among them, just as, at the crack of the bat, the mind of a skilled outfielder considers possible routes to the ball and chooses among them. (Instinct, as well as training, plays a part in this process. And writers have an advantage over athletes: We get to revise our work.) The outfielder relies on years of training, on thousands of catches made in practice, to make the choice that enables him to catch the ball. Writers, too, need to practice their "moves." If we want to develop skill in putting words together, then we need to practice paying attention to what our words are *doing* in sentences, as well as to what they mean.

Practice with content parts of speech will wake up a part of your word mind that may have been asleep all your life. And then, when you sit down to write a story, a poem, or an essay, you'll find you have new fluency in constructing sentences. You'll be amazed, I suspect, at the things you will be able to do with words, at the new techniques you have for finding just the right words and for putting those words together.

No one can write well without technique, just as no one can play music without what musicians call "chops." Technique, craft, skill— call it what you like; you must have it to keep your reader's attention. Parts of speech are one of a writer's most important tools. And the only way to make these tools your own is to practice using them.

In the next section, we turn from content parts of speech to structural words.

PARTS OF SPEECH 2: STRUCTURAL WORDS

Along with the four content parts of speech (and the pronouns and interjections) we have considered so far, English also contains another essential group of words. Traditionally, grammarians have considered these as parts of speech; today they are more likely to call them *structural words* or *function words*. These are the small—and indispensable—words that let us make connections among content parts of speech: determiners, prepositions, and conjunctions. English contains about two hundred of these words, the most frequently used words in our language.

Though these words are small and unobtrusive—who notices *an* or *the*, *in* or *on*?—they play essential roles in our language: Most important, they join content words into groups to make sentences. While we can use structural words without thinking about them, understanding what they do takes us one step further towards understanding how to compose sentences.

Structural Words 1: Determiners

Determiners are the words that indicate to readers that a noun is coming up soon in the sentence. (They are also known as *indicators.*) Determiners in English include: *the, an, a* (also known as *articles*); words like *these* and *those* (when used before nouns); and numbers used before nouns. Determiners are, to readers, what highway signs are to drivers: *Look out!* a determiner tells readers, *Noun ahead!*

You can see how determiners work in sentences like these:

> *The* girl bought a dress.
>
> *The* package was heavy.
>
> *One* boy stayed behind with *that* horse.

Determiners always come *before* the noun. It's important to note that nouns are sometimes *not* preceded by a determiner, as in these sentences:

> If snow falls, we'll have to stay indoors.
>
> Bring food with you when you visit.

Just as a sign for an upcoming exit can be a quarter of a mile or more from the exit itself, so can the determiner be separated from the upcoming noun by one or more other words. Read these sentences slowly, preferably out loud, and see if you can hear, as well as see, the distance from the determiner to its noun.

> *The* blonde girl bought *a* new green dress.
>
> *One* wide-eyed eager boy stayed behind with *that* large, shaggy, entrancing horse.

> Mrs. Jennings, Lady Middleton's mother, was *a* good-humoured, merry, fat, elderly woman, who talked *a* great deal, seemed very happy, and rather vulgar.
>
> —Jane Austen, *Sense and Sensibility*

When we add a determiner to a noun, or to a noun plus one or more adjectives, we create what's called a *noun phrase*. A noun phrase, grammarians tell us, is a group of words that "goes together" and that is headed by a noun.

Practice with Determiners: Making Noun Phrases
Experiment with putting nouns together with determiners, then add some adjectives between the two. Read your experiments out loud. How do they sound? Try putting some of them into sentences and read those out loud. What does your ear tell you?

Practice with Determiners: Reading for Noun Phrases
To continue developing your awareness of noun phrases, look for them in sentences by your favorite writers. If you wish, copy one of their sentences and then imitate the structure of the noun phrases in it, using exactly the same number of adjectives between determiner and noun as the writer did.

Structural Words 2: Prepositions

Of. At. To. With. In. These are some of the many words in English that are known as *prepositions*. Prepositions are words that show a *relationship* between two or more things and/or people in a sentence. They link the noun, noun phrase, or pronoun that follows the preposition to another word in the sentence, indicating such relationships as location (*The cat is on the table.*) and direction (*The men strolled across the room.*) and time (*I'll see you after the game.*). Native English speakers can use most prepositions without thinking about them.

What are some prepositions you're familiar with? Take a minute to jot them down.

Here are some of the most common prepositions in English:

> about, across, after, against, along, among, around, as, at,
> below, before, behind, beneath, beside, between, beyond, by,
> down, during, except, for, from, in, inside, into, like, near, of,
> off, on, onto, out, outside, over, past, since, through, toward,
> under, until, up, with, without

Except in rare instances, prepositions never stand alone in a sentence; they always function as part of a group of words, known as a *prepositional phrase*. We make prepositional phrases like this:

> preposition + noun (with or without a determiner) or pronoun = prepositional phrase

Here are some examples of prepositional phrases:

> in darkness, of home, around the town, at the beach, in the
> days, of winter, on the street, with kindness

Prepositional phrases sometimes include an adjective (or two) before the noun. For example:

> in the hot soup, on the wooden table, with a plastic spoon

Prepositional phrases can also combine to make longer phrases: *in the dark days/ of winter.* (The slash mark indicates the two prepositional phrases that make up the longer one.)

Practice with Prepositions: Making Prepositional Phrases

Collect some nouns and some prepositions, and then combine them into prepositional phrases. Read your phrases out loud. What do you notice?

Then rewrite your phrases adding some adjectives. What do you notice now, when you read these aloud?

Like noun phrases, prepositional phrases are an essential writer's tool. Take some time to build your facility in making them. Once you feel comfortable constructing prepositional phrases, select some and put them into sentences. Read your sentences out loud. What do you hear?

Practice with Prepositions: Reading for Prepositional Phrases
As you did with other parts of speech, read your favorite authors and notice the prepositional phrases they use. Copy some of these sentences, and imitate the way your chosen writer uses prepositional phrases. Some examples:

> He drummed his fingers *on the leather of the steering-wheel*, toyed *with the radio-cassette*, eased his head back *onto the padded headrest*.
> —Ian Rankin, *Knots and Crosses*

> We came *on the wind of the carnival*.
> —Joanne Harris, *Chocolat*

Structural Words 3: Conjunctions

Conjunctions are a versatile part of speech: They have several important roles to play. Overall, though, their function is to join one element of a sentence to another element. For now, let's pay attention only to how conjunctions can join content parts of speech. The conjunctions we use most frequently to perform this task are ones we use all the time: *and* and *but*. For example:

> Susie *and* Brian went to the party. (The conjunction *and* joins two nouns.)

> Susie giggled *and* laughed. (The conjunction *and* joins two verbs.)

> Susie's hat was soft *and* fluffy. (The conjunction *and* joins two adjectives.)

> Brian drove fast *but* safely. (The conjunction *but* joins two adverbs.)

Note that when we use conjunctions in this way they *must* join two parts of speech *of the same kind*. So we can use these conjunctions to join a noun and a noun, or an adjective and an adjective, but not a noun and a verb, or an adjective and an adverb. (*And* and *but* are known as known as *coordinating conjunctions*; this particular category of conjunction also includes *or, nor, yet,* and *so,* but not all of these can join two parts of speech.)

Note, too, that when we combine two (or more) nouns in this way, we are creating a *noun phrase.* Two or more verbs joined with a conjunction make *a verb phrase.* And we can make adjective phrases and adverb phrases in the same way.

Sometimes writers use pairs of conjunctions to join two parts of speech; *and/or; either/or; neither/nor; not only ... but also:*

> Joe will eat either the apples or the oranges.
>
> Joe will eat neither the apples nor the oranges.
>
> Joe ate not only the apples but also the oranges.

Practice with Conjunctions: Combine Parts of Speech

Collect some nouns. Then, using *and* or *but*, combine selected nouns into noun phrases. Then use some of these noun phrases in sentences. Read these sentences out loud. What do you notice?

Try the same thing with verbs, adjectives, and adverbs in turn.

Practice with Conjunctions: Read for Conjunctions

When you look at the writing of professionals, you will find lots of conjunctions. For now, pay attention only to how conjunctions join two nouns or two verbs (including verbals), two adjectives or two adverbs. Here's Ian Rankin again:

> She had a real inspector's eyes: they worked into your conscience, sniffing out guilt *and* guile *and* drive, seeking give.
> —Ian Rankin, *Knots and Crosses*

> I spent a long day wandering aimlessly *and* happily along residential streets *and* shopping streets, eavesdropping on conversations at bus stops *and* street corners, looking with interest in the windows of greengrocers *and* butchers *and* fishmongers, reading fly-posters *and* planning applications, quietly absorbing.
> —Bill Bryson, *Notes from a Small Island*

Then Mowgli picked out a shady place, *and* lay down *and* slept while the buffaloes grazed round him.

—Rudyard Kipling, *The Jungle Book*

Although structural words are small, and although they may seem un-important, they provide writers with a most useful tool: the ability to create phrases. In the next chapter we'll explore the craft of making and using phrases.

TAKE TIME TO REFLECT

What have you learned through the practices in this chapter. Do you need to review any techniques before moving on?

PARTS OF SPEECH: A REVIEW

When we say a word "is" a certain part of speech—for instance, "The word *home* is a noun"— we are not making a statement about the nature of that word; we are explaining what it *does* in a sentence. Parts of speech are best thought of as labels for the *kind of work* a word (or a group of words) is doing in a sentence. It's important to remember this concept, because one of the things skilled writers know about English words is that they can frequently do different kinds of work. For example: *I love my* home (*home* as a noun); *I always root for the* home *team* (*home* as an adjective); *After the game we went* home (*home* as an adverb). Skilled writers have trained their minds to consider, not only the meaning and qualities of words, but the work they do. The more you practice using words in different roles (within the limits of sense, of course), the more flexible and inventive your word mind will become.

CONTENT PARTS OF SPEECH

NOUN: A noun *names* things—people, places, other living beings, objects, ideas, emotions, etc.

VERB: A verb identifies the condition of a noun, or tells what action a noun performs. Verbs can take two forms: *finite* verbs (also known as *predicate* verbs), which have tense, and which serve as the main verb of a sentence, and *nonfinite* verbs, which do not. *Nonfinite* verbs are also known as *verbals*.

ADJECTIVE: An adjective modifies (gives more information about or limits) a noun.

ADVERB: An adverb modifies a verb (and, sometimes, an adjective or another adverb).

STRUCTURAL PARTS OF SPEECH

DETERMINER: A determiner signals a noun. When a noun is preceded by a determiner, the two words create a *noun phrase* that, in its entirety, works as a noun in its sentence.

PREPOSITION: A preposition joins with a noun or pronoun (known as the *object* of the preposition) to form a *prepositional phrase*. Prepositional phrases serve as adjectives and adverbs.

CONJUNCTION: A conjunction's work is *joining* elements of a sentence (single words, phrases, and clauses). There are two main kinds of conjunction: coordinating (*and, but, for, or, nor, yet, so*) and subordinating (see Chapter 12). A coordinating conjunction must always join elements of the same kind; for instance, *noun + noun* or *verb + verb*. When a coordinating conjunction joins two such words, the result is a *phrase* serving as a single part of speech.

OTHER PARTS OF SPEECH

PRONOUN: A pronoun substitutes for a noun.

INTERJECTION: An interjection is a word or phrase structurally unrelated to a sentence, serving to express emotion or to make an exclamation.

CHAPTER 9

MAKING PHRASES

....

When you write, you make a point not by subtracting, as though you had sharpened a pencil, but by adding.

....

—JOHN ERSKINE

One of the most important characteristics of the English language is the way we group words together and pause slightly at the boundaries between groups. In his excellent book *The Movement of English Prose*, Professor Ian Gordon calls this grouping process "segmentation"; he shows it's been part of our language since its earliest days, spoken and written by the Anglo-Saxons. These groupings—what I've been referring to as *phrases*—are not random: word-groups are created and pauses are made in order to create meaning. So, while we need to know how to choose individual words, if we want to excel as writers, we also need to know how to construct and employ phrases—not the stock phrases of ordinary speech ("nice day!"), but *phrase patterns*.

To make use of this tool, we need to understand more clearly what phrases are and how they work.

WHAT IS A PHRASE?

Making phrases, grouping words together as we speak, comes naturally to us: Our daily conversations are thick with stock phrases like "no way!" or "too bad!" But the kind of phrase writers need to know about is different: It's not a group of specific words—it's *a structural unit of spoken and written language.* When you listen to someone speak, or you read their sentences, a phrase is a small group of words that your brain processes as a single unit of meaning. A phrase is any group of words that makes sense together, a group of words that forms a coherent unit.

So far we've looked at three kinds of phrases we can make use of: noun phrases, like *the black cat;* prepositional phrases, like *in the morning;* and compound phrases (phrases using coordinating conjunctions), like *black and white.* If you read phrases like these out loud and try pausing before you get to the end of each group, you will notice that your mind demands the last word. Try it: *the black* ... ("The black *what?*" asks the mind.) Or *in the* ... ("In the *what?*" the mind wants to know.) Those incomplete phrases make no sense, and the mind wants words to make sense.

Now try reading each phrase in its entirety and notice what happens in your mind. *The black cat.* ("Okay," the mind says, "those words make sense together.") *In the morning. Black and white.*

Phrases—along with single words—are the building blocks of sentences. Consider a sentence like this: *In the morning the black cat ran away.* As we read (or listen to) this sentence, our brains automatically search for groupings of words, for words that "make sense" together. So we instantly process *In the morning* as one group, *the black cat* as another group, and *ran away* as a third group.

Our ability to put words together like this, to hear words in groups, enables us to quickly make sense of speech or written sentences. If we had to consciously add every word to the one that follows it, even the simplest utterance would take so much time to process that we would easily become lost or confused.

So grouping words together into phrases is one of the natural abilities of the language part of our brain. Skilled writers (who are always experienced readers) know this, and either through intuition or training they make deliberate use of phrases when they write. We can follow their example. To do this, we need to tune our writer's ear to phrases.

Practice with Phrases: Tune Your Ear to Phrases

Although you may feel that you've already spent quite a lot of time on phrases, I encourage you to go back to your lists of phrases (from the previous chapter) and read some of those out loud. Listen to the ways the words "go together." Experiment with reading a phrase and stopping before the end. What do you notice? Try to start getting a "feel" for the structure of phrases.

Practice with Phrases: Freewrite with Phrases

Pick a subject to write about, or just begin writing without anything particular in mind. As you write, keep your word mind focused on using noun phrases, prepositional phrases, and phrases using *and* or *but*. Afterwards read over what you've written, out loud, paying particular attention to the phrases. What do you notice?

Practice with Phrases: Read for Phrases

Take a passage from the work of a writer you like and read it out loud, slowly, noticing the phrases. (You will probably find other kinds of phrases than the ones you have learned so far; just take note of these and set them aside, for now.) Imitate the writer's use of noun phrases, prepositional phrases, and phrases with conjunctions.

Phrases as Patterns

One of the things you may notice in doing these practices is that, while every phrase you come up with makes use of different words, certain phrases do resemble certain other phrases. *The black cat,* for example, resembles *the happy boy. In the morning* resembles *on the table.* That's because, when we put words together into phrases, we are following certain patterns that are characteristic of the English language. So, rather than seeing phrases as groups of particular words (as in stock phrases), we can see that phrases are *structural patterns.*

The black cat and *the happy boy* make use of different words (except for *the*), but they share a structure: *determiner + adjective + noun.*

In the morning and *on the table* also share a structure: *preposition + determiner + noun.*

It's because these phrase patterns are so familiar to us that we can slide different words into each slot of the pattern without even thinking about what we are doing. But bringing these structural patterns into conscious awareness provides us with another extremely important tool for writing. When we are aware of the different phrase patterns available to us, we have more choices for composing sentences. We don't have to write using only those patterns we know well; we can add new ones to our repertoire. We'll be doing just that in upcoming chapters.

Practice with Phrases: Some Basic Phrase Patterns
Take the following two basic phrase patterns and play with them. How many phrases using the pattern *determiner + adjective + noun* can you come up with? How many phrases can you invent using the pattern *preposition + determiner + noun?* What do you notice in doing this?

Now try combining one or more of your phrases from the first group with one or more of your phrases from your second group? What do you notice?

One of the things you will probably notice is that you have created sentence beginnings. If you like, go ahead and complete the sentences.

Now try making some phrases using *and* or *but* between two or more content words. Then use these phrases to construct sentences.

Phrases as Content Parts of Speech
In order to make skillful use of phrases, there are several important things we need to remember. First: A phrase is a group of words that makes sense together and functions as a unit. Second: Phrases are composed using established *patterns* of content and structural parts of speech. Third: Phrases, like single words, function in sentences as *content parts of speech.*

This third characteristic of phrases is the most important for writers: *The power of phrases resides in their ability to act as nouns and verbs, adjectives and adverbs.* When we know (not intellectually, but practically) how to use phrases, we can compose sentences not just with individual words, but with single words *and* groups of words. The realm of possibilities open to us then is limitless; knowing how to make use of phrases is one of the secrets to becoming a skilled writer.

So let's review some of the basic ways in which well-trained writers use phrases as content parts of speech.

Making Noun Phrases

A noun phrase takes the role of a noun in sentences. The phrase acts as a single unit and works as a single part of speech. If we write *Boys are silly,* the word *boys* is acting as a noun. If we write *The boys are silly,* the phrase *the boys* acts as a noun. Here are some basic ways to make noun phrases:

1. The easiest way to make a noun phrase is to use this pattern:

> determiner + noun = noun phrase

2. A noun phrase can also include adjectives:

> the purple flowers
>
> a dark, cold day
>
> the long and deserted road
>
> the bright cloudless sky

Here's the pattern we use to make this very common noun phrase:

> determiner + adjective(s) + noun = noun phrase

3. Sometimes a writer will create a noun phrase by combining a noun with adjectives, without a determiner:

> Bright yellow flowers filled the garden.

Such noun phrases are made according to this pattern:

> adjective(s) + noun = noun phrase

4. We can also create noun phrases by adding nouns together using the conjunction *and:*

> Boys and girls, come out to play!

The patterns for this kind of noun phrase are:

> Noun + conjunction + noun = noun phrase
>
> Determiner + noun + conjunction + determiner + noun
> = noun phrase

5. A noun phrase can also be made by combining a possessive noun or pronoun with another noun: *John's dog* or *Mary's blue sweater*. Here's the pattern:

> Possessive noun (or pronoun) (+ adjective) + noun = noun
> phrase

6. Noun phrases can also be constructed from a gerund (a present participle acting as a noun) and from an infinitive (the "to" form of a verb) by adding more words. There are a number of patterns for using these verbals. Here the pattern is: gerund + prepositional phrase = noun phrase:

> Going to law school is her dream.

Here the pattern is: infinitive + prepositional phrase = noun phrase:

> To go to law school is her dream.

The most important thing to remember about noun phrases is that they act just like nouns: They can play any role in a sentence that a noun can.

Practice with Phrases: Playing with Noun Phrases

Here are some "games" to play with noun phrases:

1. **USE NOUN PHRASES:** Collect as many noun phrases as you can. Select from your list some phrases you like, and use them to construct sentences. Remember that noun phrases can take any role in a sentence that a noun can—try them as complements or direct objects or indirect objects. (If you don't know what these terms mean, you'll find out in the next chapter.)

2. **SUBSTITUTE NOUN PHRASES:** Write some simple sentences using only nouns, or nouns preceded by determiners. Now rewrite these sentences, substituting longer noun phrases for each noun. What do you notice in doing this practice?

3. **FREEWRITE WITH NOUN PHRASES:** Do some freewriting and keep your word mind focused on using noun phrases. What happens?

4. **READ FOR NOUN PHRASES:** When you read, notice how the writer makes use of noun phrases, then imitate those sentences. Here are some examples:

> He had *faded blue eyes, a thin melancholy nose,* and *a vague but courteous manner.*
>
> —Agatha Christie, *The Secret of Chimneys*

> *The modern Orpheus* doesn't have to be torn apart by harpies. *Their place* has been taken by *the fans* lying in wait at *club entrances and exits, the journalists and photographers, the autograph seekers, the professional and amateur Peeping Toms, the hosts of "friends and relatives"* demanding *financial assistance and favors, the blackmailers, psychopaths, and schemers."*
>
> —Wislawa Szymborska, "Blowing Your Own Horn"

Making Verb Phrases

A verb phrase is a group of words that "go together" and that, together, take on the role of a verb in a sentence. Verb phrases can be constructed according to several different patterns. Here are three of them:

1. ADD TWO OR MORE FINITE VERBS TOGETHER: *Jennifer skipped and hopped down the street. Skipped and hopped* is a verb phrase.

verb + conjunction + verb = verb phrase

2. ADD A FINITE VERB AND AN ADVERB: *Jennifer skipped happily down the street. Skipped happily* is a verb phrase.

verb + adverb = verb phrase

3. ADD AUXILIARY VERBS TO THE MAIN VERB. (Auxiliary verbs are also known as "helper verbs." If you're not sure how they work, consult your grammar book.) Auxiliary verbs provide us with more than one way of conveying a particular action. For instance, we might write *John walks down the hall,* or *John is walking down the hall.* If we decide to use *is walking* instead of *walks,* we have created a verb phrase—two words acting as one unit.

auxiliary verb + main verb = verb phrase

Practice with Phrases: Play with Verb Phrases

1. Combine verbs using *and*: Collect some verbs. Choose some you like and combine them into verb phrases using the conjunction *and.* Now put these verb phrases into sentences. What do you notice?
2. Combine a verb and one or more adverbs: Make a list of verbs. Make a list of adverbs. Combine one verb with one or more adverbs. Now put these verb phrases into sentences.
3. Use auxiliary verbs: Write some sentences in which you use only single-word verbs. Now try adding auxiliary (helper) verbs to make verb phrases. What do you notice?
4. Read for verb phrases, and note which pattern the writer is using, then imitate his sentence. For example:

> There was nobody there, nor any trace of anybody, but I *shuttered and bolted* all the windows ...
> —John Buchan, *The Thirty-Nine Steps*

Making Adjective and Adverb Phrases

We can also make phrases that take on the roles of adjectives or adverbs in sentences. Here are three basic ways to do this:

1. We can combine two adjectives, or two adverbs, using the conjunction *and.* (We can't combine an adjective and an adverb, though.) For example:

The day was *bright and sunny*.

Joe ran *quickly and easily* down the street.

Here are the patterns we use:

adjective + *and* + adjective = adjective phrase

adverb + *and* + adverb = adverb phrase

2. We can make use of prepositional phrases in the role of adjective or adverb, giving us another important tool for adding information to nouns and verbs. For instance:

The man *in the blue hat* stood up. *(in the blue hat* is a prepositional phrase serving as an adjective.)

Joe ran quickly and easily *down the street*. (*Down the street* is a prepositional phrase serving as an adverb.)

Typical patterns for using prepositional phrases as modifiers are:

noun + prepositional phrase used as adjective

verb + prepositional phrase used as adverb

3. We can use verbals—present and past participles, and infinitives—as adjectives and adverbs. For example:

The teddy bear, *forgotten in the rush*, lay in a heap on the floor. (*Forgotten in the rush* is a participial phrase serving as an adjective, modifying the noun *teddy bear*.)

The pattern for using participial phrases as adjectives is:

present or past participle + prepositional phrase = participial phrase

Here's an example of using an infinitive as a modifier:

Tom reached out his hand *to touch her face*. (*To touch her face* is an infinitive phrase serving as an adverb, modifying the verb *reached*.)

In this case, the pattern is:

infinitive + noun or noun phrase or pronoun = infinitive phrase

The use of verbals as adjectives and adverbs is an extremely useful technique, but it's also a little tricky. You may need to review the information on verbals in Chapter 8.

Practice with Phrases: Play with Adjective and Adverb Phrases

1. Construct phrases made up of adjectives (or adverbs) joined by *and*.
2. Construct prepositional phrases you can use to modify nouns or verbs. Select some of these adjective or adverb phrases and use them to make sentences. Read the sentences out loud. What do you notice?
3. Construct participial phrases, using present or past participles or infinitives, according to the patterns above.
4. Read some sentences by your favorite writer out loud. Notice how he makes use of adjective and adverb phrases, and imitate those sentences. Here are some examples:

The sun blazed *in the bat's eyes*, so that everything looked *blurred and golden*.

—Randall Jarrell, *The Bat-Poet*

The taxi vanished *into the black tunnel of the main souk with a jarring of gears and another yell of its horn.*

—Mary Stewart, *The Gabriel Hounds*

Here there was a considerable colony of houseboats—boats *ancient and modern, bright and drab,* barges and landing craft and converted lifeboats—all *huddled together in tatty confusion* and all *approached across the salting by an old and rickety wooden footbridge.*

—Andrew Garve, *The Cuckoo Line Affair*

COMPOSING WITH PHRASES

If making and using phrases is new to you, take time to become comfortable with doing it before you continue. While it's easy to understand this material intellectually, if you don't give yourself the opportunity to grasp it fully by doing the practices (many, many times!), the techniques won't be available to you when you sit down to a work-in-progress.

Once you've mastered phrase making, you will have more freedom of choice as you write. Do you want to write a certain sentence using only single content words? Or would you rather replace some of those content words with phrases? Listen, for instance, to these different ways of constructing one sentence:

> Mr. Forbes is evil. (*proper noun + verb + adjective*)
>
> Mr. Forbes is an evil man (*proper noun + verb + noun phrase*)
>
> Mr. Forbes is evil in every way. (*proper noun + verb + adjective + prepositional phrase serving as adverb*)
>
> Mr. Forbes is a man of evil heart. (*proper noun + verb + noun phrase that includes a prepositional phrase serving as an adjective*)

These examples illustrate three possible ways to replace a single content part of speech with one or more phrases:

1. Replace one word with a phrase. In the second example above, the adjective *evil* becomes a noun phrase, *an evil man*. The adjective could also be replaced with an adjective phrase, such as *evil and scary*.
2. Add one or more phrases to a single content word. In the example above, *evil* becomes *evil in every way*.
3. Embed a phrase within another phrase: *a man of evil heart* is a noun phrase that has a prepositional phrase embedded within it.

Practice with Phrases: Substitute Phrases

Begin with a short sentence. Then experiment with each of the above ways of using phrases instead of single content parts of speech. How many ways can you find to say the same thing?

As you practice making phrases, two things will eventually happen. First, you will find that when you write or revise, your word mind will now provide you with more options for putting words together. It will say to you things like *Remember to try noun phrases.* Or *What about adding another verb here?* And, second, you will begin to make certain kinds of choices consistently, because you like them, because they feel right to you, because they sound good to your ear. In this way, you will continue to develop your own writing style.

And so I encourage you to try different ways of naming, showing action, and adding information to nouns and verbs. The more you play, the more you are practicing the craft of creating sentences. And the more you practice, the sooner you will get to the place where, as you write, phrases will come easily to your mind.

Here are some more ways to practice using phrases:

Practice with Phrases: Free Play with Phrases

Collect some content words. Collect some structural words. Select some of each and make phrases. Add some of these phrases together to make longer phrases. Use some of these phrases to make sentences. Read your sentences out loud. What do you notice?

Practice with Phrases: Review Kinds of Phrases

Repeat the above practice, but this time, once you have collected words, give yourself some specific kind of phrase to compose. For instance, you might say, "I'm going to make some noun phrases, using the pattern *determiner + adjective + noun*," or "I'm going to make verb phrases using the pattern *verb + and + verb*."

Practice with Phrases: Free Play with Phrases

In separate lists, collect some noun phrases, some adjective phrases, some verb phrases, and some adverb phrases. From each list select one phrase and put these together into a sentence. For example, from your noun list you might select a phrase like *The boy.* From your list of adjective phrases you might select a phrase like *in the blue jacket* (a prepositional phrase acting as an adjective). From your list of verb phrases you might select a phrase like *laughs and sings.* Put them together and you get this: *The boy in the blue jacket laughs and sings.* Your sentences don't have to make sense. Pay attention to the *function* of each phrase; that is, to the role it is playing in the sentence: noun, adjective, verb, adverb.

As you do these practices, keep your writer's ear open. *Listen* to your words and phrases. *Listen* to what happens when they are selected and combined: to the phrase *patterns,* to their shapes and rhythms. Listen to the meaning the words make, and to their music. Notice when you come up with a combination of words you like and try to identify why these words work well together.

Practice with Phrases: Revise for Phrases

Take a passage from your own work and examine how you use phrases. Are there any ways in which you could replace single words with phrases, or add phrases to your sentences to make them clearer or more powerful?

Practice with Phrases: Read for Phrases

Most of all, learn from the professionals. When you are reading a writer you like, slow down as you read. Let your ear, not just your mind, be involved in your reading and *listen* to this writer's phrases. Read out loud the sentences you like. See if you can take them apart, phrase by phrase, and identify the kinds of phrases being used. Then, once you have identified the phrase structure of a sentence, use that structure to write your own sentences.

Here are some examples you might like to imitate:

> A silver cloud of pigeons swirled and settled.
> —Helen MacInnes, *The Venetian Affair*

His hands were large and very long, with stained fingers, but he used them with simplicity and grandeur.
—Mary Norton, "Mr. Sequeira"

In a hole in the ground there lived a hobbit. Not a nasty, dirty, wet hole, filled with the ends of worms and an oozy smell, nor yet a dry, bare, sandy hole with nothing in it to sit down on or to eat: it was a hobbit-hole, and that means comfort.
—J.R.R. Tolkien, *The Hobbit*

It may be that you find that hearing and making phrases comes naturally to you. That's a good thing: It means that you are naturally attuned to this primary characteristic of the English language. But if you can't quite get a grip on phrases, don't despair. Remember to *slow down* as you read for phrases, and as you compose them. Read out loud—put some breath into those words—and really *listen* to how the phrases unfold.

Phrases Create Natural Pauses

When you read aloud, paying attention to phrases, you'll notice that you're making tiny pauses between phrases; that is, between the groups of words that "go together." These pauses in fact delineate the phrases. Much of the time writers use punctuation marks to indicate these pauses. For instance:

Our president, Joe Harris, could not attend the meeting.

The comma after the word *president* tells readers to *pause here;* so does the comma after the word *Harris.* These commas make certain that we read *Our president* as one phrase and *Joe Harris* as another phrase. Doing so means we won't mistakenly run the words together.

Sometimes writers feel that readers will understand how to phrase the words without the guidance of punctuation marks. For instance:

By morning the snow was falling heavily.

Readers can tell that *by morning* is a phrase without the need of a comma after *morning*.

Practice with Phrases: Phrases and Punctuation
Read out loud a passage from a favorite writer, paying particular attention to pauses as directed by the punctuation marks. Notice which punctuation mark is being used in each case, and see if you can figure out why the writer used it. Then see if you can imitate the phrase structure of the sentence, including exactly the same punctuation marks.

Phrase Length

As you continue to train your word mind in composing phrases, you'll soon be able to make choices about how many phrases you want to have in a sentence, and how long you want your phrases to be. Do you want your sentences to be full of phrases like *in the long-lived, lingering, mist-filled and eloquent evening?* Or does your preference run more to phrases like *the misty evening?* Your choices will play a part in determining your style.

Practice with Phrases: Phrase Length
Read sentences out loud from the work of different writers and listen to the phrases. How many phrases does each sentence contain? Are the phrases long or short? Simple or complex? Try imitating some of these sentences to get a feel for each writer's use of phrases.

THE POWER OF PHRASES

Once you've developed your skill with phrases, you'll have at your disposal one of the most important tools a writer can possess.

First, making use of phrases helps us communicate. It produces writing that is consistent with the fundamental nature of the English language. The brains of English speakers are conditioned to expect phrases; when a writer provides them, he makes it easier for readers to process his sentences. The pauses created by phrases give our readers' brains the chance to take in one group of words and make sense of it before moving on to the next word-group. Phrases encourage our readers to slow down as they move through our sentences, so they are more likely to take in our meaning and to fully experience the effects of the words we've chosen.

Second, making use of phrases enables us to write more easily, and in a more natural way. When we compose sentences with an awareness of phrases, we're more likely to slow down and to be able to think more clearly about what we want to say. At the same time, because making phrases is natural to English speakers, we will probably find it easier to put sentences together when we compose phrase by phrase.

Third, making use of phrases gives us many different ways to say the same thing. With so many more choices available to us, we can vary the way that we build our sentences. Variation in phrase length and structure will please our readers and help to keep their attention. And the choices we make contribute to own individual style, or voice, on the page.

Using phrases also gives life to our writing. Phrases enable our writing to breathe, and to move in natural and graceful ways. They give rhythm to our sentences and make them more pleasurable to read; they help our sentences sing. Making use of phrases is one of the techniques that helps our writing "flow."

Finally, skillful use of phrases enables us to create powerful effects with our words, to make things happen in our readers. We can, for instance, use the staccato rhythm of short phrases to create a sense of tension, or the more relaxed rhythm of longer phrases to create a sense of ease.

From Phrase to Sentence

To read, in English, is always to engage in a process of *addition:* Our minds process sentences one bit at a time, adding a word or group of words to the ones that came before it. If we are native English speakers, or well-trained in English as a foreign language, we will engage in this process of addition without thinking about it. And as we take in a piece of writing, bit by bit, two things are happening: We are trying to understand what the writer is saying, and we are being affected (if the writer is skillful) by words.

If we want to create sentences that will work magic on readers, we need to know how to choose the right words and phrases. We also need to know how to *order* those words and word-groups with an awareness of the process of addition our readers will go through. Whether in composition or in revision, we need to master the skills of making sentences. In the next chapters we turn to those skills.

 ## TAKE TIME TO REFLECT

Do some reflecting on what you have learned through the practices in this chapter. Are there any practices you want to do regularly?

SECTION 4

The Power of Syntax: Ordering Words

I wish our clever young poets would remember my homely definitions of prose and poetry, that is, prose—words in their best order; poetry—the best words in their best order.

—SAMUEL TAYLOR COLERIDGE

No matter what kind of words you choose when you write—abstract or concrete, discursive or representational—if you want to make magic with them, you need to know how to arrange them into effective sentences. While finding the right words for our purpose is crucial, it's only when we get those words into the right order that they can create the spells we intend. "Open, Sesame!" makes the door to the treasure-cave creak open; "Sesame, open!" may not have the same effect. Magic can happen only when we have put the right words into "their best order." And just as knowing how words work enables us to make choices in diction, knowing how sentences work empowers us to construct exactly the kind of sentence that we need at any given moment in our writing. So now, on our learning journey, we enter the territory of *syntax,* the craft of ordering words into sentences.

We'll begin with what I'm calling "the basic sentence," a structure that is simple in construction yet rich in possible uses. The basic English sentence is a beautiful thing. Even in its simplest form, it can communicate; and, elaborated by the mind of a master, it is capable of infinite variety and effects both subtle and profound. If you have never given much thought to how basic sentences work, you may be surprised at how easy they are to construct.

After we play with the basic sentence, we'll turn our attention to elaborating and extending them. If you have never consciously tried to elaborate or extend a basic sentence, you will—I hope—be amazed at how many possibilities exist and how much fun you can have fooling around with them. You can expand your repertoire of sentence construction techniques very quickly, and once you have developed a feel for the available techniques, you'll be able to choose the ones you want. Without this understanding of how sentences work, your writing will be doomed to plod along in the same old ruts. With it, though, you'll be able to do just about anything you want to do on the page, developing your own individual style and voice.

A word of caution: There's a great deal of material here, so don't expect to master it all at once. You'll probably find it helpful to go slowly, so you don't feel overwhelmed, and to spend time with each group of practices before moving on. Remember that an intellectual knowledge of how sentences work will not, by itself, help you become a better writer. You've got to dig in and actually *make* those practice sentences, over and over, before what you have learned becomes a part of you. And so (once again!) I urge you to devote yourself to these practices and to make them an ongoing part of your writing life.

CHAPTER 10

MAKING SPELLS: THE MAGIC OF SENTENCES

••

Thus I got into my bones the essential structure of the ordinary British sentence—which is a noble thing.

••

—WINSTON CHURCHILL

In arriving at sentences, we have come to the heart of the craft of writing, to the place where writing differs from ordinary conversation. In the rush of daily life we often talk in phrases. If your spouse asks, *Where's my book?* you can reply, *On the table,* and your meaning will be clear. But while such fragments have their place in speech, and even in some informal writing, they don't allow us to make complete statements. And making complete statements is what sentence expertise is all about.

So, once we've learned how to choose words and combine them into phrases, we now have to master the choices available to us for gathering those words and phrases into sentences. If you studied grammar in school, you may think sentences are boring. But the truth is far different: Sentences are the key to making magic with writing. Sentences help us make our meaning clear, and—even more important—they give us tools to command the attention of our readers and to shape their experiences as they read our work. Writers who have mastered a wide range of sentence structures can choose just the right one for their purpose, whether it be to ratchet up (or down) the suspense, to make readers laugh, to surprise them, to make them cry, and much more. Mastery of sentence structures gives us a whole repertoire of techniques we can use to create the effects we want inside our readers.

Inexperienced or unskilled writers often don't even know there are choices to make in composing sentences. So we begin our exploration of sentences by looking at some of our choices.

KINDS OF SENTENCES

What do sentences do, anyway? A sentence can do one of four things:

1. **MAKE A STATEMENT:** *The small boy ran down the street,* or *John won't be at school today because he is ill.* Sentences like these are called *declarative sentences.*
2. **ASK A QUESTION:** *Are you coming to the game? Who scored the final run?* Sentences that ask questions are called *interrogative sentences.*
3. **MAKE A COMMAND:** *Tell me the truth!* or *Don't touch that package.* Such sentences are called *imperative sentences.*
4. **MAKE AN EXCLAMATION:** *How hot it is today!* or *What delicious cookies you make!* Sentences like these are called *exclamatory sentences.*

You don't need to remember the grammatical names for each kind of sentence, but your ability to make sentences will improve if you remember that you have these four kinds of sentences available to you when you write. You can do more than simply put down one declarative sentence after another. Professional writers make use of the four kinds of sentences: statement, question, command, exclamation. In the following example, from Lewis Carroll's *Alice's Adventures in Wonderland*, notice what each sentence is doing.

"… I wonder [said Alice to herself] if I've been changed in the night? Let me think: was I the same when I got up this morning? I almost think I can remember feeling a little different. But if I'm not the same, the next question is, Who in the world am I? Ah, that's the great puzzle!" And she began thinking over all the children she knew that were of the same age as herself, to see if she could have been changed for any of them.

Practice: Four Kinds of Sentences

Experiment with making different kinds of sentences. Then write a passage using only declarative sentences. Rewrite substituting other kinds of sentences for some of the declarative ones. Read the two versions out loud. What do you notice?

The Wonderful World of Declarative Sentences

Now that you have a feel for the different kinds of sentences available to you, let's turn to investigating the type of sentence writers use most frequently: the declarative sentence. Why this one? Because most of the time, when we write, we are telling our readers things, and it is the declarative sentence that allows us to do that. The declarative sentence lets us tell them *There was a black shadow upon the moon,* or *Beckett struck out ten in a row last night,* or *Jane wore a dress of green silk and a single strand of pearls.* From now on, anytime I use the word "sentence," I mean "declarative sentence."

And now … let's play with making sentences!

Practice: Make Sentences

Write a very short noun phrase. Write a very short verb phrase that makes sense with your noun phrase. Combine the two. Do this a few times, just to get the feel of it.

And now (drum roll …): What have you just created?

Sentences!

Making a sentence, then, involves *adding* together two or more phrases (or, occasionally, two single words or a single word and a phrase).

Remember that we created phrases out of single words added together; now we're making sentences using that same principle of addition.

But we can't use just any kind of phrase to make sentences, for sentences in English are constructed according to a certain basic pattern:

noun (or noun phrase) + verb (or verb phrase) = sentence

The Basic Sentence Pattern

Notice that in making sentences in the last practice you *added* two phrases together. Notice that one of the two is a noun phrase and that one of them is a verb phrase that contains a finite verb. And notice that when you put them together, the noun phrase comes first.

I call your attention to these things because, if you are a native English speaker, composing sentences in this way probably comes so naturally to you that you may not be aware of what you are doing. You may never have realized that, when you write, speak, and read sentences, you are putting words together according to a particular *pattern*, one that has been part of the English language since its beginnings. Here's the pattern again:

noun phrase (or single noun) + verb phrase (or single verb) = sentence

You may be more familiar with seeing the pattern expressed in these words:

subject + predicate = sentence

And here's the amazing thing: *All declarative sentences in English are constructed according to this basic sentence pattern, or one of its variations.*

Just think about this for a moment: Every declarative sentence in English is built upon this one basic pattern (and its variations, which we'll get to shortly). Just one single basic pattern for poetry and prose, fiction and nonfiction, professional writers and amateurs. One single basic pattern for best-selling authors and beginners, for Shakespeare and Stephen King, Benjamin Franklin and William Faulkner.

Because we know this pattern, says one expert on language, we can "comprehend literally millions of spoken or written sentences we have never heard or seen before—simple sentences and complicated ones, fact and fiction, prose and poetry."[22] Because we know this pattern, we can write sentences that will dazzle and delight our readers, that will inform and entertain and move them.

So if we want to write well, one of our most important tools is a solid grasp of the basic sentence pattern.

Sentence Kernels

The simplest and shortest of all sentences are called *kernels* (also known as *base clauses* or *core statements*). Some kernels are made up of a single noun (with or without a determiner) and a single finite verb. *Joe laughed* is an example of a sentence kernel; so is *The dog died.* Kernels can also be made with very short and simple noun and verb phrases: *The wolf chased the deer* is a kernel sentence; so is *The black sheep wandered away;* so is *All the boys were sick that day.*

Kernels are the most basic declarative sentences we can make: simple, unadorned, and straightforward. Before we can make elaborate sentences, we need to know how to make kernels.

Practice: Make Kernels

Write as many kernels as you can, first using single nouns and verbs and then very short noun and verb phrases. These sentences may sound silly to you; that's okay. Concentrate, not on the words, but on the *pattern:* noun or short noun phrase + verb or short verb phrase.

What do you notice in doing this?

The Rhythm of Kernels

Practicing kernels gives us an opportunity to get the underlying rhythm of English sentences into our writer's ear and our bones. It's a duple rhythm, like the rhythm of walking: *left-right, left-right.* With kernels we can name this rhythm as *noun phrase-verb phrase* or as *subject-predicate, subject-predicate.* It's crucial that we get to know this rhythm in our bodies, as well as our minds, for it is the ground rhythm of all English sentences.

Here are a few ways to play with this rhythm:

Practice: Subject-Predicate Rhythm
Start writing kernels again. Keep your sentences short and simple, and don't try to make them perfect. Now, as you write, turn part of your attention to the rhythm of subject and predicate: *subject—pause—predicate*. Try to feel this rhythm in your body, as well as your mind. *Left-right, left-right; subject-predicate, subject-predicate.*
What do you notice in doing this?

Practice: Subject-Predicate Rhythm
Now read your sentences out loud, pausing between the subject and the predicate. Try to feel the rhythm: These-words-are-naming-the-subject/ these-words-are-saying-something-about-the-subject. If you like, try this with a passage from a favorite writer or from a piece you are working on. What do you notice?

The Importance of Kernels
When we practice making kernels, we are training our brains in the basic pattern of English sentences, so I consider practice in making kernels to be an *essential* writing practice. The more we practice, the more easily we can make use of this pattern without conscious thought when we are writing, just as a catcher who practices throwing to second base a thousand times will be able to nail a base stealer during a game.

As with making things in any craft, the construction of sentences can be done with immense skill and subtlety. But we have to have the basic sentence pattern totally wired into our brains so that we can make use of it to write more elaborate sentences. So let's consider this basic pattern more carefully.

What the Basic Pattern Does 1: Provide Purpose

Making use of the basic sentence pattern when we write enables us to do some essential things. First, it lets our sentences have *purpose*. A sentence written according to the basic pattern does two things:

1. It gives the reader someone or something who is the subject of the sentence. That is, it *names* who or what the sentence is about; it gives the sentence an "actor."
2. It says something—makes a statement—about the subject of the sentence, gives us the "action" of the sentence.

To repeat: The *subject* of the sentence consists of a noun or a noun phrase; the verb or verb phrase that conveys the action is known as the *predicate* of the sentence.

Practice: Naming and Saying

Write a few more kernels, keeping your attention first on asking, "What am I naming?" then on asking, "What do I want to say about whatever I just named?" If you like, try writing longer sentences; sentences using concrete language; sentences using abstract language. Then read your sentences aloud. What do you hear?

What do you notice in doing this?

What the Basic Pattern Does 2: Make Meaning

To construct sentences, as I've said, is to enter the realm of *syntax*. While that word may sound forbidding, its meaning is simple: It means the way we *order* our words and phrases in sentences. The basic sentence pattern provides us with a way to do this, with an established template. Imagine what would happen if we didn't have this pattern, and writers could throw words onto the page in any old order: No one would be able to understand them!

A sentence is a particular way of ordering words and phrases to make sense. The key words here are "order" and "sense." English is a language in which we make meaning, not only by the particular words we choose and the phrases or images we create, but also by the way we order those words and phrases.

Take, for instance, this sentence: *The cat ate the cream.* Now, what would happen if we took the same words and arranged them into different orders? We could write *Ate the cat the cream.* We could write *The cream ate the cat.*

Each of our three sentences uses exactly the same words; the only difference is the order in which we receive them. But what a difference that order makes!—quite literally the difference between sense and nonsense.

This example illustrates the basic reality that, in English, word order helps create meaning. Not all languages work this way, though. In Latin, for instance, there exists a group of endings, called inflections, that attach to words and enable them to play different roles in sentences. If we take, as an example, the ending -*um,* and if we decide that adding this ending to a noun will make it play the role of an *object* (that is, someone or something that receives an action), and if we then attach our -*um* to the end of the word *cream* in our third example, we'd get this:

> The creamum ate the cat.

Because we know that, in our invented language, the ending -*um* turns the word *cream* into the receiver of the action, rather than the doer of the action, we know that what this sentence really means is *The cat ate the cream,* even though it's not using that particular order of words.

For anyone who has grown up speaking and reading English, the idea of having to process sentences in this way is mind-boggling. In English we make sense through syntax, through the way we order our words in sentences.

So strong is the power of syntax to help make meaning that writers who know how to make use of the basic syntactic patterns of English sentences can make even nonsense at least partly intelligible. Listen to these lines from Lewis Carroll's "Jabberwocky":

> 'Twas brillig, and the slithy toves
> Did gyre and gimble in the wabe;
> All mimsy were the borogroves,
> And the momeraths outgrabe.

We may not know what "slithy toves" are, but the syntax tells us that those words are the subject of the kernel "the slithy toves did gyre and gimble in the wabe" and that "did gyre and gimble in the wabe" make up the predicate. So we can guess that "slithy" is an adjective that modifies the noun "toves," and that whoever or whatever "toves" are, they are doing some action conveyed by the words "gyre and gimble."

What the Basic Pattern Does 3: Create Movement from Known to Unknown

Because the basic pattern gives us a structure for ordering our words and phrases, it helps us make meaning, as we've seen. The basic pattern also gives *forward movement* to our sentences. How does this movement happen?

It happens because English sentences have a characteristic movement built into their basic structure: They move "from known to unknown." This movement of English sentences "from known to unknown" is an essential feature of the language. It has been described by one language expert as "probably one of the most important grammatical observations to be made about English prose style."[23]

A typical English sentence begins with the subject, then continues with a predicate that says something about that subject. So the reader now knows two things: what the subject of the sentence is, and what is said about it. To move from what is "known"—that is, what is known to the *reader*—to what is "unknown," a skilled writer will *repeat* an element from her first sentence in the one that follows. Most often she will repeat the subject (*Joe was hungry. He ate a banana.*). Sometimes she will repeat a different sentence element (*Joe ate a banana. It tasted delicious.*). In writing her third sentence, and any following ones, she will use the same technique of repeating an element from a previous sentence: In this way her sentences will move the reader forward smoothly from one statement to the next, from what he already knows to what is unknown.

Writing in Time

This movement of sentences from known to unknown can also enable our sentences to have drama. Within the limits imposed by the basic sentence structure, we can choose *when* we want to give our readers bits of information. We can use syntax to create suspense and anticipation, to keep our readers reading.

That's because while we are, in a sense, ordering our words visually (whether from one side of the page to the other in prose, or in some other arrangement in poetry), what we are actually doing is ordering them in *time*. Our readers' brains will not approach our writing as if it were a painting, whose many elements can be taken in almost simultaneously. Rather, they will come to those little black marks on the page in a way very similar to the way the brains of trained musicians come to a musical score: They will process one group of words, and then the next, and then the next … until they "get" our meaning. Through the way we arrange our words into sentences we can control how readers understand what we have to say. We can also manipulate their emotional reactions.

I want to stress this point, because to fully realize that writing (for the reader) unfolds in time is the gateway to getting a practical, rather than a merely mechanical or intellectual, understanding of syntax. *Sentences are auditory patterns, which happen in time,* so *when* in our sentences we give readers certain words is just as important as the specific words we choose. When we have a command of sentence patterns, we can make exactly the right choice to "get the spell right" and keep our readers enthralled from the beginning of a piece of writing to the end.

To explore syntactic possibilities does not necessarily involve writing long and complex sentences. It's amazing how many possibilities simple kernels can give us to play with.

The Types of Kernels: Four Variations on the Basic Pattern

Once you've mastered the basic sentence pattern and can easily write simple sentences with clear subjects and predicates, you're ready to refine your understanding of how sentences work and give yourself more possibilities to play with. The basic sentence pattern has four types, each making use of a different kind of verb in its predicate.

Remember that the subject of the sentence tells readers what the sentence is about. The verb tells what the subject is doing. Every sentence has an actor and an action.

Sometimes the action conveyed by the verb is indeed full of energy: *He heaved the packages into the car.* Other times the verb gives a state of being: *Joe is sad.* Or *Sally appears happy.*

The important things to remember are: 1) main verbs (also known as finite verbs) can convey different kinds of action or energy; and 2) main verbs are categorized by the amount of energy they convey.

With this in mind, let's take a look at the four variations on the basic sentence pattern:

- **TYPE 1:** Subject + *be* verb (some form of the verb *be*) with a noun (or noun phrase), adjective (or adjective phrase), or adverb (or adverb phrase) as predicate;
- **TYPE 2:** Subject + a *linking* verb (such as *seem, become, feel, remain, appear)* with a noun (or noun phrase) or adjective (or adjective phrase) as predicate;
- **TYPE 3:** Subject + an *intransitive* verb (such as *laugh, jump, walk*), which may or may not be followed by an adverb or adverb phrase;
- **TYPE 4:** Subject + a *transitive* verb (such as *throw, drop, make)* with a noun or noun phrase as *direct object.*

The noun or adjective constructions that follow *be,* or a linking verb, are known as the *complement* (or *subject complement)* of the verb.

Any of these patterns may also include an adverb or short adverb phrase, such as a prepositional phrase. (For example: John is happy *at last.*) The Type 4 kernel, using a transitive verb, can also include an *indirect object* or an *object complement.* (For example: Joe gave

Mary *the apple*.) We'll explore these options in more detail later in the chapter.

You may notice that the kernel types progress from a verb that expresses little action (*be*) to verbs that convey a great deal of action. Remember that all verbs are not created equal: Some can express only a state of being or a condition; others are full of energy and activity. If you know how to use all of these different kinds of verbs, you can choose the kind that best suits your purpose as you construct sentences. Suppose, for instance, the subject of your sentence is a frog. *The frog,* you might write, *is on the rock.* (He's there; that's all.) Or perhaps you'd rather write *The frog remains on the rock.* (A little more activity is implied here, perhaps; the frog seems to be *deciding* to stay on the rock.) Or this: *The frog sits on the rock.* (The frog still isn't moving, but he is engaged in an activity: sitting there.) Or this one: *The frog embraces the rock.* (Can you feel the frog's muscles moving now?)

Notice that the substitution of verbs in these examples is not just a matter of finding synonyms; it's about considering the amount of activity each type of verb conveys. Knowing how to use all four types will expand enormously your options for making sentences.

Let's look at each one of these a little more closely.

SENTENCE KERNELS

Type 1 Kernels: To Be or Not to Be?

The *be* verb has taken a lot of abuse in recent years from those who give advice about writing: Many of them tell us we should never use this verb. Although, like any other word, forms of *to be* can be overused, in the hands of skilled writers, *be* is an important tool. Listen to this example:

> Mariposa is not a real town. On the contrary, it is about seventy or eighty of them. … To the careless eye the scene on the Main Street of a summer afternoon is one of deep and unbroken peace. The empty street sleeps in the sun-

shine. There is a horse and buggy tied to the hitching post in front of Glover's hardware store. ... But this quiet is mere appearance. In reality, and to those who know it, the place is a perfect hive of activity. ...

  — Stephen Leacock, *Sunshine Sketches of a Little Town*

In these sentences, the *be* verb becomes almost invisible, directing the reader's attention to the nouns and noun phrases that bring Main Street alive. To use some form of *be* is not necessarily the mark of a poor writer; what's important in such sentences is what lies on either side of the verb.

Four Ways to Write Kernels with "Be"

Here are four ways of using forms of *to be* in kernel sentences, which you may like to add to your repertoire of sentence-making techniques. As you practice these techniques, notice how familiar they are to you already.

We can use kernels with *be*:

1. To State (and Perhaps Emphasize), Identity:

Use the kernel pattern: noun or noun phrase + *be* verb + same noun or noun phrase (as complement):

> Boys will be boys.

> Manny is Manny.

> A rose is a rose is a rose. (Gertrude Stein)

2. To Rename the Subject:

Use the kernel pattern: noun or noun phrase + *be* verb + new noun or noun phrase as complement.

> Canadians are not Americans.

> Jason Varitek is the Red Sox captain.

> Hell is other people. (Jean-Paul Sartre)

You can also use this pattern to create metaphor and simile; for instance:

> Ted Williams is God.
>
> Time is a river.
>
> Juliet is the sun. (Shakespeare, *Romeo and Juliet*)
>
> The snow is like butterflies.

Note that all of these constructions are built on *nouns*.

3. With a Complement (What Comes After the Be Verb) That is an Adjective or an Adjectival Phrase:

> Joe is cute.
>
> Tomorrow will be fine.
>
> All is well.

4. With a Complement That is an Adverb or an Adverbial Phrase:

> Joe is far away.
>
> The apples are on the shelf.
>
> You are in big trouble.

Practice: Kernels with the Be Verb

Write some kernels using various forms of the *be verb*. What do you notice?

Type 2 Kernels: Using Linking Verbs

The linking verbs include *seem, appear, feel, become, look, turn, get, grow, remain*. Remember that these are "state-of-being" or "condition" verbs, not action verbs. Kernels with linking verbs use one of two patterns:

1. *subject + linking verb + noun or noun phrase as complement*

> Jennifer became a doctor.
>
> Jonathan remains a judge.

2. *subject + linking verb + adjective or adjectival phrase as complement*

> The monkey grew sad.
>
> Everything became clear.
>
> Susie looked very beautiful.
>
> He appeared angry.

Practice: Kernels with Linking Verbs

Make some kernels with linking verbs. What do you notice?

According to some experts on sentences, the most important information in a sentence tends to come at the end of the sentence, especially when the pattern is a kernel with *be* or a linking verb. That's because we don't usually write sentences in isolation, but one after another, and so the subject of a sentence often refers to a person or thing the reader is already familiar with. (See above for the discussion of moving from known to unknown.)

In the two patterns we've just played with, the kernels usually have little activity. To create more activity in a sentence, we need to use intransitive or transitive verbs.

Type 3 Kernels: Using Intransitive Verbs

Intransitive verbs are those that convey action, without requiring additional words to complete the action. The kernel pattern is subject + intransitive verb, possibly followed by an adverb or a short adverbial phrase.

> Birds sing.
>
> The boys laughed.
>
> The dog barked loudly.
>
> Susie giggled uncontrollably.
>
> She skated with ease.

Practice: Kernels with Intransitive Verbs
Make some kernels using the pattern for intransitive verbs. What do you notice?

Type 4 Kernels: Using Transitive Verbs

Transitive verbs also convey action, but they require another word or phrase to complete the action. This word or phrase is known by grammarians as the *direct object*. The kernel pattern is: subject + transitive verb + noun (or pronoun) or noun phrase as direct object.

> Joe hated the woman. (*direct object = the woman*)
>
> The dog bit the postman.
>
> Jeff read the newspaper.
>
> Anna ate the spaghetti.

This pattern can also be varied as follows: subject + transitive verb + noun phrase (or pronoun) + adverb or prepositional phrase.

> She threw the ball hard.
>
> His question shattered the silence like glass.
>
> Susie's mother drove her to the party.

One additional variation of the pattern adds a noun or noun phrase serving as an *indirect object*. For example:

> Jack gave Amanda a present. (*indirect object = Amanda*)

Practice: Kernels with Transitive Verbs
Make some kernels with transitive verbs. What do you notice?

Practice: Play with Kernels
Take some time to practice each type of kernel in turn. Read your sentences out loud, and notice what you hear. Try rewriting a sentence using different kinds of verbs. It's also fun to freewrite using one kind of kernel after another.

Practice: Tell a Story with Kernels

Using the kernel patterns in the order in which they are explained above, one at a time, tell a story. Your first sentence will use a Type 1 kernel, your second sentence a Type 2 kernel, and so on. When you've completed four sentences, write another four sentences using the kernel types in the same order. Continue until your story ends.

Kernels Provide Choices

I hope you will notice how becoming aware of the different kinds of kernel patterns gives you more choices in how to say something. For instance, do you want to write *Sam is strange,* or *Sam seems strange,* or *Sam acts strangely?* Do you want to write *That fly is annoying* or *That fly annoys me?*

As you play with kernels I encourage you to try different ways of saying the same thing so that you build in your word mind a repertoire of sentence-structure possibilities.

Practice: Learn from the Professionals

Study writers you like for how they use kernels. Imitate what they do. Here are a few examples to consider.

The Pros Use Kernels

"Don't do anything daft, sons," said one of the uniforms. But they were just words. Nobody was listening. The two teenagers were against the rails now, only ten feet or so from the crashed car. Rebus walked slowly forward, pointing with his finger, making it clear to them that he was going to the car. The impact had caused the trunk to spring open an inch. Rebus carefully lifted it and looked inside.

There was nobody inside.

—Ian Rankin, *Let It Bleed*

I'm one for routine. I like to get on with my job, and then when the day's work's over settle down to a paper and a smoke and a bit of music on the wireless, variety or something of the sort and then turn in early. I never had much use for girls …

—Daphne Du Maurier, "Kiss Me Again, Stranger"

He would have given up that hope [of vengeance] for Flavia's sake, if she had come with him, because the quest for vengeance was a trail that no man should follow with a woman and a child dependent on him. But Flavia had not come.

—Rosemary Sutcliff, *The Lantern Bearers*

Now it was the twenty-fourth of December, and just such a morning. Christmas tomorrow. She was alone, and she would spend tomorrow alone. She did not mind. She and her house would keep each other company.

—Rosamunde Pilcher, "Miss Cameron at Christmas"

I could not help it. I burst into a shout of laugher as I looked at George's wrathful face, I rolled in my chair, I very nearly fell on the floor. George never forgave me. But Tom often asks me to excellent dinners in his charming house in May-fair, and if he occasionally borrows a trifle from me, that is merely from force of habit. It is never more than a sovereign.

—Somerset Maugham, "The Ant and the Grasshopper"

Using Kernels for Effect

As the preceding examples demonstrate, kernels can create powerful effects. So they are an important part of every skilled writer's sentence repertoire. You can, for instance, use kernels in the following ways:

1. To vary the length of your sentences and create rhythm. One writer on style says, "The better the writer, of fiction and of nonfiction alike, the more he tends to vary his sentence length. And he does it as dramatically as possible. Time and again the shortest sentence in a professional paragraph is brought up against the longest, or at least lodged among some much longer. This smallest sentence is often a kernel, or a near-kernel."[24]

2. To create movement by using different kernel-structures in sequence. (Remember that each kernel type has a different amount of energy because each uses a different kind of verb.)
3. To create emphasis or drama or surprise. Professional writers, like the ones above, often begin a paragraph with a kernel to grab the reader's attention (see the Du Maurier example), or end a paragraph with one to create emphasis or climax (see the Rankin and Sutcliff examples). Sometimes they use a kernel in the middle of a paragraph, to create a transition or change direction— and sometimes they even use kernels in all three positions (see the Maugham example).

Practice: Play with Kernels

Fool around with using kernels to create different effects, either by writing a few sentences or paragraphs on a subject of your choice, or by revising some of your own writing. What do you notice?

Kernels and Fragments

Contemporary writers make frequent use of sentence fragments to replicate how people talk, either in dialogue or in internal monologue. Such fragments differ from kernels in that they are not complete sentences: They lack subject or predicate, or both. Can you find the fragments in this example?

> Badgworthy was in a seventh heaven. A murder! At Chimneys! Inspector Badgworthy in charge of the case. The police have a clue. Sensational arrest. Promotion and kudos for the aforementioned inspector.
>
> —Agatha Christie, *The Secret of Chimneys*

Number of words is not a useful indicator of whether a given utterance is a sentence fragment or a kernel. Sometimes a sentence fragment can be longer than a kernel, as in the following example, spoken by a police officer (compare the second and third sentences):

"Basil Blake was at a party at the studios that night. You
know the sort of thing. Starts at eight with cocktails and
goes on and on until the air's too thick to see through and
everyone passes out."
—Agatha Christie, *The Body in the Library*

Practice: Play with Kernels
Write some kernels, remembering the basic subject-predicate rhythm.
Now write some sentence fragments. Can you feel the difference? Experiment with combining kernels and fragments in the same passage.
(You may find it helpful to use dialogue or internal monologue.)

The Benefits of Practicing Kernels

Though kernels are short, they are an exceptionally useful writer's
tool. Beyond their ability to create effects, they are important because the more we practice them, the more we train our writer's
mind to get a solid grip on the basic structure of the English sentence.
Naturally we're not going to fill our pages only with kernels—that
would bore us, and bore our readers. But when we have really learned,
through practice, how kernels work, when we can write them with
ease, then we can learn to elaborate them into more complicated
structures. The sentences we write then will be longer, but they will
always be grounded in the basic structure of the kernel—which is
the fundamental structure of the English sentence, the structure
our readers expect.

So I hope you will not disdain kernels as "too simple." In the next
chapter we'll begin our exploration of ways to elaborate and extend
them into more complex sentences. Having a solid grip on kernels
will enable you to take in this new material more easily.

If you feel ready to take on the making of more complex sentences, proceed to the next chapter. But if you'd like to play with kernels
a while longer, here's another way to understand the basic patterns
of English sentences.

SYNTACTIC SLOTS

"And the words slide into the slots ordained by syntax, and glitter as with atmospheric dust with those impurities which we call meaning,"[25] writes British author Anthony Burgess. These "slots ordained by syntax" are, in an English sentence, the subject and the predicate: what is named, and what we say about what is named. If you are a visually minded person, you might find this notion of "syntactic slots" helpful in visualizing how syntax works.

Into the subject "slot" can go nouns or pronouns, or noun phrases (that is, any group of words functioning as a noun) and any words or phrases modifying the noun. Into the predicate "slot" go the main verb of the sentence and any words or phrases serving to modify that verb, as well as any complements or objects. You may find it helpful to create a mental image of these slots, so that, as you produce sentences, one after another, you keep in mind that first you must fill the subject slot, then the predicate slot. As you begin your next sentence, you must fill the subject slot again, and then the predicate slot, and so on.

If you like this idea, here are some practices to try.

Practice: Sentence Slots
Write sentence kernels, using a mental image of the subject and predicate "slots," and fill them with the appropriate words. Read your kernels out loud. What do you notice?

Practice: Sentence Slots
Do some freewriting, trying to keep the mental image of the subject and predicate "slots" alive in one part of your mind. What happens when you do this? Afterwards read your sentences aloud. What do you notice?

Practice: Sentence Slots
Revise some of your writing by reading it out loud and trying, at the same time, to keep in mind the mental image of the syntactic "slots."

Syntactic Slots: More Details

If you find it helpful to visualize the "slots" words must slide into, here is a more detailed picture of the basic English sentence: The subject takes up only one "slot," while the predicate can contain from one to three slots. How can that be? It all depends on what kind of verb is being used. *Be* or a linking verb will require two slots for the predicate: the verb and the complement. (*George// is/ sad.*) An intransitive verb requires only one slot for the predicate. (*Philip// laughed.*) A transitive verb will require two slots for the predicate: the verb and the direct object. (*Melissa// read/ the book.*) A transitive verb will require three slots for the predicate when there's an indirect object (*Mary// gave/ Alice/ a book.*): subject (slot 1) + verb (slot 2) + indirect object (slot 3) + direct object (slot 4): slots 2–4 make up the predicate. A transitive verb will also require three slots for the predicate when there's an object complement. (*Joe// considers/ my brother/ a friend.*)

With any kind of verb, the predicate can include an adverb or adverb phrase. For example:

> Rebecca is sleepy *in the morning.*

> Joe laughed *loudly.*

SUMMARY OF THE BASIC SENTENCE PATTERNS [26]

SLOT 1	SLOT 2	SLOT 3	SLOT 4
1A. Subject	Be	Subject Complement	
1B. Subject	Be	Adverbial	
2. Subject	Linking Verb	Subject Complement	
3. Subject	Intransitive Verb		
4A. Subject	Transitive Verb	Direct Object	
4B. Subject	Transitive Verb	Indirect Object	Direct Object
4C. Subject	Transitive Verb	Direct Object	Object Complement
4D. Subject	Any Verb	Complement/ Object, if necessary	Adverbial (optional)

Practice: Sentence Slots

Using the information in the sidebar, play with writing different kinds of kernels.

Notice the kinds of verbs you are using and the particular part of speech you are sliding into each slot.

The Value of Sentence Patterns

The more we practice sentence patterns—like a musician practicing scales and intervals—the more options we have at our command when we are in the midst of composition and revision. I encourage you to play as much as you can with these basic patterns, and, if you like, to invent your own practices.

 TAKE TIME TO REFLECT

What have you learned from this chapter? What sections (if any) might you need to revisit? What practices do you want to make a part of your practice repertoire?

CHAPTER 11

ELABORATING
THE BASIC SENTENCE

....

If art is the bridge between what you see in your mind and what the world sees, then skill is how you build that bridge.

....

—TWYLA THARP, *The Creative Habit: Learn It and Use It for Life*

While mastery of sentence kernels is an essential writing skill, limiting your sentence-making to kernels alone will probably bore both you and your readers. If you imagine that creating a basic kernel sentence structure is like building a small, plain house, then elaborating that structure is like adding details and decoration to that house. The kernel sentence, just like the unadorned house, does the essential work it needs to do; the act of adding details and decoration, to either sentence structure or house structure, can move both of them beyond the basic. In both cases, though, you need to know *how* to elaborate the elemental structure so that your additions enhance that structure rather than detract from the work it already does well.

The techniques of making more complex sentences are all based on the process of *adding* to basic sentences. To write a sentence that is more complex is to add more "stuff"—more information, more details, more words—to a basic sentence. Many writers get into trouble when they try to construct complicated sentences because they lose track of the basic sentence pattern. If you keep a firm grip on that pattern (or one of its variations), you're less likely to lose your way (and to lose your readers).

The techniques of making complicated sentences fall into two main categories:

1. You can add more words and phrases to a single basic sentence (kernel). I call this process *elaborating the basic sentence*.
2. You can also *combine* one or more basic sentences, in a process I call *extending the basic sentence*.

Skilled writers make use of both of these techniques, both separately and together. In this chapter, we'll explore elaboration; in Chapter 12, we'll turn to extending sentences.

ELABORATING THE BASIC SENTENCE PATTERNS

When we want to add more material to a kernel, we have to keep in mind two things. First, readers *expect* the basic sentence pattern to provide a foundation for every declarative sentence, so we don't want to thwart that expectation unless we're doing it on purpose and for good reason. In other words, we have to make sure that when we elaborate a kernel we don't mess up the basic kernel structure. We need to add our material to sentences in ways that don't confuse our readers—unless we have some good reason for wanting to disorient them. We need to make sure that when we add more material to a kernel, our sentences still *make sense*.

Second, elaborating kernels is one of our most useful tools for making things happen inside our readers' minds and for keeping their attention. When we learn how to add material to kernels, we have unlimited options for creating the effects we want.

There are two primary ways we can elaborate kernels: We can create *compound subjects or verbs*; and we can add *modifiers* to the subject or the predicate, or both. Some of these techniques will be familiar to you from the chapter on phrases. Here, we'll go over them again—this time thinking about them a little differently, from the point of view of elaborating kernels. Then we'll examine some other techniques.

How to Elaborate a Kernel 1: Compound Subjects and Predicates

You'll remember that we can combine two or more nouns (or noun phrases) using the conjunction *and*. When this construction serves as the subject of a sentence, the result is called a compound subject. For example:

> *The Sharks and the Jets* eyed each other with suspicion.

> *Joe and Mary* have never met.

We can also use *and* to combine verbs. When two or more verbs (or verb phrases) serve as the predicate of a sentence, they are called a compound predicate. For example:

> Joe *opened the window and looked out.*

> The dog *barked at the postman and growled fiercely.*

Sometimes compound subjects or predicates take the form of a list:

> Joe *jumped out of bed, grabbed his clothes, and dressed hurriedly.*

If you vaguely remember something called "compound sentences" from a grammar lesson, please note that there is a big difference between a compound predicate and a compound sentence: a sentence with a compound predicate has only one subject (though that subject may contain more than one noun). If you feel confused about this, read over the sentences above and pause after the subject, then notice how it's the same subject engaging in every one of the actions conveyed by the verbs. As for compound sentences, we'll get to them in the next chapter.

Practice: Compound Subjects and Predicates
Write some short sentences using compound subjects and predicates
(or both). What do you notice?

You probably remember that a predicate can often contain more
than one "slot"; when it does, the constructions in those slots can
also become compound. (See Chapter 10 for an explanation of slots.)
For example:

> *Joe threw the apples and oranges into a bag.* (Compound
> direct object)
>
> *Mary gave Steve and Suzanne a list of tasks to do.* (Com-
> pound indirect object)
>
> Mary is *a liar and a thief.* (Compound complement)

Play around with using the compounding technique with these constructions. As you do this, keep in mind that whenever you join two
words or phrases with *and*, those constructions must be the same part
of speech; that is, you must join nouns and nouns, adjectives and adjectives, but not nouns and adjectives.

The Pros Use Compound Structures
Compound structures are a useful tool, one that enables writers to con-
dense a great deal of information into a single sentence. For example:

> "All the frustration and bitterness and fascination of the
> years I spent [in Moscow] during the war came rushing
> back at me …"
> —Andrew Garve, *Murder Through the Looking Glass*
>
> By seven o'clock the orchestra has arrived, no thin five-
> piece affair, but a whole pitful of oboes and trombones
> and saxophones and viols and cornets and piccolos, and
> low and high drums.
> —F. Scott Fitzgerald, *The Great Gatsby*

The Rat brought the boat alongside the bank, made her fast, helped the still awkward Mole safely ashore, and swung out the luncheon-basket.

—Kenneth Grahame, *The Wind in the Willows*

Compound predicates also enable writers to infuse their sentences with the energy of activity:

He threw his head down and gnashed his teeth, and allowed a murmur of suppressed anger to sweep the crowd.

—Chinua Achebe, *Things Fall Apart*

The skipping-rope was a wonderful thing. [Mary] counted and skipped, and skipped and counted, until her cheeks were quite red ...

—Frances Hodgson Burnett, *The Secret Garden*

Practice: Learn from the Pros

Search the work of one of your favorite writers for compound subjects, verbs, direct objects, and other structures, then imitate those sentences.

What do you notice in doing these practices?

How to Elaborate a Kernel 2: Modifiers

The second way we can elaborate a kernel is by adding modifiers. As you undoubtedly remember, a modifier is a word, or a group of words, that adds some information to a noun or a verb; a modifier makes its noun or verb more specific, more precise, more vivid. When a word or a group of words modifies a noun, it is functioning as an adjective. When a word or a group of words modifies a verb (or, sometimes, an adjective or another adverb), it is functioning as an adverb.

Any noun or noun phrase can have modifying words added to it; so can any verb or verb phrase, including verbals.

When we come to elaborate our kernels with modifiers there are two main things we have to pay attention to. First, within the limits imposed by the need to make sense, we can make choices about *what* material we want to add; second, we can make choices about *when* we want to add that material.

Elaborate a Kernel with Modifiers 1: The "What"

There are three verbal structures we can use as modifiers: single content words, phrases, and clauses. For the time being, let's focus on the first two. (We'll get to clauses later.) You'll remember this material from the practices on making phrases; I want you to revisit it here so you can focus on modification as a technique for elaborating kernels.

Modifiers as Single Words

When a noun is modified by a single word, most of the time that word comes between the determiner and the noun:

> The boy laughed.
>
> The *small* boy laughed.
>
> The *small, timid* boy laughed.
>
> The dog was a *long-eared, friendly* mutt.

Single adjectives in between a determiner and a noun can be combined with *and*:

> The dog was a *long-eared and short-haired* mutt.

Anytime you put a noun into an appropriate place in a sentence—as, for instance, object or complement—you can, if you like, add modifiers:

> The *small* boy reached out with *timid* fingers to pat the *long-eared, friendly* mutt.

Like nouns, verbs can (and often are) modified by single words—in this case, adverbs:

> The small boy walked *softly*.

Practice: Modify Nouns with Single Words

Write some kernels. Now rewrite them, adding single-word modifiers to the nouns. What do you notice? (Of course, adding an adjective or two in between a determiner and a noun makes the noun phrase longer. Do you like the sound of longer noun phrases?)

Practice: Modify Verbs with Single Words

Write some kernels. Now rewrite them, adding single-word modifiers to the verbs.

What do you notice? If you like, try writing kernels and then adding single-word modifiers to both nouns and verbs.

Modifiers as Phrases

One of the most important things to know about modifiers is that they can be single words—*or* they can be phrases. For instance:

> The boy laughed.

> The *small* boy *in the blue hat* laughed *loudly at the clown.* (The modifiers, in order: single adjective; prepositional phrase acting as an adjective; single adverb; prepositional phrase acting as an adverb.)

Practice: Modify with Phrases

Write some kernels, then elaborate them with adjectival or adverbial *phrases.* Use these two phrase patterns: 1) two adjectives or two adverbs connected by *and*; 2) prepositional phrases.

Read your sentences out loud: How do they *sound* to you? What do you notice doing this? (If you struggle with this practice, you may want to review Chapter 9.)

Now experiment with taking a kernel and modifying it, first, with single words, then with phrases, then with both single words and phrases. What do you notice?

The Pros Elaborate Kernels with Modifiers 1: Single Words and Prepositional Phrases

> Tears rolled slowly down Mrs. Packington's middle-aged cheeks.
>
> —Agatha Christie, "The Case of the Middle-Aged Wife"

Note the single modifiers: *slowly* (modifying *rolled*), *Mrs. Packington's* and *middle-aged* (both modifying *cheeks*), and the phrase *down Mrs. Packington's middle-aged cheeks* (modifying *rolled*).

> The house had *roughcast* walls and a roof *of mossy stone tiles* and stood *at the far end of the farmyard in the shade of an old Scots pine.*
> —Bruce Chatwin, On the Black Hill

> Mary touched [the branch of the tree] *in an eager, reverent way.*
> —Frances Hodgson Burnett, The Secret Garden

> Just then they heard the *intimate, dramatic, triumphant, wheedling* voice of the radio …
> —Nadine Gordimer, "The Gentle Art"

Practice: Imitate the Pros

Use the sentences above, or choose a passage from a writer of your choice. First, identify the kernel of each declarative sentence. Notice what kind of modifiers the writer used: single words or phrases. Now imitate each sentence by writing a kernel and then using modifiers in the same way as the professional writer did; in other words, place single modifiers and modifying phrases exactly where she did. Read your sentences aloud. What do you notice?

One of the things you'll probably notice is that single word modifiers are often a *part* of prepositional phrases, as in *of an old Scots pine,* where *old* and *Scots* modify *pine.* You may also find the writer using structures that you can't yet identify; just set these aside, for now.

Participial Phrases as Modifiers

In addition to using single words and prepositional phrases as modifiers, we can also use participial phrases. You'll remember from our discussion of verbals in Chapter 8 that we have two participial forms of verbs that we can use as modifiers: the present participle (which commonly ends in *-ing*), and the past participle (which often, though not always, ends in *-ed*). It's essential to be aware of the difference between a participle that is taking the role of main verb in a sentence—Stephen *was singing* loudly in the car— and a participle used as an adverb or adjective—Stephen listened to the *singing* bird. In the example from Nadine Gordimer, the word *wheedling* is a participle serving as an adjective. (If you feel confused about participles, review Chapter 8 or consult your grammar book.) Here we will talk only about participles used as modifiers.

Like other modifiers, participles can be inserted into an existing phrase, as the word "singing" is into the noun phrase "the bird" in the above example; they can also have other words added to them and become participial phrases. For example:

> We listened for a long time to the sparrows *chirping in the trees.*

Participles can be confusing because they are very adaptable and can do a number of different things in sentences. To make sure you know what a participle is doing in a particular sentence, try this: First identify the single parts of speech and the phrases in the sentence, and name the role each is playing. This will show you that, in a sentence like this one, for instance—*Joe hit the barking dog*—the phrase *the barking dog* has a participle (*barking*) in it, but it's not a participial phrase (an adjective construction) because it's functioning as a direct object and so must be a noun phrase.

The Pros Elaborate Kernels with Modifiers 2: Participles and Participial Phrases

> … the lines of *trembling* monkeys *huddled together on the walls and battlements* looked like *ragged* shaky fringes of things.
>
> —Rudyard Kipling, *The Jungle Book*

> They had left him, and now they were going to bed. Uncle Alan took a bath, and Tom lay *listening to him* and *hating him.*
>
> —Philippa Pearce, *Tom's Midnight Garden*

> [He] had dwindled now simply into a nice-looking young
> man *standing in the sunshine*, with doubt *melting on his face*
> into *horrified* apology.
>
> —Mary Stewart, *The Ivy Tree*

Practice: Imitate the Pros

Find examples of participles or participial phrases in a passage by your favorite writer, or use the examples above. Imitate how your chosen writer uses these structures as modifiers. What do you notice? Then invent some sentences of your own, using these structures.

Elaborate a Kernel with Modifiers 2: The "When"

When we elaborate a kernel, we need to remember that sentences unfold for readers in *time*: To make sense of what they are reading, readers *add* each element in a sentence to the one that came before it. So one of the keys to successful elaboration lies in knowing *when* in a kernel we can add modifiers.

We have three choices:

1. We can add words and phrases to one of the two primary "slots" in a sentence; that is, to the subject, to the predicate, or to both.
2. We can add words and phrases *before* the subject, *between* the subject and predicate, or *after* the predicate.
3. We can do some of both.

If you skipped the section on slots (it's in Chapter 10), all you need to know here is that a declarative sentence has two main parts—the subject and the predicate—and that each of these can be considered as a syntactic "slot" into which we slide words.

The "When" of Elaborating a Kernel 1: Elaborating Within Slots

Suppose we have a basic sentence kernel like, *The dog barks.* We've got a subject, *The dog,* and a predicate, *barks.*

This sentence communicates something ... but perhaps it doesn't get across all the details we'd like to include. As we saw above, we can add modifiers within the noun phrase "the dog": *The little brown dog barks.*

Suppose we still want to add more information to our subject, *the little brown dog.* We can do that by adding more modifiers within the subject slot:

> The little brown dog with the injured foot / barks.

In general, when we add modifiers to a noun, single adjectives come between the determiner and the noun; adjective phrases come after the noun.

If we want to, we can also add single words or phrases, as adverbs, to the predicate slot:

> The little brown dog with the injured foot / barks loudly.

> The little brown dog with the injured foot / barks loudly until dusk.

Practice: Elaborate Within Subject and Predicate Slots

You just did this practice above; nonetheless, I encourage you to do it again. This time, though, as you do it, be aware that you are sliding your words into sentence "slots."

Write a kernel, then add single words or phrases—only prepositional phrases, for now—or both, to the subject or the predicate slots, or both. Try to pay attention to the boundary between the subject and the predicate slots.

Bound Modifiers

When we add modifiers *within* a syntactic slot—that is, to the subject or predicate of the sentence—those modifiers are known as *bound modifiers.* They are called "bound" because they are fixed in place in a sentence; they cannot typically be placed elsewhere in the sentence without distorting its meaning.

You probably remember from Chapter 10 that, depending on the verb being used, the predicate slot can often contain one or two slots in addition to the one containing the main verb. Each one of these slots can also be elaborated with bound modifiers. For instance, here's a kernel:

> Joe gave Jenny a bracelet.

Now here's the kernel with elaboration in the fourth slot:

> Joe// gave/ Jenny/ a silver bracelet from his grandmother's jewelry case.

In this second version the fourth slot contains the direct object, "bracelet," which is modified in two ways: with the single adjective *silver* inserted into the noun phrase (*a bracelet*) and with the prepositional phrase (*from his grandmother's jewelry case*) placed after the noun phrase, *a silver bracelet*.

Like prepositional phrases, participial phrases can be bound modifiers, as in this example: *He was a timid man hiding behind a brave smile.* (*Hiding behind a brave smile* is an adjective phrase modifying *man*.)

Practice: Elaboration Using Bound Modifiers in All Slots
Write some kernel sentences making use of two, three, or four slots. Then elaborate each one with bound modifiers, using both single words and phrases, as you like.

What do you notice?

Bound Modifiers and Punctuation
One of the things you may have noticed in fooling around with bound modifiers is that they don't require you to use internal sentence punctuation. Why is this so?

We don't use internal punctuation (unless there's a list involved) because our brains can recognize the boundary between one slot and another without punctuation. As we've seen, our brains are used to taking in sentence material, not one word at a time, but in groups of words that "go together." Our brains recognize that the boundaries of slots mark the main segments of a sentence. So even if, in reading aloud, we might pause between the subject or the verb, or between the verb and the direct object, we don't need to put punctuation at those boundaries unless we are adding other words or phrases *between* the boundaries—a technique we'll get to in just a moment. We can trust that our readers will know that one slot has ended and another one has begun; that's because, like us, they are totally familiar with the basic sentence patterns of English.

Bound Modifiers: The Flexible Adverbial

Something else you may have noticed in playing with bound modifiers is that some adverbial modifiers can, in fact, be moved to a different place in the sentence without changing its meaning. In fact, adverbials so frequently appear at the end of a sentence, or at the beginning—that is, not inside the verb slot—that some writers on syntax suggest there is a fifth syntactic slot, which they call the optional adverbial slot. If you prefer to consider adverbials in this way, go right ahead.

Here's an example:

> I ate lunch *at noon.*
>
> *At noon* I ate lunch.

Flexible adverbials are an important tool for creating sentence drama, a subject we'll explore later in this chapter.

The Pros Use Bound Modifiers

To elaborate sentences with bound modifiers comes naturally to us, and this technique can often give powerful results, especially when we choose our added modifiers with care.

> Jacob Saint was sitting at his *ultra-modern* desk in his *ultra-modern* chair. A *cubistic* lamp lit up the *tight* rolls *of fat at the back of his neck.* ... Wreaths *of cigar smoke* rose above his *pink* head.
>
> —Ngaio Marsh, *Enter a Murderer*

All that the *unsuspecting* Bilbo saw that morning was an *old man* *with a staff.* He had a *tall pointed blue* hat, a *long grey* cloak, a *silver* scarf ... and *immense black* boots.

—J.R.R. Tolkien, *The Hobbit*

The smell *of mothballs* came *from a pyramid of hatboxes piled up beside the washstand.*

—Bruce Chatwin, *On the Black Hill*

Can you name these modifiers as single words or phrases? One of the things you will notice is that phrases often "nest" inside other phrases. For instance, in the first example, *of fat at the back of his neck* is an adjectival phrase modifying *rolls,* while *at the back of his neck* is an adjectival phrase modifying *fat* and *of his neck* is an adjectival phrase modifying *back.* If this seems confusing to you, try extricating one of the phrases and applying it to one of the other nouns and you'll see that the sentence no longer makes sense. *A cubistic lamp lit up the tight rolls of his neck?* No, our minds can't make sense of that.

Practice: Using Bound Modifiers
Imitate the use of bound modifiers in the above sentences (or sentences from your favorite writer). Remember that, for the time being, we are considering only single words and phrases as modifiers. What do you notice in doing this?

The Limitations of Bound Modifiers
Bound modifiers are useful tools; and, like any tool, they can be relied upon too much. These days it's common for writers (especially of academic or bureaucratic prose) to "load their slots" (especially the subject slot and the complement/direct object slot) with modifiers. Here's an example:

> An element of a shared symbolic system which serves as a criterion or standard for selection among the alternatives of orientation which are intrinsically open in a situation may be called a value ...[27]

If we try to strip this sentence down to a basic kernel (difficult to do!), we get *An element may be called a value.* Aside from the abstract and general language being used here, the main problem with the original sentence is the way words and phrases are "stuffed" into the subject slot: Just look at how long it takes this sentence to get to its verb!

If you add bound modifiers to a noun phrase or a verb phrase, you make that slot longer. Because there is no punctuation (except between items in a list, as in the Tolkien example above), there are no places in the slot where the reader can take a mental breath. The longer a slot is, the longer a reader has to wait to get to the next slot; therefore the longer she has to wait to put the whole sentence together: *The boy in the blue hat who lives next door in the white house with the green shutters and the red roof is very nice.*

Skilled writers never write like this. Instead, they use another technique for modification: *free modifiers.*

The "When" of Elaborating a Kernel 2: Elaborating with Free Modifiers

While elaborating your kernels with bound modifiers is a useful technique, being able to use another kind of modifier—called *free modifiers*—is even more useful. That's because free modifiers enable us to add information to a sentence, not by "stuffing the slots," but by keeping the kernel (also known as the *base clause*) relatively intact and elaborating it. Free modifiers can do this because they are almost always set off from the slots of the sentence by punctuation. You can remove free modifiers (also called nonrestrictive modifiers) from a sentence and be left with a structurally sound and meaningful kernel. Free modifiers can modify a single word or a phrase acting as a single content part of speech; less frequently, they modify an entire kernel.

The key to working with free modifiers is to keep in mind the basic structure of kernels: noun or noun phrase + verb or verb phrase. (When free modifiers are added to a kernel, usually the subject of the sentence is a phrase, and the predicate is a phrase.) Free modifiers do not interrupt these phrases; they *add* to them.

There are a number of verbal structures that can be used as free modifiers. Here we will concentrate only on phrases, especially prepositional phrases and participial phrases. (Single words can also be used as free modifiers, but more rarely than phrases and other structures.) Later on, we'll look at other structures as free modifiers.

Where Free Modifiers Can Go

In the basic kernel pattern—noun phrase (subject) + verb phrase (predicate)—there are three places where we can place free modifiers:

1. before the subject, to set up the core statement made by the kernel
2. between the subject and the predicate
3. after the predicate, to keep the sentence moving forward

When we elaborate a kernel sentence with free modifiers, we are adding these modifying words or phrases *outside of* syntactic slots. So, unlike bound modifiers, which are stuck *inside* slots, free modifiers can often be moved around to different places in a sentence. Free modifiers thus give writers the freedom to construct a sentence in a number of different ways, depending on the effects they want to create. Free modifiers, then, are one of a writer's most useful tools.

How Free Modifiers Work

Suppose you have this kernel sentence: *The cows stand in the field.* Suppose you want to add more information, like the fact that the cows are chewing their cud. You could rewrite the sentence adding that new information in a participial phrase: *The cows stand in the field, chewing their cud.* You might also rewrite the sentence placing the participial phrase before the subject: *Chewing their cud, the cows stand in the field.* It's even possible to put the participial phrase in between the subject and the verb: *The cows, chewing their cud, stand in the field.*

Some writers on grammar call a sentence that opens with one or more free modifiers a "left-branching sentence," one that ends with free modifiers a "right-branching sentence," and one with the free modifiers between subject and verb a "mid-branching sentence." I prefer to think of free modification in terms of time: What do you want the reader to take in first? What do you want him to take in second? Third?

Free modifiers, like other sentence elements, can only be arranged in ways that make sense, so it isn't always possible to place any particular free modifier in any one of the three positions (before the subject, after the verb, between subject and verb). Nonetheless, free modification opens up a world of possibilities for sentence construction.

Practice: Free Modifiers

Write some kernels, noting the subject and predicate for each one. Now try adding some adjective or adverb phrases to your kernels, as free modifiers. Experiment with different kinds of phrases. Try putting your free modifiers into different places in your sentences. Do the sentences still make sense? How do they sound? Which arrangement do you prefer? Why?

Free Modifiers from the Pros

Skilled writers make frequent use of free modifiers. Here are some examples:

> *Lazy and indifferent, shaking space easily from his wings, knowing his way,* the heron passes over the church beneath the sky.
> —Virginia Woolf, "Monday or Tuesday"

> "You surprise me," said Frank, *yawning drearily, wanting a drink more than anything in the world.*
> —Elizabeth Bowen, "The Needlecase"

> [The snow] had come from the north, *in the mist, driven by the night wind, smelling of the sea.*
> —John le Carré, *The Looking Glass War*

> *With a rattle of chains, a tremble of engines, a blast of siren,* the liner swept round in a half-circle to point into the Straits once more.
>
> —Helen MacInnes, *Decision at Delphi*

Practice: Identify and Imitate Free Modifiers

Select one or more of the examples above (or some sentences from a writer of your choice). Read each sentence aloud, listening first for the kernel of the sentence. Read it again, listening now for the free modifiers. Notice, first, the kind of free modifier being used (single word or phrase; compound phrase, prepositional phrase, participial phrase). Then notice where in the sentence the free modifiers are added.

Now see if you can rewrite the sentence, putting its free modifier(s) in a different place. Does the sentence still make sense? (If not, then you can't write the sentence that way.) How does it sound to you now? Which version do you prefer?

Now take one or more of these sentences and imitate its structure: That is, imitate the kind of free modifier being used and the place in the sentence where the writer has added it.

Understanding the technique of elaborating basic sentences in between syntactic slots will dramatically expand your repertoire of ways to construct sentences. I encourage you to spend as much time as you can investigating and practicing this technique. The more you study and practice, the easier it will be for your word mind to make choices when you write and revise.

Practice: Write Sentences with Free Modifiers

Write a kernel sentence.

Write it again and add one or more free modifiers at the beginning.
Write it again and add one or more free modifiers at the end.
Write it again and add one or more free modifiers in the middle.
What do you notice?

Free Modifiers and Punctuation

In order to make clear that a phrase is serving as a free modifier, it must be set off by punctuation: typically commas or dashes; sometimes parentheses or ellipses.

Those flexible adverbial phrases discussed above can also be considered free modifiers because they can be moved around in a sentence. But, unlike other free modifiers, which must be set off by punctuation, these adverbials sometimes don't have to be. For example, in the sentence *At last the day arrived,* we could add a comma after the word "last," but we don't have to, because, even without the comma, readers will still know how to phrase the sentence.

Free Modifiers and Clear Communication

Free modifiers enable us to add more information and details to our sentences in a way that makes it easy for our readers to process them. Remember that the reader is always moving *forward* through a sentence. You do not want her to have to go back and reread (unless she's thinking *What a great sentence that was! I just have to read it again!*). Free modifiers let us write longer sentences without confusing our readers.

So when we are deciding where in a sentence to place our free modifiers, the most important thing we need to consider is this: Does our sentence make sense?

Because free modifiers are so mobile, writers sometimes fail to keep this principle in mind.

The Dangers of Free Modifiers

Here are some sentences using free modifiers. Read them and note your reaction:

> At the new Chinese restaurant, you can try a delicious pork dish. Thinly sliced and topped with a special sauce, food lovers won't be disappointed.

> After eating a four-course dinner, a concert was given.

Did these sentences make you laugh? Why?

The answer is that in each sentence a modifying phrase has been added in the wrong place, creating the impression that it modifies a word that common sense tells us it can't possibly modify. Food lovers can't be "thinly sliced," nor can a concert eat a "four-course dinner."

When a modifier is placed in the wrong spot in a sentence, grammarians call it a "misplaced modifier" or a "dangling modifier." To avoid such grammatical errors, make sure to read your sentences out loud, slowly, and notice whether you have inserted your free modifiers in a place that creates nonsense. Remember that modifiers, to make sense, need to be placed so that their connection with the noun or verb they modify is absolutely clear.

Free Modifiers and Sentence Drama

Our options for placing any given free modifier in a particular kernel are always limited by common sense: There's no point in trying to put a modifier someplace in a sentence where it distorts the meaning. But within the limits imposed by meaning, free modifiers provide us with options for moving our sentences forward and creating drama through sentence structure.

For instance, take this kernel:

The dog ran away.

Now, suppose we wanted to add an adverbial phrase: *one cold night.*

We could place that phrase before the subject: *One cold night the dog ran away.*

Or we could place it at the end of the sentence: *The dog ran away one cold night.*

We might even be able to put it in between the subject and the predicate: *The dog, one cold night, ran away.*

All these sentences make sense. But which one creates the most drama? Which one do you think will best keep a reader's attention?

Naturally our choice depends on our focus, and on the sentences that precede and follow our sample sentence. But let's assume that we're writing about the dog. To my ear, then, the version of our sample sentence that has the most drama is the one that uses the free modifier to set the scene:

One cold night the dog ran away.

Try reading the three versions of the sentence out loud. Which one sounds most dramatic to you?

In this example we're dealing with that flexible adverbial construction we looked at earlier. (Grammarians don't consider this structure a free modifier, but in its mobility, it acts like one.)

There are other ways, too, that we can create drama in our sentences using free modifiers. Suppose we have this sentence: *They struggled along the rocky, winding, treacherous path.* If we want to, we can take these adjectives (bound modifiers) and combine them into an adjective phrase, and then rewrite the sentence, using the adjective phrase as a free modifier: *They struggled along the path, rocky and winding and treacherous.* Read these sentences out loud. Which one has more drama, to your ear?

Participial phrases as free modifiers can also give us a tool for creating drama. Consider this sentence: *Holding out his hand, smiling broadly, the stranger approached her.* Now consider this version: *The stranger approached her, holding out his hand, smiling broadly.* These sentences are both grammatically correct, but they present the same information in different orders. Read the two versions aloud, listening to the order of the information. Which one sounds better to you? Which one is more dramatic?

Now, creating drama in our sentences may not always be our goal. But, if it is, free modifiers are one of our best tools. Through free modifiers we can decide *when* to give readers information; we can build suspense and anticipation.

Practice: Write Sentences with Free Modifiers

Write some kernels and elaborate each one with free modifiers, aiming to create drama in the sentence.

Free Modifiers and "Flow"

Free modifiers also help us create "flow," or cohesion, in our writing. In other words, they help us move our readers' minds forward from one sentence to the next.

Take, for instance, these three versions of the same sentence:

> With the grace of a ballerina, the cat leaped onto the table.
>
> The cat, with the grace of a ballerina, leaped onto the table.
>
> The cat leaped onto the table with the grace of a ballerina.

Listen to these possibilities. Use your writer's ear. Which one do you prefer?

Listen for sense. Listen for drama. And now, listen for movement—for how each sentence might move the reader's mind forward to another sentence. What might that sentence say?

Remember the principle mentioned earlier that sentences move from known information to unknown information. According to that principle, the "new" information in a sentence comes at the end, which makes the end of a sentence a place of emphasis. Following this principle, it seems to me that the first two sentences, ending up with "the table" direct the reader's mind there. I would expect the following sentence to say something more about the table, or about what the cat found, or did, there. The third sentence, though, ends with "ballerina," and so I would expect the following sentence to say more about the cat's ballerina-like qualities or behavior.

I should caution you that what we are discussing here is very much outside the realm of writing "rules." All three ways of writing the sentence are "correct." Which one is "right," though, depends on the particular purpose of the individual writer.

Free modifiers give you a tool to make your own choices, choices that will contribute to your own style. I urge you to experiment, and to study how writers you like use free modifiers to move the reader's mind from one sentence to the next.

Practice: Write Sentences with Free Modifiers

Write a kernel and elaborate it with one or more free modifiers. Rewrite the sentence, putting the free modifiers in different places (within the limits of sense). Now take a few of these sentences and write a sentence or two after each of them. Does your writing go in a different direction, depending on where you put the free modifiers in your original sentence?

Free Modifiers and Sentence Rhythm

There are many tools to create sentence rhythm, and free modifiers are one of them. The length of a free modifying phrase, and where it's inserted into a sentence kernel, both contribute to the rhythm of a sentence; so does how many modifying phrases the sentence contains. To borrow a term from music composition, free modifiers enable us to "phrase" our sentences. They let our writing breathe. (We'll spend more time on this later.)

Practice: Write Sentences with Free Modifiers

Write some kernels and elaborate them with free modifiers, using your ear to listen to the rhythms you are creating. What do you notice?

Now copy some sentences using free modifiers from one of your favorite writers. Read the sentences out loud, paying attention to the rhythm that is created by the number of free modifiers, their length, and where they are placed in the sentences. Write your own sentences imitating this rhythm.

Practice: Write Sentences with Free Modifiers

Write some sentences using free modifiers, without constructing kernels first. (Keep the kernel pattern in mind, though). Experiment with putting the modifiers in different places in the sentences. Try using more than one free modifier in a sentence. Play, and see what happens!

Practice: Revise with Free Modifiers

Take a passage from your own work and rewrite it using free modifiers.

Practice: Write Sentences with Bound and Free Modifiers
Practice making sentences that contain both bound and free modifiers. Play with using both bound and free modifiers as you write and rewrite a piece of your own.

The Value of Free Modifiers
The use of free modifiers is one of the marks of a skilled writer. One writer on style says, "[The] preservation of the kernel, or a succinct base clause of some kind, amid elaborate free modification, is one of the most important lessons any writer can master." She adds, "Free modification is absolutely essential."[28] When you can use free modifiers as well as bound modifiers, you avoid the pitfall of "loading the slots," and all kinds of stylistic choices become available to you. You have more than one way of saying what you want to say; you have a powerful tool for creating drama and rhythm with your sentences. And, in making these choices, you create your own individual style.

Later on, we'll examine some other sentence elements that can be used as free modifiers. Now, though, we'll take a look at two especially useful ones: the appositive and the nominative absolute.

What Is an Appositive?
An appositive is a different kind of free modifier from the ones we've been playing with so far. Unlike the adjective and adverb phrases we've explored, this kind of free modifier is usually a noun phrase. (Skilled writers also use adjective or even verb phrases as appositives, but we'll stick with noun phrases to begin with.)

So far we've encountered noun phrases in five roles in sentences: as the subject (*My brother's name* is Joe.); as the complement of *be* or a linking verb (Joe was *the happy kid in the family*.); as the direct object of a transitive verb (The cat ate *the leftover pizza*.); as the indirect object of a transitive verb (Dick gave *the black cat* the leftover pizza.); as the object of a preposition or a verbal (We went to *our grandfather's farm*, where we practiced milking *a cow*.). To act as an appositive gives noun phrases one more role to play.

When a noun phrase takes on the role of an appositive, it usually arrives very soon after another noun phrase. The first noun phrase is known as the *antecedent* of the appositive. Most of the time, the appositive serves to rename the antecedent, as in this example:

> Cindy Alexander, my best friend, won the scholarship.

Here the noun phrase *my best friend* follows the noun phrase *Cindy Alexander* and renames it. Note that the appositive is set off by commas—and that it can be removed from the sentence and the sentence will still make sense.

Appositives give us an opportunity to insert more information about nouns into our sentences without having to "load slots." It also gives us another option for where to place information. Apposition is a kind of juxtaposition, a placing of one thing next to, or near, something else. Skilled writers spend time considering where in a sentence information is best placed; apposition provides another tool for making meaning clear and for creating effects.

Appositives need to be set off from the rest of the sentence with punctuation—usually commas or dashes, but sometimes by parentheses or a colon. Sometimes writers make use of sentence fragments as appositives. (See the Christie example in "Other Kinds of Appositives.")

Some Uses of Apposition

What can we do with apposition?

We can use apposition as a form of repetition, to emphasize or call attention to something:

> Steve made a bad joke, a really terrible joke.

In addition to creating emphasis, apposition used in this way can act as a springboard for the writer to add more details:

> Steve made a bad joke, a really terrible joke, a joke so offensive that Cindy decided to break up with him right then.

We can also use the appositive as a kind of synonym for the antecedent. This is particularly helpful when the subject of the sentence is a pronoun. For instance:

> He walked into the room, a man full of his own importance.

Sometimes we can use an appositive at the beginning of a sentence, to set it up:

> The last kid to make the team, Tommy never played a single game.

Appositives can sometimes be placed in the middle of a sentence, too. For instance:

> The dog Julie found—a cocker spaniel with sad eyes—is devoted to her.

As with other free modifiers, we can use appositives to create drama, cohesion, and rhythm in our sentences.

Practice with Appositives

Write some kernels. Now add appositive noun phrases to each of them. Experiment with the placement of these appositives. What do you notice?

The Pros Use Appositives

1. Appositive as synonym

> When she left England the lawyer, *an old man and an old friend*, had patted her hand.
> > —W. Somerset Maugham, *Up at the Villa*

> Everywhere he saw signs of il boom—*the surge in wealth and literacy that was transforming Italy.*
> > —Jess Walter, *Beautiful Ruins*

> Beyond the open window she could see the pale, cloudless sky, *herald of a perfect day.*
> > —Rosamunde Pilcher, "Spanish Ladies"

2. Appositive as a springboard for development

> Once upon a time there was a bat—*a little light brown bat, the color of coffee with cream in it.*
>
> — Randall Jarrell, *The Bat Poet*

> This was the generation whose girls dramatized themselves as flappers, *the generation that corrupted its elders and eventually overreached itself less through lack of morals than through lack of taste.*
>
> —F. Scott Fitzgerald, *The Crack-Up*

Practice Appositives with the Pros

Use the examples above (or find some of your own from professional writers) to get ideas about how to use appositives. Imitate the way in which your chosen writer has used an appositive.

Other Kinds of Appositives

Sometimes writers use structures other than noun phrases as appositives. For instance, a writer may use as appositives adjective or adverb phrases. (Appositive adjectivals are placed *after* the noun they modify.)

> Mrs. Bantry's voice, *breathless and agitated*, came over the wire.
>
> —Agatha Christie, *The Body in the Library*

> She had a round and freckled face, dark brown eyes, and reddish hair, *abundant and thick and windblown.*
>
> —Rosamunde Pilcher, "Miss Cameron at Christmas"

> They stood by the door, the four of them, *waving and waving* until the pedlar, with his pack, his cudgel and his mastiff, had walked out of Swaffham; *out of sight.*
>
> —Kevin Crossley-Holland, "The Pedlar of Swaffham"

Sometimes writers even use verbs as appositives:

> He'd had enough, *could stick it* no longer.
>
> —J.L. Carr, *A Month in the Country*

> Without it she would be lost, *would probably burst into tears*
> *and be unable to stop crying for the rest of the day.*
> —Rosamunde Pilcher, "Spanish Ladies"

More Practice with Appositives
Experiment with different kinds of appositives. Look at writers you like to see how they use appositives, and imitate what they do. Try putting appositives before the subject, in between the subject and predicate, after the predicate. What do you notice? One of the things you may notice is that appositives let you open up a sentence and move it forward, especially when placed after the predicate.

Once you've become comfortable using appositives, you may want to try out another effective technique, the nominative absolute.

What Is a Nominative Absolute?

A nominative absolute (also known as an absolute) is a noun phrase used as a sentence modifier. One of the most useful of the modifying structures, it is almost a complete sentence, so it lets you add a lot of information or detail to a kernel. A nominative absolute must begin with a noun, which cannot be the same as the subject of the sentence to which it's added. Here are five ways to construct nominative absolute phrases:

1. **NOUN OR NOUN PHRASE + ADJECTIVE:** The man, *his head bowed,* muttered to himself.

2. **NOUN OR NOUN PHRASE + PRESENT PARTICIPLE:** The dog, *its tail wagging madly,* ran to meet him.

3. **NOUN OR NOUN PHRASE + PAST PARTICIPLE:** The cat, *claws unsheathed,* hissed at the puppy.

4. **NOUN OR NOUN PHRASE + PREPOSITIONAL PHRASE:** *Hands in his pockets,* the boy stared at her.

5. **NOUN OR NOUN PHRASE + NOUN OR NOUN PHRASE:** The woman, *her hair an unruly mass of curls,* sat before the mirror.

Like other free modifiers, absolute phrases can often be moved to another place in the sentence; like other free modifiers, they can help you create drama, suspense, and rhythm.

Practice with Nominative Absolutes

Following the formulas given above, try constructing short sentences that contain absolute phrases. If you find this difficult, concentrate on one formula at a time, until you've mastered it. Experiment with moving an absolute phrase to different places in your sentence. What happens?

The Pros Use Nominative Absolutes

I had come out of the dark shop doorway into the dazzle of the Damascus sun, *my arms full of silks.*
—Mary Stewart, *The Gabriel Hounds*

She waited, *the lines in her face deepened by her annoyance*, and at last she swung the door fully open to let Fenner step inside.
—Helen MacInnes, *The Venetian Affair*

Practice Nominative Absolutes with the Pros

Find examples of nominative absolutes in the work of your favorite writer, or use the ones above, and imitate these sentences.

Mixing It Up with Modifiers

Make a list of all the kinds of modifiers you've learned about in this chapter. Now write some sentences using more than one kind. Experiment with using modifying words and phrases to create drama, suspense, and rhythm. Find sentences you like from the works of your favorite writers and imitate their structure. (See sidebar.)

I have mentioned that we can use structures other than phrases as modifiers. Before we explore how to do that, we will temporarily leave modifiers and the techniques of elaborating a single kernel and turn, in the next chapter, to techniques of combining kernels.

◾️ TAKE TIME TO REFLECT

Before you turn to the next chapter, take some time to think about what you have learned in this one. What do you want to practice now? Are there any techniques you need to review before moving on? Remember that you are on your own learning journey, and you may want to spend more time with the material in this chapter before moving ahead.

HOW TO IMITATE THE STRUCTURE OF A SENTENCE

You can, if you like, imitate a sentence by a professional writer entirely by ear: Read it aloud several times and then imitate the rhythm of the sentence structure. But you'll learn a lot more if you first consciously take the model sentence apart and name its constituent structures, like this:

Model sentence: *Mrs. Bantry's voice, breathless and agitated, came over the wire.*

1. IDENTIFY THE KERNEL: *Mrs. Bantry's voice came over the wire.*

2. IDENTIFY THE PARTS OF THE KERNEL: *S = Mrs. Bantry's voice, P = came over the wire* (S identifies the subject of the sentence; P identifies the predicate. Usually the predicate can be broken down further, as here: *P = V [verb=came] + ADV [adverbial phrase = over the wire]*)

If you are at the stage in your practicing where you want to practice only kernels, then forget about the rest of your model sentence and imitate the kernel pattern it exemplifies: *S + V + adverbial*. In this case, you can, if you wish, enhance your practice by looking more closely at the components of the kernel sentence. You'll see that here the subject of the model sentence is a noun phrase consisting of a possessive proper noun and another noun, and that the adverbial is a prepositional phrase. You might then write the pattern you want to practice this way:

Noun phrase (possessive proper noun + noun) + verb phrase (verb + prepositional phrase as adverb)

Now you have a more specific pattern to practice.

3. IDENTIFY THE BOUND MODIFIER(S): In this case, *Mrs. Bantry's*.

4. IDENTIFY THE FREE MODIFIER(S): Here, *breathless and agitated*—and name the construction and the role the modifier is playing (in this case, a compound adjective phrase serving as an appositive and modifying *voice*). Notice whether the free modifier is located before the subject, between the subject and predicate, or after the predicate.

5. WRITE THE PATTERN YOU WANT TO PRACTICE: For example, based on this model, you could extract this pattern:

Subject + two appositive adjectives in a compound phrase + predicate

6. REMEMBER THAT YOU HAVE CHOICES ABOUT HOW SPECIFIC YOU WANT YOUR IMITATION TO BE: You should make your choice based on what you need to focus on in your practicing right now. So, if you are just starting to work with appositives, you might want to use the pattern in #5. Your sentence will then imitate the overall structure of your model but perhaps not the details. For instance, following the pattern in #5, you might write something like this: *The boys, laughing and shouting, chased the dog.* If you wanted your sentence to be a more exact copy of the model, then you would need to make the pattern you extract from your model more detailed, like this:

Subject (noun phrase = possessive noun as adjective + noun) + appositive adjectives in compound phrase + predicate (verb + adverbial prepositional phrase)

But most of the time, you can learn the skills you need by focusing on the larger elements of sentence structure (as in #5).

7. DON'T GET AHEAD OF YOURSELF: Make sure that you have a solid grasp of the simpler structures before moving on to more complex ones.

CHAPTER 12

EXTENDING
THE BASIC SENTENCE

....

Only connect.

....

So far we have been fooling around with techniques that allow us to elaborate a single kernel sentence by adding to it words or phrases that act as modifiers, either bound or free. Now let's turn to another essential way of adding more material to a single sentence: by combining it with other sentences. In order to learn how to do this, we need to add one more grammatical term to our vocabulary: the word *clause*.

EXTENDING THE BASIC SENTENCE 1:
ADDING TOGETHER INDEPENDENT CLAUSES

An independent clause is a group of words that can stand alone as a complete sentence; that is, it contains both a subject and a predicate. The sentences we have been constructing so far are all independent clauses: Kernels and elaborated kernels are both independent clauses. (A sentence made up of only one independent clause is also known as a *simple sentence*.)

Independent clauses can be added together to make longer sentences:

> "There were two brothers of mine fishing and one day they
> went away to the States. I went down to the pier one morning,
> and I had an old bag of books, and I had no use for books at
> that time, or schooling. You know what I did? I threw them
> inside the fence and went out in the curragh, the canoe, and
> when I came home in the evening, I had a bag of pollocks—
> the pollocks was my exchange for the books."
>
> —Irish storyteller Tomas Walsh, quoted by Lawrence Millman,
> *Our Like Will Not Be There Again*

To add sentences together in this way comes naturally to us—just listen to any young child telling a story: *And then the lion came and then the lion growled and then the lion ate the pig.* To create longer sentences by adding together two or more independent clauses, we need to use a particular group of conjunctions called *coordinating conjunctions: and, but, for, or, nor, yet,* and *so.*

Coordinating conjunctions join words or groups of words that are equal in structure: two nouns, for instance, or two prepositional phrases. So these conjunctions are the ones we use when we want to combine independent clauses.

Writers of fiction and narrative nonfiction often use *and* to join independent clauses, thus creating forward motion, a narrative pace.

> There was a crowd of kids watching the car, and the square
> was hot, and the trees were green, and the flags hung on their
> staffs, and it was good to get out of the sun and under the
> shade of the arcade that runs all around the square.
>
> —Ernest Hemingway, *The Sun Also Rises*

They also frequently make use of *and* at the beginning of sentences, to create cohesion.

> [Honolulu] is the meeting place of East and West. The very
> new rubs shoulders with the immeasurably old. And if you

have not found the romance you expected you have come
upon something singularly intriguing.

—W. Somerset Maugham, "Honolulu"

Practice: Join Independent Clauses

Write a number of independent clauses. Then, using coordinating
conjunctions, join them together, two or three at a time. Read over
these longer sentences. What do you notice?

Perhaps you noticed that you had to stop and think about which
coordinating conjunction to use. Do you want to write *It was raining, and we stayed home?* Or *It was raining, but we stayed home?* Or
It was raining, so we stayed home? Your choice depends on your intended meaning.

Conjunctions like *and* or *but* may appear to lack meaning, but
you may find as you play with them that this is not the case. It's
been suggested that *and* indicates "continuous and repeated action,"
while *but* suggests "contrast, opposition, or negation." A number of
writers (Oscar Wilde, Edgar Arlington Robinson, and others) have
been named as the source of a quote that says, in effect, "I spent the
entire morning putting an *and* into my manuscript, and the entire
afternoon taking it out." Coordinating conjunctions may be short
words, but they have a lot of power!

You may also have noticed that combining the same independent clauses in different orders sometimes results in different meanings. For example: *The two dogs growled at each other, and then
they fought.* This is not the same as *The two dogs fought, and then
they growled at each other.* Remember, always, that you are putting
groups of words into your readers' minds one group at a time. The
order in which you present these groups helps determine the sense
readers make out of them. Keeping this principle in mind enables
you to craft sentences that take your readers exactly where you
want them to go.

Grammarians tell us that when we join two independent clauses, we must punctuate the resulting sentence with a comma after
the first independent clause (before the conjunction). Profession-

al writers, especially writers of fiction, often choose to ignore this rule, omitting the conjunction or using other punctuation marks.

Joining Independent Clauses Without Conjunctions

Sometimes professional writers will choose to join independent clauses by using punctuation alone, without a conjunction. This technique is called *asyndeton*. (Asyndeton can also be used with single words or phrases.)

When a writer makes use of asyndeton, he can juxtapose two images or ideas without making explicit the connection between them; he can create emphasis; and he can create an effect of accelerated motion or intensity, or a sense of things happening simultaneously. For instance:

> I cannot rest, I cannot stay, I cannot linger anywhere.
>
> —Charles Dickens, *A Christmas Carol*

> I hurried through the greenwood. I kicked leaves and they crackled, I stroked grass and it was silk.
>
> —Kevin Crossley-Holland, "The Green Children"

Often clauses put together without conjunctions are kernels, or kernels only slightly elaborated. Trying to put together longer clauses using asyndeton is trickier, and, if you attempt this, you may find yourself accused of having made a grammatical error known as the comma splice. (Asyndeton with clauses and the comma splice refer to exactly the same thing, so grammar snobs may object no matter what!) To decide whether you are using asyndeton well, you need to read your sentences out loud and listen to them. If you have a good reason for omitting the conjunction between two independent clauses, then you will be able to justify your choice.

Asyndeton can also be used with compound predicates, as in this example:

> He had removed his gray jacket, hung it carefully over the back of his chair, slackened his dark-blue tie, loosened his white collar.
>
> —Helen MacInnes, *The Venetian Affair*

Joining Independent Clauses with Other Punctuation

Ordinarily, grammatical convention demands that independent clauses connected by punctuation alone must be joined not with a comma, but with a semicolon, a dash, or a colon. Most writers, especially of nonfiction, follow the convention—at least most of the time. For example:

> Bill adjusted his tie; he settled his hat more firmly on his head.

> He knew he would find Elaine at work—she never left early.

> He planned to tell her what was on his mind: She might be the murderer's next victim.

The Pros Combine Independent Clauses
1. USING COORDINATING CONJUNCTIONS:

> Once it was the middle of winter, and the snowflakes fell from the sky like feathers.
>
> —Randall Jarrell, *Snow-White*

> Jimmy Sinclair was there meeting us at the end of his own branch road. It is a lyrical little road to Lyking, with a good deal of winding in it and ups and downs, and that afternoon it was gay with trefoil and buttercups, daisies, cotton and springy heather.
>
> —George Mackay Brown, *Northern Lights*

2. USING COMMAS:

> The color subsided in her cheeks, her eyes could meet his, her pretty hands … were relaxed as he lit her cigarette, she even laughed.
>
> —Helen MacInnes, *The Venetian Affair*

3. USING DASHES:

> As if in a dream, [Newton] walked towards the German with only one option—he hit the soldier hard in the face with his

fist and the man crumpled and fell unconscious.
—John Nichol and Tony Rennell,
Home Run: Escape from Nazi Europe

4. USING SEMICOLONS:

The loudspeaker was humming; it blared suddenly, faded
out and began again, properly tuned.
—John le Carré, *The Looking Glass War*

5. USING SEMICOLONS AND CONJUNCTIONS:

Everyone thought this was a very auspicious beginning; and
they were right.
—Robin McKinley, *The Door in the Hedge*

6. USING COLONS:

The transition from pagan to Christian is the point at which
the ancient world still touches ours directly. We are heirs to
its conclusion: on either side, participants shared an education which, until recently, we widely maintained.
—Robin Lane Fox, *Pagans and Christians*

Practice: Use Punctuation to Join Independent Clauses
Experiment with writing independent clauses and joining them together in the ways discussed above.

The Value of Joining Independent Clauses

When we join independent clauses, we create *a compound sentence*.
Knowledge of different ways of joining independent clauses will provide you with more options for making sentences. Now you'll be able to
make sentences of different length, to create rhythm and variety. You'll
also be able to create effects by using short and long sentences together.

Compound sentences, like simple sentences, can be plain or elaborated with modifiers. Now you have four kinds of sentences at your
disposal: the plain kernel (or independent clause); the elaborated kernel; the compound sentence; and the elaborated compound sentence.

Practice: Elaborated Compound Sentences

Write some kernel sentences and then combine two or more of them into compound sentences. Now rewrite one or more of these compound sentences, elaborating them using any of the techniques you learned in the last chapter. Try writing some elaborated compound sentences without starting from kernels. What do you notice in doing this practice?

EXTENDING THE BASIC SENTENCE 2: ADDING DEPENDENT CLAUSES

There's another way to extend the basic sentence besides joining two or more independent clauses. You can add to your basic sentence a different kind of clause: a *dependent clause*.

To add together two independent clauses is to join two groups of words of equal importance, two structures that each have a subject and a predicate: in other words, two kernels or two elaborated kernels, or one plain kernel and one elaborated one. To join an independent clause and a dependent clause is to do something a little bit different: namely, to make one clause "depend" (grammatically speaking) on another.

This process may sound confusing, but in fact we make sentences containing dependent clauses all the time in ordinary speech: *If she doesn't get here soon, I'm leaving.* Or *The man you want is the one who is wearing the brown coat.* Let's see if we can get a better understanding of what we are doing when we construct such sentences.

A dependent clause, like an independent one, has to contain a subject and a predicate; otherwise it couldn't be a clause. But while it's easy to identify the subject and the predicate in an independent clause, and to understand at once that an independent clause can stand alone as a complete sentence, such identification is harder to do with dependent clauses. That's because dependent clauses are *altered* independent clauses, and it's this alteration that makes them "dependent" on—or subordinate to—independent clauses.

There are two main ways that we turn independent clauses into dependent ones: by using subordinating conjunctions, and by using relative pronouns. When we take the first approach, the dependent clauses we create are known as *subordinate clauses*. When we take the second approach, the dependent clauses we create are known as *relative clauses*.

Making Dependent Clauses 1: Using Subordinating Conjunctions

Suppose we have two independent clauses: *Bill failed his exam. His father was disappointed.* If we join these two clauses with the coordinating conjunction *and*, we will have this sentence: *Bill failed his exam, and his father was disappointed.* By joining the clauses in this way we have made a connection between the meaning of the first sentence and the meaning of the second. Try reading the sentence out loud. How does it sound to you? Perhaps to your ear it sounds fine. And certainly, according to the rules of grammar, there are no grammatical errors in this sentence. And yet …

One of the things that professional writers do is to try, as best they can, to make the meaning of their sentences absolutely clear to their readers. One way they do that, as we saw in the sections on word choice, is to select exactly the right words that convey their meaning. Another way they create clarity for readers is to arrange words and phrases in sentences in exactly the right order. And a third technique they use, when they combine two or more clauses into a single sentence, is to show exactly how the statement one clause makes connects with the statement another clause makes.

To make connections between one statement and another is not, as so many inexperienced writers assume, the responsibility of the reader; it is the duty of the writer. The work of writing requires us to *think* about these connections, if not while we are getting our first ideas down on the page, then certainly as we revise. That's because a large part of the meaning of a piece of writing resides, not in individual words or phrases or clauses, but in the ways word is *connected* to word, phrase to phrase, clause to clause. When a writer fails to make clear the connection between the elements in a sentence, the reader will not know what he is trying to say.

Dependent clauses give writers another tool to make their meaning clear to readers. *Bill failed his exam, and his father was disappointed.* An experienced writer will read that sentence and think to herself, *If I write the sentence that way, I won't be making clear to the reader exactly what the relationship is between the two parts of the sentence.* And so, she will rewrite, perhaps like this: *Because Bill failed his exam, his father was disappointed.* Now the exact relationship, the specific connection, between the two statements is clear, and her readers will be able to understand her meaning.

Practice: Make Subordinate Clauses

Write some independent clauses. Now turn them into subordinate clauses by adding to each one a subordinating conjunction: *if, though, because, before, after, since, as, while, when, where, unless, although.* (These are some of the most commonly used subordinating conjunctions; if you want a complete list, consult a good grammar book.) You may not be able to turn all your independent clauses into dependent ones; use your ear and your common sense.

Note the pattern for creating this kind of dependent clause:

subordinating conjunction + independent clause = subordinate clause

Now select some of those subordinate clauses and turn them into complete sentences by adding one or more independent clauses. Read your sentences out loud. What do you notice?

Making Dependent Clauses 2: Using Relative Pronouns

The other most common way to construct dependent clauses also begins with an independent clause. But in this approach, instead of adding something to the independent clause, we take something away: We substitute a *relative pronoun* for the word or phrase that is the subject of the clause.

Suppose you have two independent clauses: *The man is laughing loudly. He is wearing a brown coat.* It's possible to combine them using a coordinating conjunction, but the result may not be satisfactory: *The man is laughing loudly, and he is wearing a brown coat.* Your ear will tell you, *That construction doesn't sound right!* If you try to use a subordinating conjunction, your ear will again object. *Because the man is laughing loudly, he is wearing a brown coat.* Nope. That makes no sense. Those of you who have practiced phrases will immediately see a way to rewrite the sentence so it does make sense: *The man in the brown coat is laughing loudly.*

Here's another option: *The man who is wearing a brown coat is laughing loudly.* To construct this sentence we have replaced the pronoun *he* with the relative pronoun *who*, thereby turning the independent clause *he is wearing a brown coat* into a particular kind of dependent clause known as a *relative clause.* Now the clause reads *who is wearing a brown coat.*

You will see right away that the clause *who is wearing a brown coat,* while it has a subject (*who*) and a predicate (*is wearing a brown coat),* can't stand alone as a sentence; it has to "depend" on another independent clause, in this case *The man is laughing loudly.*

Practice: Make Relative Clauses

Write some short independent clauses. Now turn them into relative clauses by replacing the subject with a *relative pronoun,* such as *who, whom, whose, which,* or *that.* Note the pattern for creating relative clauses:

> relative pronoun (replacing noun or pronoun) + predicate = relative clause

Now complete each sentence by combining the relative clause with an independent clause. Read your sentences out loud. What do you notice?

Note that the word *that* is sometimes omitted from relative clauses, especially in informal writing: *The dress [that] I wore was green with white trim.* Sometimes writers feel confused about relative pronouns;

if you're not sure whether to use *that* or *which,* for example, or *who* or *whom,* consult your grammar book.

What Dependent Clauses Do

Now that we've explored how to make dependent clauses, let's take a look at some of the things they can do in sentences. There are three main roles that dependent clauses can play: They can serve as adverbs, as adjectives, and as nouns.

The Role of Dependent Clauses 1: Adverbs

Most of the time, dependent clauses created with subordinating conjunctions take the role of adverbs in their sentences. In this role they are known as *adverb clauses.* For example:

> Joe took an umbrella with him because the weather forecast promised rain.

The subordinate clause *because the weather forecast promised rain* explains why Joe took the umbrella, and modifies the verb, *took*; therefore, the subordinate clause—*in its entirety*—is serving as an adverb. Many other sentences follow this pattern:

> independent clause + subordinate clause (as adverb)

Most of the time, sentences that follow this pattern don't require punctuation between the independent and subordinate clauses.

Sometimes, though, writers like to reverse the order of the two clauses, putting the subordinate clause first:

> Because the weather forecast promised rain, Joe took an umbrella with him.

In this case, a comma follows the subordinate clause.

An adverb clause can also modify a verbal. For example:

> I needed to do my homework before the game started.

Practice: Subordinate Clauses as Adverbs

Try writing sentences using subordinate clauses as adverbs, following either of the preceding patterns. Try using verbals other than infinitives, if you like.

The Role of Dependent Clauses 2: Adjectives

When we make dependent clauses using relative pronouns, these clauses usually function as adjectives in their sentences; in this case, they are known as *adjective clauses*. For example:

> The man who stopped by last night is my cousin.

The dependent clause *who stopped by last night* serves—in its entirety—as an adjective modifying the noun phrase *The man*.

Writers sometimes feel confused about the punctuation of adjective clauses. Here are some tips to help.

The words *who, whom, which,* and *that* are the most commonly used relative pronouns. When you begin an adjective clause with one of these words, you need to decide whether or not the information the clause contains is essential to the meaning of the noun being modified. For instance, suppose you have the sentence *The woman walked down the street.* You want to add more information about the woman in an adjective clause: *who was carrying a cocker spaniel.* Perhaps you'll write the new sentence like this: *The woman who was carrying a cocker spaniel walked down the street.* Or perhaps you'll write it like this: *The woman, who was carrying a cocker spaniel, walked off down the street.* Your decision should be based on whether the information in the adjective clause is—or is not—essential to naming the woman. If you need that information to identify this particular woman and to distinguish her from others (perhaps another woman carrying a different breed of dog), then you will write the sentence without punctuation. If, however, the information in the adjective clause is *not* essential to identifying the woman, then you write the sentence with commas around the adjective clause. (When you have a sentence using an essential relative clause, sometimes it's possible to omit the relative pronoun and turn the verb into a participle, creating an adjective phrase: *The woman carrying a cocker spaniel walked down the street.*)

Grammarians also tell us that the word *that,* when used as a relative pronoun, always indicates an essential dependent clause. Adjective clauses beginning with *which, who,* or *whom* may or may not be essential, depending on their meaning.

At the risk of creating hopeless confusion, I will add one more technique here: the use of words such as *when, where, after, before, since, while,* and *why* to create clauses that function as adjectives. You'll remember you encountered these words just a little while ago, in their role as subordinate conjunctions, beginning clauses that function as adverbs. But through the mysterious ability of English words to take on many different roles in sentences, these same words can also act as *relative adverbs;* in this role they drive adjective (not adverb) clauses—like so:

> They moved to a small Ohio town where Alice's parents
> own a house.

In this sentence, the clause that begins with *where* modifies town, thus serving as an adjective clause.

Without punctuation, relative clauses function as bound modifiers; with punctuation, as free modifiers.

Practice: Relative Clauses as Adjectives
Experiment with using relative clauses as adjectives. If you get confused about "the rules," consult a good grammar book.

The Role of Dependent Clauses 3: Nouns
Dependent clauses can sometimes serve as nouns. Here's how:

> I know where he is.

Can you name the elements of this sentence? There's a subject, the pronoun, I; there's a main verb, know; and there's a dependent clause, where he is—which is taking on the role of a noun serving as the direct object of the verb.

A noun clause can do almost anything a noun can do in sentences. For instance:

Noun clause as subject: *What he said* baffled me.

Noun clause as complement: My apple pie is *what he loves best.*

Noun clause as object of transitive verb: I know *where he is.*

Noun clause as object of a preposition: We'll go to *whichever store you prefer.*

Noun clause as appositive: I want you to know a secret: *that I solved the problem.*

Practice: Noun Clauses

Noun clauses are a little tricky, but they can be fun to fool around with. Try writing some kernels and then see if you can replace any of the nouns with noun clauses. Or choose one of the structures above and imitate it to write a sentence using a noun clause. What do you think of this particular sentence structure?

The Options Provided by Dependent Clauses

Do I Want to Use a Word, a Phrase, or a Clause?

Like phrases, dependent clauses are groups of words that "go together," that function as a unit. Like phrases, these word-groups can also take on the roles of nouns, or of adjectives or adverbs, in sentences. And so dependent clauses provide us with yet another way of saying things; along with single words and phrases, they give us limitless choice in constructing our sentences. For instance, do we want to write: *Mike kicked the cat hard*? Or would we rather write *Mike kicked the cat onto the floor* (adverb phrase instead of single adverb)? Or perhaps we'd rather write this *When Mike got angry, he kicked the cat onto the floor* (adverb clause added)?

So the first kind of option we have is whether to use single words, phrases, or clauses (or some combination thereof) for adjectives, adverbs, and nouns.

Practice: Choose Single Words, Phrases, or Clauses

Write some kernel sentences. Then take one of these and see if you can add single adverbs or adjectives (or both). Now rewrite the sentence substituting phrases as adjectives or adverbs, or including them in addition to single-word modifiers. Now rewrite the sentence again, using clauses instead of phrases, or adding clauses (if your sentence still makes sense this way). Now try substituting noun phrases or noun clauses for single nouns. What do you notice? Try this whole process again with more kernels.

And now rewrite your sentences, making choices among all these options.

Where Do I Put My Dependent Clause?

The second choice we need to make is where in our sentences dependent clauses should go. Often dependent clauses, like phrases, can serve as *free modifiers*. We can choose where in a sentence to put them: at the beginning, before the subject; at the end, after the main verb of the sentence; perhaps, sometimes, even in the middle, between the subject and the main verb.

How do we make these choices?

You'll find it easier to make such choices as you train your word mind with practice and study, and as you imitate the sentences of professional writers; with this practice comes facility with single words, phrases, and clauses. And then, in the heat of composition, or—more likely—in revision, you'll need to listen to your sentences and pay attention to what your ear is telling you. Do your sentences make sense? Will they be clear to your readers? Have you created enough movement and drama, or do you need to try another way of saying what you are trying to say? What about the rhythm of each sentence, the rhythm of all the sentences in a paragraph working together? These are the kinds of questions you can ask yourself as you revise (and revise, and revise …).

The most important things to hold onto in writing sentences are these: Always be aware of the basic kernel structure of English sentences; and keep in mind at all times the necessity for *ordering* the elements of your sentences. Look, for instance, at how these writers use all of the structures we've been talking about to create fairly long sentences that, however, never confuse the reader:

> Father Wolf listened, and below in the valley that ran down to a little river, he heard the dry, angry, snarling, singsong whine of a tiger who has caught nothing and does not care if all the jungle knows it.
>
> —Rudyard Kipling, *The Jungle Book*

> Fat women, gross women, stumpy women, bony women, shapeless women, old women, plain women, sat in the spacious armchairs and because Lisette looked so sweet bought the clothes that so admirably suited her.
>
> —W. Somerset Maugham, "Appearance and Reality"

> A woman who can toss you a check for a hundred grand without blinking hasn't had much practice listening to reason from a hireling, but she managed it.
>
> —Rex Stout, *The Doorbell Rang*

> We drove over to Fifth Avenue, so warm and soft, almost pastoral, on the summer Sunday afternoon that I wouldn't have been surprised to see a great flock of white sheep turn the corner.
>
> —F. Scott Fitzgerald, *The Great Gatsby*

> Our garden was the center of my world, the place above all others where I wished to remain forever.
>
> —Esther Hautzig, *The Endless Steppe*

Practice: Place Dependent Clauses

Write some sentences using dependent clauses (subordinate or relative). Experiment with rewriting these sentences, placing the dependent clauses in a different place in the sentence (if the sentence still makes sense that way). What do you notice?

NEW SENTENCE STRUCTURES

When we use subordinate and relative clauses, we are doing two things. One of these—using clauses as nouns, adjectives, and adverbs—we have just explored. At the same time, when we use dependent clauses, we are creating new sentence structures.

Complex Sentences

When we combine one (or more) dependent clauses and an independent clause, we are creating what's known as a *complex sentence*. Here's the pattern for this kind of sentence:

> dependent clause(s) (can be subordinate or relative) + independent clause = complex sentence
> When the thunder crashed, we ran screaming into the house.

Practice: Make Complex Sentences

Write some sentences according to the pattern for complex sentences. Try some with only one dependent clause; try some using more than one dependent clause. Read your sentences out loud. What do you notice?

Compound-Complex Sentences

There's another common sentence pattern you'll want to have in your repertoire: the *compound-complex sentence*. Here you add two or more independent clauses together along with one or more dependent clauses.

> Jane wanted to talk, but because Joe was tired, he refused.

Practice: Make Compound-Complex Sentences

Write some sentences according to the pattern for compound-complex sentences. What happens when you do this? Read your sentences out loud. How do they sound to you?

The Pros Combine Independent and Dependent Clauses
1. WITH SUBORDINATING CONJUNCTIONS:

In the neighboring court, where the Lord Chancellor of the rag and bottle shop dwells, there is a general tendency towards beer and supper.
—Charles Dickens, *Bleak House*

Although the roots go back decades, the 2000 and 2004 presidential elections marked the transformation of the GOP into the first religious party in U.S. history.
—Kevin Phillips, *American Theocracy*

On to the pigs' house, where four grunters—one yellow, with a dainty white head—romped playfully, while, led by the Skea boys, I picked my way through gilded pools and that strong sweet gorge-raising smell peculiar to pigs, into an inner sanctum, where a really immense porker lay on her side and a dozen week-old piglets with curly tails scampered round her.
—George Mackay Brown, *Northern Lights*

He lay in the soothing water utterly at ease for the first time since his long journey home had begun eight weeks before.
—Marjorie Allingham, *Coroner's Pidgin*

2. WITH RELATIVE PRONOUNS:

She was a child whose father and mother were dead and who lived around with various uncles and aunts.
—Lucy Maud Montgomery, *The Road to Avonlea*

In the county of Gloucestershire there lived with his father, who was a farmer, a boy called Dick.
—Walter de la Mare, "Dick and the Beanstalk"

3. WITH BOTH KINDS OF DEPENDENT CLAUSE:

[Gran'ther Pendleton] ignored them, this naughty old man, who would give his weak stomach frightful attacks of indigestion by stealing out to the pantry and devouring a

whole mince pie because he had been refused two pieces
at the table ...
—Dorothy Canfield Fisher, "Heyday of the Blood"

Practice: Learning from the Pros
Look at the work of writers you like for how they use dependent clauses in constructing sentences, or go back and study the preceding examples. Copy out some of these sentences and imitate their structure
(that is, use the same number of relative/subordinate and independent
clauses in each sentence, and in the same order). Read your sentences
out loud. What do you notice?

Practice: Combine Kernels in Different Ways
Write five or six kernels that all have the same subject. Now practice
different ways of combining them. (Add new words if necessary.)

Making Choices in Sentence Structure
As you are undoubtedly realizing now, the use of dependent clauses can
dramatically expand the possibilities for sentence construction. You
can write kernels—short and syntactically simple. You can elaborate
your kernels with bound or free modifiers, sometimes single words,
sometimes phrases. You can add independent clauses (kernels or elaborated kernels) together via coordination. You can turn some of your
independent clauses into dependent clauses and combine the two via
subordination. You can make use of all these possibilities.

The choices you make in sentence structure help create your own
style. They also create variations in rhythm, and they contribute to (or
obscure) readability. With a command of sentence structures you can
control the movement and drama of your sentences, thereby heightening
suspense, shaping your readers' experience, and riveting their attention.

As I've said, I recommend that you spend a good deal of time studying how professional writers use syntactic structures; then experiment
with different sentence structures to see which ones you like.

Practice: Make Choices in Sentence Structure

Experiment with the sentence structures you've learned in any way that appeals to you. You may want to revise a passage of your own writing to make use of your new learning.

 # TAKE TIME TO REFLECT

What has stood out for you in this chapter? Which techniques do you want to spend more time with? You may want to revise your practice list to give priority to these new techniques.

TWO IMPORTANT NOTES

If you feel confused as you do these practices, don't fret! It isn't all that important to know the right labels for elements of sentences; I have included the labels so that, if you like, you will be able to look up these terms in a grammar handbook. More important than knowing the correct grammatical names is being able to make use of these techniques to compose sentences. You may find it easier to learn how to do this by listening to sentences (yours and those of professional writers) rather than using the grammatical terms.

Remember, too, that you can take as much time as you need to learn these sentence constructions. There will be no test at the end of this book to see whether you have learned everything! Keep checking in with yourself to see how much of all this information about sentences you can actually use right now. For instance, I have found it very helpful to concentrate on kernels for a long time (and to keep coming back to them in my practice) before moving on to practicing more complex structures. There's absolutely nothing wrong with reading through some of this information, trying the practices, and then saying to yourself, "I'm not ready for this yet."

Also, when you imitate sentences by your favorite writers, look first for sentences that contain the structure each practice is focusing on. You may find that these sentences also contain structures that you're not yet familiar with. You can do your best to imitate the entire sentence anyway, or you can omit the unfamiliar structure from your imitation.

SECTION 5

The Power of Composition: Putting It All Together

Don't study an art; practice it.

—JAPANESE PROVERB

GETTING THE SPELL RIGHT

I hope by now you are feeling excited (and not too overwhelmed) by all the options we have for constructing English sentences. With all these options in your repertoire, you can make *choices* when you write and revise, in the process developing your own writing style.

Even more important, when you have a command of sentence structure, as well as of diction, you have power: the ability to cast a spell over your readers, to grab and keep their attention, to make things happen inside them. Readers are fickle creatures, with many other demands on their time and energy. We writers need all the linguistic resources we can find to keep them reading our words.

This does not mean that our sentences must be long and complex. It means, rather, that we must know what we are doing when we write and revise our sentences. The more we practice, the more we study the work of skilled writers, the more we will learn about how sentences affect readers, and the easier it will become for us to make our syntactic choices.

When we make our choices, we can consider a number of different things. In this section we'll examine a few of them. First, we'll review the basics of syntactic structures and some of our options for using them. Then we'll see how these options enable us to produce writing that is clear, writing that contains the energy of movement, writing that has the quality of flow: all characteristics that grab and keep our readers' attention. Finally, we'll do some playing with sentence rhythm, to add variety and interest to our sentences.

In all these practices, we'll be working in the realm of composition, where we draw on everything we have already learned about diction and syntax to create sentences powerful enough to transfer what we want to say into the minds of others, powerful enough to keep them spellbound.

CHAPTER 13

MAKING SENTENCES MOVE

....

Essentially style resembles good manners. It comes of endeav-
ouring to understand others, of thinking for them rather than
yourself—or thinking, that is, with the heart as well as the head.
....

—SIR ARTHUR QUILLER-COUCH

A COMMAND OF SYNTACTIC STRUCTURES

Most inexperienced writers believe that what makes a person a good writer is her ability to come up with words. As we've seen, though, skilled writers know how to choose words *and* they know how to arrange those words effectively in sentences. Skilled writers, then, have a command of syntactic structures. This doesn't mean they necessarily know the grammatical names for every structure they use; it does mean that they have those structures so completely embedded in their word mind, in their writer's ear, that they can make effective choices every time they write or revise a sentence. If you want to raise the quality of your writing, to make it more powerful, then I urge you, once again,

234

to practice, practice, practice the syntactic structures you learned in the last section, until you can use them without thinking about them.

If you have practiced faithfully, by now you have learned these things: the elements of syntax (parts of speech, phrases, clauses), how to make kernel sentences, how to construct more complex sentences, and how to imitate sentence structures in the work of professional writers. In case you need it, you'll find in the sidebar a quick review of syntactic constructions.

SYNTACTIC CONSTRUCTIONS: A REVIEW

When we compose sentences, we must use nouns and verbs, and we usually use adjectives and adverbs as well. All of these content parts of speech may be single words, or they may be phrases. Nouns, adjectives, and adverbs can often be clauses. (Verbs cannot.)

Nouns can play the following roles (among others)[29] in a sentence:

1. Noun as subject of a sentence or a clause:

   Jane spoke loudly.

   Because *Bob* was late, we missed the plane.

2. Noun as direct object of a verb:

   Bob patted *the dog.*

3. Noun as subject complement of a *be* verb or linking verb:

   Joe is *my friend.*

4. Noun as indirect object:

   We gave *Amy* all the apples.

5. Noun as object complement:

   The club made Susan *president.*

6. Noun as object of a preposition:

   He drove to *the store.*

7. Noun as object of a verbal:

> Bowing *their heads*, the congregation prayed.
>
> To catch *the thief*, they set a trap.

8. Noun as adjective:

> They sat on the lawn in the fading *summer* light.

9. Noun as adverb:

> Steve went *home*.

10. Noun as appositive:

> John, *my friend*, spoke up for me.

11. Noun as nominative absolute:

> Sally, *her lips* pressed together, shook her head.

PRACTICE: NOUN CONSTRUCTIONS

Practice using nouns in the ways outlined above. Start with single nouns, then experiment with noun phrases and noun clauses.

PRACTICE: VERB CONSTRUCTIONS

Verbs, as we've learned, can take two roles in sentences: They can be the main verb of a sentence or a clause (finite verbs) or they can be verbals (nonfinite verbs).

Practice using finite and nonfinite verbs. Review Chapter 8 if you can't quite remember how verbals work.

PRACTICE: ADJECTIVE AND ADVERB CONSTRUCTIONS

Adjectives, as you know, modify nouns. They can also follow, as subject complement, a *be* verb or a linking verb. Adverbs modify verbs, and sometimes they modify nouns or adjectives. Adjectives and adverbs can be single words, phrases, or clauses; they can be used as bound modifiers or free modifiers.

OPTIONS FOR COMPOSITION

If you take the time to explore all the syntactic constructions in English, and the ways in which they can be used, you'll undoubtedly be amazed at how many options we have for composing sentences. Add to these the immense word hoard of the English language, and it's clear that the possibilities for writing sentences are infinite. Perhaps you find all those options exhilarating, or perhaps they make you feel overwhelmed. Either way, it's important to remember that while all those options exist, we don't have to make use of every single one of them. As we write and revise, we make choices about which ones to use. Exploring the options through practice makes our word mind stronger and more flexible, less stuck in the same old ruts of sentence construction. At the same time, when we work on a piece of writing others will read, our choices are constrained by our need to communicate. We can't throw in a verbal here, or an appositive there, just because we feel like it. We need to use all the options of diction and syntax to make ourselves clear to readers and to keep their attention.

Composing for Effect: Clarity

A couple of thousand years ago, the Greek philosopher Aristotle recorded some of the earliest instructions in writing. "The most important goal of writing," he said, "is to be clear without being boring." His instructions still hold true today. Writing that is confused, unnecessarily complex, or just plain hard to understand will not hold the attention of readers. Unless they are forced into it, most people will not continue reading sentences that do not convey clear meaning. That doesn't mean that we must write only simple thoughts; it means that, no matter how complex our thoughts are, we must present them in such a way that readers can understand what we are saying. So, as we write and rewrite, we always need to be asking ourselves, *What am I trying to say here?* and *Will somebody who isn't me understand what I am saying?*

Choosing just the right word or phrase instead of settling for the almost-right synonym is one way we create clear, readable writing. Another way is to make effective use of the language of the imagination. Perhaps our most important tool for creating clarity, though, is the way we use syntax.

As you've learned in previous chapters, readers process our sentences one bit at a time, adding each word or phrase to the ones that precede it. A command of syntax enables us to order our words so they *say* something to readers; it ensures that our writing makes sense to them. The work of composition, then, is largely the work of ordering our material into sentences, for the order in which words, images, and ideas come to us as we write is not necessarily the order in which we want to present them to our readers.

As anyone who has done the practice of freewriting knows, our minds do not naturally work in a linear fashion. Rather, they give us thoughts, ideas, and words in what feel like free-associative clusters. So when we try to get those ideas, thoughts, and words down on paper as they have occurred to us, we may not be concerned with the order in which we record them. In fact, it may not even feel like these thoughts *have* an order; they may feel more like networks of connection. If we wanted to make a representation of these networks of thought, as they happen in our minds, we could probably do that visually, because a visual representation allows us to work in space and therefore to show a picture of more than one thing at the same time.

But writing, like speech, does not happen in space; it happens in *time*. And the time we must concern ourselves with—not necessarily as we try to get down on paper our first, fleeting thoughts or visions, but most definitely at some point before we finish a piece—is the experience, in time, that our readers will have as they process our sentences. Because of the nature of the English language, readers will *have* to take in what we tell them, one word-group at a time, one sentence at a time, one paragraph at a time. As they read, they will add each "bit" of information to the bits that have come earlier. Knowledge of syntax provides us with established linguistic structures that enable us to order our thoughts and words so that readers can add them together and make sense of them. Much of the revision that a skilled writer does involves tinkering with the order of elements in her sentences so that readers can process them with ease and extract from them the meaning she intends.

One of the best ways to ensure that we have successfully ordered our sentences for the minds of readers is to read our work out loud. When we read aloud, we come closer to the experience a reader will have of our words. When we read our words silently, it's very easy to "read into" them what we mean to say: We have our intended meaning in mind, and we project that into the words on that page. But the reader, as I always tell my students, is not inside the head of the writer. When we get our words out of our own heads and into the air, we can really hear them; and then it's much easier to understand them as our readers will.

Practice: Reading as a Reader

Take some passages from your own writing, or some of your practice sentences, and read them out loud slowly, pretending that you are someone who has never seen them before. Try to *listen* to them, receive them, as a reader, rather than as a writer. Take in these words and sentences as a reader would, one "bit" at a time. Notice whether your imaginary reader will be confused by anything in your writing. Is your meaning clear? Mark all the places where clarity is lacking.

Practice: Using Syntactic Structures in Revision

Now, using what you have learned from earlier sections in this book, as well as from the review above of syntactic structures, revise your marked passages for clarity. Read them aloud again. How do they sound now, to your imagined reader? If they're still not clear, revise again.

Composing for Effect: Purpose

Clear communication is a kind of successful magic. When we write with clarity, we transfer meaning from our minds into the minds of other people—people we don't know and will probably never meet. But our words and sentences make another kind of magic, too, which gives them even more power: They make things happen; they *do* things to people. The words we choose have different kinds of power; so do our sentences.

What are some of the things sentences can do? You'll remember that they can make a statement, ask a question, make a command, or make an exclamation.

When we consider declarative sentences (which make statements) more closely, we find that this kind of sentence can also do many different things. For instance:

It can *narrate*; that is, tell what happened, convey an action or an event: *Joe walked slowly down the street, thinking hard.*

It can *describe*; make a picture: *The street was lined with apple trees, all covered with white blossoms and giving off a sweet smell.*

It can give someone's reactions to happenings or pictures: *But Joe didn't notice.*

It can give someone's thoughts: *"If only I hadn't said that,"* *Joe thought.*

OR: *Joe wished he had said nothing.*

It can give someone's spoken words: *"What a fool I am!" he said.*

It can give someone's feelings: *Joe felt sad.*

OR: *As Joe spoke, a tear ran down his face.*

It can state a fact or report a piece of information: *Joe was fifteen years old; he hadn't cried since he was a kid.*

It can convey an idea or explain something: *His father had always told him that men don't cry.*

It can state an opinion or make a comment: *But sometimes what our fathers tell us turns out not to be true.*

Practice: What Declarative Sentences Do

Try writing some declarative sentences, using any of the techniques you have learned so far, and think about each sentence's purpose, what you want each sentence to do. Experiment with sentences that do different things.

Practice: What Declarative Sentences Do

Now take a look at a passage or two by one of your favorite writers. See if you can figure out what each sentence is doing, and jot that down. For instance, you might write: sentence 1—gives a piece of information; sentence 2—gives a picture; and so on. Then imitate the passage by writing sentences that imitate, in order, what each sentence in your chosen passage is doing.

Practice: What Declarative Sentences Do

Pick a subject and write some sentences on it, thinking not only about what you want to say, but also about what you want each sentence to do. Keep in mind your options for syntactic structures.

Composing for Effect: Movement

When we write and revise sentences, there's another thing we can pay attention to: sentence movement. Thinking about what our sentences are doing (as in the previous exercises) is one way to enliven our sentences with movement.

Even more important to sentence movement is the actual structure of our sentences. Forward movement is embedded in the basic structure of the English sentence: the S-V, or S-V-C (subject-verb-complement or object) kernel pattern. In this pattern, as we saw in earlier lessons, the subject of the sentence—the "actor"—usually comes first, then comes the predicate—the "action." With the use of this pattern, every sentence is a story. And so sentences written according to this basic pattern, either as kernels or with the careful use of modifiers, move forward. This forward movement helps to sustain our readers' attention.

As we have seen, we can also hold our readers' attention through the way we place our modifiers, whether they are single words, phrases, or clauses. We can choose when to pass on information in a sentence; our choices can create flow, suspense, drama, surprise, and other effects. One of our main tools for creating these effects is free modifiers.

Remember that we have three possibilities for placing free modifiers: before the subject, after the main verb, between the subject and the main verb. Grammarians sometimes call these three kinds of sentences, respectively: left-branching sentences, right-branching sentences (also known as cumulative sentences), and mid-branching sentences. Let's take a look at these from the point of view of sentence movement, beginning with the most straightforward: right-branching (cumulative) sentences.

Once we have the basic pattern of English sentences in our minds, it becomes quite easy to write sentences that begin with the subject, continue with the verb ... and then keep going. Professional writers make use of this kind of sentence all the time:

> My great-uncle Silas used to live in a small stone reed-thatched cottage on the edge of a pine-wood, where nightingales sang passionately in great numbers through early summer nights and on into the mornings and often still in the afternoons.
>
> —H.E. Bates, "The Lily"

One of the great advantages of the right-branching sentence is that it lets you move your reader forward into the next sentence:

> The guard, eight little Dyak soldiers, stood to attention as [Mr. Warburton] passed. He noted with satisfaction that their bearing was martial, their uniforms neat and clean, and their guns shining. They were a credit to him.
>
> —W. Somerset Maugham, "The Outstation"

To create a left-branching sentence, we place free modifiers (or flexible adverbials) *before* the subject of a kernel. This structure creates movement in a different way: It helps us set a scene or delay the action of the sentence.

A tiny brown, glittering creature, the fly soared up to the ceiling, sped like a bullet past the child's ears, collided with the walls, and rebounded in noisy spirals.

—J. Kessel, "The Doll"

At police headquarters, at the National Gallery, at Oslo's newspaper and television and radio stations, phones rang day and night.

—Edward Dolnick, *The Rescue Artist*

Whenever a situation gets so ticklish that he wishes he were somewhere else, he can walk over to the globe and pick spots to go to.

—Rex Stout, *The Doorbell Rang*

The mid-branching sentence inserts useful information into the middle of a sentence while keeping the movement of the sentence going:

The flames—and theirs was a strange music—roared loud in the wintry air—red, greenish, copper and gold—licking and leaping their way from strand to strand up and up …

—Walter de la Mare, *Dick and the Beanstalk*

But Charlie, the bank-clerk on twenty-five shillings a week, who had never been out of sight of a made road, knew it all.

—Rudyard Kipling, "The Finest Story in the World"

It's also possible to insert additional material between the two clauses of a compound sentence:

One [television monitor] screen suddenly flickered with life. The black-and-white picture was shadowy—the sun would not rise for another ninety minutes—but the essentials were clear enough.

—Edward Dolnick, *The Rescue Artist*

And finally, skilled writers often make use of two or three of these options in a single sentence:

Though old when I made his acquaintance, he was still a powerful horse of a man, always dressed in well-pressed

Irish tweeds, heavy countryman's boots and a fawn, flat-topped bowler-hat set squat above a big, red, square face, heavy handlebar mustaches and pale-blue, staring eyes of which one always saw the complete circle of the iris, challenging, concentrated, slightly mad.

—Sean O'Faolain, "A Touch of Autumn in the Air"

Charmed by the sober beauty of the house, fascinated by the seclusion of its setting, your refined taste tickled by the good manners of the noticeboard, you will decide that here at last is the country hotel of your dreams, where good cheer and comfort await the truly discriminating traveller.

—Cyril Hare, *Suicide Excepted*

If it was inevitable that Rose Birkett should marry a naval man, it was equally inevitable that the day of her wedding should be the most perfect day of unclouded sun tempered by a breeze not powerful enough to disarrange her hair or her veil.

—Angela Thirkell, *Cheerfulness Breaks In*

Rare, exotic, strangely lovely, the red lily had blossomed there, untouched, for as long as I could remember.

—H.E. Bates, "The Lily"

Practice: Sentence Movement

Study the examples above—or choose others you prefer—for how each writer constructs his sentence to create—or delay—forward movement. Then imitate the structure of the sentence. Draw on your knowledge of syntactic sentences to experiment with combining single words acting in various roles and with different kinds of phrases and clauses.

Composing for Effect: Sentences into Paragraphs

When we talk about the movement of sentences, we leave the realm of single sentences and enter that of sentence-groups—otherwise known as paragraphs. How do we arrange our sentences into paragraphs? How do we keep the movement of our thoughts and images going from one sentence to the next?

Sometimes the technique of freewriting, or focused freewriting, will enable us to write sentences that flow naturally one into the next. But often this approach doesn't work. Here's something else to try: Write a fairly simple sentence. Then identify the elements of the sentence, as follows:

Sentence: *The woman walked to the store.*

Elements: *the woman / walked / to the store*

Now choose one element and develop it to create a paragraph, like this:

1. The woman walked to the store. She was tall, maybe five-eight, and her body had the taut look that comes with long hours at the gym. Her blonde hair gleamed in the sun, and her painted nails flickered like tiny red lights.

2. The woman walked to the store. She moved slowly and tentatively, as if she were taking each step for the first time. Her feet, in battered sneakers, appeared to be not quite touching the pavement, and she kept glancing around as she walked as if she were looking for something to hold on to.

3. The woman walked to the store. Once it had been a real general store, where you could find anything you needed. Nails, bandages, cola, cigarette papers, a quart of milk, a half-dozen eggs—they had it all. The owner, Mr. Johnson, would even give you credit, if you went there often enough. But then one day Mr. Johnson died, and his relatives sold the place to some yuppies from the city who turned it into one of those upscale bakeries where they don't even sell doughnuts. She didn't like the way the store was now, but she went there anyway, because they would let her have day-old bread at half-price.

Practice: Developing Elements
Write a simple sentence as in the example above. Take one element and develop it through several sentences to create a paragraph. Then take a different element and develop that one. What do you notice in doing this?

Paragraphs, like sentences, are a tool we use to grab and keep our readers' attention and to make things happen inside them. Paragraphs, like sentences, begin and end with "pauses." In the case of sentences, those pauses are indicated by periods; with paragraphs, we use white space on the page. That white space, like punctuation, gives readers time to take a mental breath, to assimilate what they have just taken in, and to ready themselves for what is to come. So how we construct our paragraphs depends in large part on how we want to use them to create a certain kind of experience for our readers.

Just as readers process sentences by adding one word-group to the one they just read, so they process paragraphs by adding sentences together. When we write and revise, we may want to consider what will happen inside our readers as they finish one sentence in a paragraph and then move into the next one. Is this what we want to have happen at this particular moment?

Composing for Effect: Creating Continuity or "Flow"
When we think about how to move our sentences forward, one to the next, one of the things we can consider is how to create continuity or "flow"—a sense of one thing connecting naturally to what preceded it and what follows.

As we learned earlier, linguists tell us that the typical English sentence has a characteristic movement, from known to unknown. Keeping that concept in mind can help us create continuity in our writing. One of the most useful techniques for creating continuity is to repeat a word or phrase from one sentence in the next (or in a nearby sentence). Sometimes writers repeat the subject (or use a pronoun that refers to it):

> *Dusko Popov*, the Serbian playboy, was not as feckless and apolitical as he seemed. The invitation from *his* old friend

Johnny Jebsen to work for German intelligence was an attractive one.

—Ben Macintyre, *Double Cross: The True Story of the D-Day Spies*

Sometimes a writer will repeat a word other than the subject (or use a pronoun that refers to it):

"This is what you take to Paris," the gray-uniformed man said. He had opened his toolbox and drawn out an envelope. It was a medium-sized opaque envelope, unaddressed, sealed, not much bulkier than if it contained a three-page airmail letter. He threw it across the desk.

—Helen MacInnes, *The Venetian Affair*

Other techniques for creating continuity include opening a sentence with an adverbial phrase or clause (*An hour later ...* or *When we had finished dinner ...*) or a coordinating conjunction. Professionals also use appositives, nominative absolutes, and other syntactic techniques to bring related material close together.

Practice: Creating Flow
Write a few sentences, experimenting with using one or more of the techniques explained above to create flow.

The Pros Create Continuity
Read through the following excerpt (from a recent nonfiction book), and notice your reactions. Then read through it again, seeing if you can discover how the writer keeps the narrative continuous, while moving us around.

... A motion detector triggered a second alarm. This time the guard, 24-year-old Geir Berntsen, decided that something was wrong. Panicky and befuddled, he thrashed about trying to sort out what to do. Check things out himself? Call the police? Berntsen still had not noticed the crucial television monitor, which now displayed a ladder standing unattended

against the museum's front wall. Nor had he realized that
the alarm had come from room 10, where The Scream hung.

Berntsen phoned his supervisor, who was at home in
bed and half-asleep, and blurted out his incoherent story …
At almost precisely the same moment, a police car making
a routine patrol through Oslo's empty streets happened to
draw near the National Gallery. A glance told the tale: a dark
night, a ladder, a shattered window.

The police car skidded to a stop …

—Edward Dolnick, *The Rescue Artist*

Practice: Creating Flow

Take a look at a passage from a writer you like and see if you can figure
out what she did to create continuity. Then imitate that technique. You
might also like to try revising some of your own writing to increase
your reader's sense of continuity.

Composing for Effect: Steps and Leaps

When we write to create continuity, we are, in a sense, encouraging the
reader to proceed in a particular direction, step-by-step. But sometimes
what we want is not continuity, but temporary discontinuity: We want
our readers to take mental leaps.

There are almost always places in our writing where we must invite
our readers to take these leaps: when we take a new view of a subject,
change a scene, move back or forward in time, etc. When we change
directions in these (and other) ways, we need to remember to bring our
readers along with us. Skilled writers know how to make such leaps easy
for their readers by carefully ordering images, ideas, and syntactic elements, by using transitions, by making a new paragraph at just the
right point, or by a skilled use of free modifiers. They also use some of
the same techniques that create flow: repetition of a word or phrase, or
beginning a sentence with an adverbial.

The Pros Take Leaps

In the predawn gloom of a Norwegian winter morning, two men in a stolen car pulled to a halt in front of the National Gallery, Norway's preeminent art museum. They left the engine running and raced across the snow. Behind the bushes along the museum's front wall they found the ladder they had stashed away earlier that night. Silently, they leaned the ladder against the wall.

A guard inside the museum, his rounds finished, basked in the warmth of the basement security room …

—Edward Dolnick, *The Rescue Artist*

[Stephen's] first excited reaction to London—its shops, its restaurants, its well-dressed attractive women—had faded. He saw it now as a glittering rhinestone set in a dingy setting.

Supposing he were back in South Africa now … He felt a quick pang of homesickness. Sunshine—blue skies—gardens of flowers—cool blue flowers—hedges of plumbago—blue convolvulus clinging to every little shanty.

And here—dirt, grime and endless incessant crowds—moving, hurrying, jostling…

—Agatha Christie, *A Holiday for Murder*

Practice: Making Leaps

Use the above examples as a model, or find some examples of your own. Notice how the writer enables our minds to take a leap; notice where the paragraph breaks come. And notice, as well, what technique(s) the writer uses to keep us oriented as we leap. Imitate the examples in a way that feels useful to you.

Now take a passage of your own writing that contains at least one leap, and see if you need to rewrite it to ease your reader's path. (Leaps demand more of a reader than moving step-by-step.) You can also try this exercise by seeing if there's a way to tighten a sprawling passage in your work by omitting some steps and taking a "leap" instead.

Paragraphs by Ear

Paragraphs, as you no doubt learned in school, are tools for organizing sentences. *How* you do that depends on the kind of writing you are doing: A formal essay requires formal, logical organization; paragraphs in fiction require organization of images and narrative events. As you study and imitate paragraphs from your chosen models, remember to use your writer's ear to listen to where the paragraph breaks go. Experiment with breaking a paragraph in different ways, read your work out loud, listen for the version that works best, that has the effect you want.

Stephen King has called paragraphs the "beat" of a story. Listening for that beat is one way into the realm of rhythm in writing—the subject of the next chapter.

 ## TAKE TIME TO REFLECT

What stands out for you in this lesson? Are there any practices you want to revisit?

CHAPTER 14

WRITING IN RHYTHM

—IRA GERSHWIN

In this chapter, we'll be entering the realm of sentence rhythm. So far I have encouraged you to use your writer's ear in a number of different ways: We have listened for the meanings of words and their connotations, for the different qualities of words, for parts of speech, and so on. In this chapter, we'll be exploring yet another way to use our writer's ear: to listen to the rhythms our sentences make. We'll concentrate, not on the meaning (or the pictures) our words are making, but on their music.

THE MUSIC OF LANGUAGE

Often when people talk about "the music of language," they make it sound like a mere frill, something we add to "dress up" plain writing. I don't agree with this view. At the heart of language, I hear music—word-music, akin in many ways to instrumental music or song. I agree with the poet Robert Pinsky, who has said, about ordinary speech, "We sing to each other all day long."

How, then, are music and language similar? You can think of it this way: Spoken language, like music, is a stream of sound; writing, like speech, can make use of the musical characteristics of that stream of sound. In this world of verbal music there's much to explore. English, like every language, is made up of certain sounds; these sounds have certain qualities and can be arranged according to musical principles.

In one chapter we can't cover all of the techniques of making music with language, so here we'll confine our explorations to the rhythm of sentences. Rhythm in writing, just like rhythm in music, comes to us through our ears. So, if you are interested in sentence rhythm, I encourage you to get into two important habits: one, *slow down* as you read and write; and two, *listen* to words with your writer's ear.

The Rhythm of Sentences, Part 1: Rhythm Patterns

When we speak or write in English, our words are grounded in rhythm because, to pronounce words correctly, we stress certain syllables and not others. *APP-le*, we say, not *app-LE*. Poets working in traditional forms find ways to organize the stressed and unstressed syllables of English into regular patterns. Prose writers don't tend to work this way: Instead of organizing syllables, we use syntactic elements (words, phrases, clauses, sentences) to create rhythm patterns, patterns that extend, like musical patterns, in *time*. To create these patterns we make use of a technique that is fundamental to musical composition: repetition and variation.

Creating Rhythm with Repetition and Variation: Single Words

When we use single words to create rhythm, we have two options:

1. We can repeat a word exactly.
2. We can repeat a part of speech.

In school we're often taught that we should never repeat a word in a sentence, or in adjacent sentences. But just listen to what the pros do with simple repetition:

> The rain is ever falling—drip, drip, drip—by day and night
> upon the broad flagged terrace-pavement, the Ghost's Walk.
> —Charles Dickens, *Bleak House*

... he knew that this day was going to be different. It would be different also, because as his father explained, driving Douglas and his ten-year-old brother Tom out of town toward the country, there were some days compounded completely of odor, nothing but the world blowing in one nostril and out the other. And some days, he went on, were days of hearing every trump and trill of the universe. Some days were good for tasting and some for touching. And some days were good for all the senses at once. This day now, he nodded, smelled as if a great and nameless orchard had grown up overnight beyond the hills to fill the entire visible land with its warm freshness.

—Ray Bradbury, *Dandelion Wine*

Oh, I should never have come, never. I'm here against my better judgment ...

—Dorothy Parker, "But the One on the Right"

The war had made him famous. Not as famous as Murrow, the voice of London, and not as famous as Quent Reynolds, now the voice of the documentaries, but famous enough to get a promise from *Collier's* ... and then the press pass to Berlin.

—Joseph Kanon, *The Good German*

Repetition, rather than being something to be avoided at all costs, is actually a very useful technique. When we repeat something, we emphasize it: We focus the reader's attention; we encourage her to dwell in that particular place; we intensify an experience; and we make rhythm.

In addition to repeating single words exactly, writers also make use of the principle of repetition and variation by *repeating a part of speech while varying the word*. We can, for instance, repeat adjectives, or nouns:

Poor Mr. Arabin—untaught, illiterate, boorish, ignorant man!

—Anthony Trollope, *Barchester Towers*

Once there was a sailor-girl and her name was Josslyn Abel-sea. On land she had tried this and that; she had been a waitress, and a bus-conductress, she had been a postwoman and a taxi-driver, but none of these jobs suited her.

—Joan Aiken, "A Basket of Water"

Practice: Rhythm with Single Words

Play with making sentences in which you repeat a single word or a single part of speech. What do you notice?

Creating Rhythm with Repetition and Variation: Phrases

I'm sure you remember phrases—those groups of words that "go together," but that do not contain a subject and predicate. Writers repeat and vary phrases, too, in order to give rhythm to their sentences.

Occasionally they repeat an entire phrase exactly:

Changed days, Fenner thought, as Ballard paid their driver, changed days from New York and Ballard's dogged news coverage over at the United Nations when he had always looked as if he needed a good square meal, a haircut, and still more information.

—Helen MacInnes, *The Venetian Affair*

More often, though, they will repeat a certain phrase *structure* or phrase type (noun phrase, adjective phrase, prepositional phrase, and so on) while varying the words. For example:

This is the story of John Segrave—of his life, which was un-satisfactory: of his love, which was unsatisfied; of his dreams, and of his death …

—Agatha Christie, "The House of Dreams"

Tired of walking, pushed about, stunned by the noise and confusion, anxious for her brother and the nurses, terrified by what she had undergone; perplexed and frightened alike by what had passed and what was yet before her, Florence went upon her weary way with tearful eyes …

—Charles Dickens, *Dombey and Son*

His incredible untidiness, his addiction to music at strange
hours, his occasional revolver practice within doors, his
weird and often malodorous scientific experiments, and the
atmosphere of violence and danger which hung around him
made him the very worst tenant in London.

—Sir Arthur Conan Doyle,
"The Adventure of the Dying Detective"

Practice: Rhythm with Phrases
Play with making sentences in which you repeat a single phrase exactly
or repeat a phrase pattern or kind of phrase while varying the language.
What do you notice?

Creating Rhythm with Repetition and Variation: Clauses

A clause, as you remember, is a group of words that "goes together"
and contains a subject and finite verb. Writers use clauses, too, to
create rhythm.

Exact repetition of a clause (that is, repetition of both clause structure
and the words filling the structure) is rare, but it can be done:

The sky was still dark when he opened his eyes and saw it
through the uncurtained window. He was upright within
seconds, out of bed, and had opened the window to study
the signs. It looked good to him, the dark just beginning
to fade slightly, midnight blueblack growing grey and
misty, through which he could make out the last light
of a dying star. It looked good to him, a calm, pre-dawn
hush without a breath of wind, and not a shadow of cloud
in the high clear sky.

—Eva Figes, *Light*

Writers usually repeat a clause *structure* while varying the language in
the clauses. For instance:

There was a crowd of kids watching the car and the square
was hot, and the trees were green, and the flags hung on their

staffs, and it was good to get out of the sun and under the shade of the arcade that runs all the way around the square.
—Ernest Hemingway, *The Sun Also Rises*

Still, he was grateful for the current of air even if it was stale, even if the sudden coolness was only an illusion made by motion.
—Helen MacInnes, *The Venetian Affair*

Lay these lives alongside one another, bang them together, hold them up to the light and you could open an entire time.
—Shawn Levy, *Ready, Steady, Go!*

Practice: Rhythm with Clauses

Play with making sentences in which you repeat the structure of clauses while varying the words. What happens when you do this?

Practice: Learning from the Pros

Study a writer you like for the ways he creates rhythm through the use of repeated single words or parts of speech, phrase structures, and clause structures. Try imitating the rhythm of a sentence or two.

The Effects of Syntactic Repetition

When we repeat a syntactic structure while changing the words, we create a regular kind of rhythm, a sense of balance. (The grammatical term for this technique is *parallelism*.) Through the repetition of a structure, the reader begins to anticipate, and then to enjoy, the pleasure of fulfilled expectation. When we then vary the syntactic structure, we throw the reader off-balance a little: We surprise her. Skilled writers don't use these techniques at random: They choose them to create particular effects. In addition to creating rhythm, syntactic repetition can make a sentence easier to understand; it can subtly connect the *content* of the repeated structures; it can emphasize something, creating an emotional effect; it can create a sense of abundance or overload, of suspense or resolution, and more.

Practice: Repetition of Syntactic Structures for Effect

Study the examples above (or some of your own choosing), and consider the effect they have on you. Then experiment with using repetition and variation of syntactic structures to create some effects of your own. Take a look at some passages from your work-in-progress to find places where you might revise to create effects using exact repetition or syntactic repetition. Ask yourself, *What do I want my readers to* feel *right here?* and see if repetition will help you make that happen.

Creating Rhythm Through Repetition and Variation: Sentence Structures

Perhaps the main way that writers create sentence rhythm is by repeating and varying the basic kernel structure of English sentences. You'll remember that the basic structure of all declarative sentences in English is *subject—main verb—complement/direct object*. (If you want to reacquaint yourself with this structure, take some time now to write some sentence kernels.)

The basic structure of English sentences creates a fundamental rhythm that underlies most sentences we write. You may want to write a few more sentences, keeping that subject-predicate rhythm in mind. Read your sentences out loud, hearing and feeling the rhythm in your body.

Making Patterns with the Basic Sentence Structure

When we write one sentence after another using the basic subject-predicate structure, we are creating a rhythm pattern: We are repeating a particular structure while varying the words each time. Listen to the repeated kernel structure in these sentences from a children's book:

> Toad did not answer.
> He had fallen asleep.
> Frog looked at Toad's calendar.
> The November page was still on top.
> Frog tore off the November page.
> He tore off the December page.
> —Arnold Lobel, "Spring," in *Frog and Toad Are Friends*

After a certain number of repetitions of the simple subject-predicate structure, many writers instinctively want to vary it. Here, for instance, is how Lobel, writing for beginning readers, continues his story:

> Frog looked at Toad's calendar.
> The November page was still on top.
> Frog tore off the November page.
> He tore off the December page.
> And the January page,
> the February page,
> and the March page.
> He came to the April page.
> Frog tore off the April page too.
> —Arnold Lobel, "Spring," in *Frog and Toad Are Friends*

Can you hear how the sentence rhythm changes, then returns to its original subject-predicate "beat"?

This technique may seem so simple as to be useless, but when you have it down, the effects can be masterful. Read out loud the following passage (also from a children's book), listening for the rhythms. Then see if you can recognize the techniques the writer uses to vary the basic kernel structure. (The easiest way to do this is to reduce each sentence to a kernel, then to notice what has been added: an appositive, for instance, or a compound subject or predicate. You'll also notice that Crossley-Holland uses exclamations and a question in addition to declarative sentences.)

> It was an empty, oyster-and-pearl afternoon. The water lipped at the sand and sorted the shingle and lapped round the rock where the girl was sitting.
>
> Then she saw a seal, like a mass of seaweed almost, until she gazed into those eyes. It swam in quite close, just twenty or thirty water-steps away.
>
> She looked at the seal; the seal looked at her. Then it barked. It cried out in a loud voice.
>
> She stood up on her rock. She called out to the seal: not a word but a sound, the music words are made of.

The seal swam in a little closer. It looked at the girl. Then it cried. Oh! The moon's edge and a mother's ache were in that cry.

The girl jumped off the rock. Her eyes were sea-eyes, wide and flint-grey. "Seal!" she cried. "Sea-woman! What do you want?"

—Kevin Crossley-Holland,
"Sea-Woman," in *British Folk Tales*

Repeating and Varying the Basic Sentence Structure

We have only a handful of syntactic structures to play with—but by repeating and varying them we can create an infinite variety of rhythms. Let's review the sentence structures we can use, listening to the differences in the way the structures sound:

1. FRAGMENT: Sometimes a sentence can be a mere fragment, made up of only one word or phrase. For instance (an example you've seen before):

Rats! There was a ruin of rats. A rat-attack! A plague of rats.
—Kevin Crossley-Holland

2. KERNEL: (also known as a simple sentence or independent clause)

Toad did not answer. He had fallen asleep.
—Arnold Lobel

3. KERNEL: (simple sentence) with compound subject, verb, or object/complement

Bob and I buried the Game Chicken that night …
—John Brown, "Rab and his Friends"

Sometimes Father Macdowell mumbled out loud and took a deep wheezy breath as he walked up and down the room …
—Morley Callaghan, "A Sick Call"

The houses looked poor and small …
—Eva Ibbotson, "A Place on the Piano"

4. KERNEL: (elaborated with bound or free modifiers, or both)

His pride and joy, a Nakamichi tape-deck, was tastefully broadcasting one of his collection of late-night-listening jazz tapes: Stan Getz or Coleman Hawkins.

—Ian Rankin, *Knots and Crosses*

5. COMPOUND SENTENCE: two or more independent clauses (elaborated or not) joined by coordinating conjunctions, asyndeton, or other punctuation:

He had a cape on, soaked with rain, and the rain was in beads in his hair.

—V.S. Pritchett

6. COMPLEX SENTENCE: one independent clause and one or more dependent clauses:

The pain in his eyes was the pain of a man who has begun to lose one of the great pleasures of life in the discovery that we can never truly remember anything at all, that we are for a great part of our lives at the mercy of uncharged currents of the heart.

—Sean O'Faolain, "A Touch of Autumn in the Air"

7. COMPOUND-COMPLEX SENTENCE: two or more independent clauses with one or more dependent clauses:

They jolted out to the main road, and as they ambled along they talked, and it seemed to him that it was very serious talk, but he forgot every word of it.

—Sean O'Faolain, "A Touch of Autumn in the Air"

We can apply the principle of repetition and variation to sentence structure in two main ways:

1. By repeating a syntactic structure using different words each time.
2. By varying the structure of sentences.

For example:

I came. I saw. I conquered.

—Julius Caesar

Mrs. Mooney was a butcher's daughter. She was a woman who was quite able to keep things to herself: a determined woman. She had married her father's foreman and opened a butcher's shop near Spring Gardens. But as soon as his father-in-law was dead Mr. Mooney began to go to the devil. He drank, plundered the till, ran headlong into debt. It was no use making him take the pledge: he was sure to break out again a few days after ...

—James Joyce, "The Boarding House"

The young man looked up. His eyes were bloodshot, dark-rimmed. A lean, angular face, bristles on the unshaved chin. His name was David Costello. Not Dave or Davy: David, he'd made that clear.

—Ian Rankin, *The Falls*

Practice: Learning from the Pros

Take a look at a passage by one of your favorite writers. Read it out loud, listening to the rhythms of the sentences. What kind of effect does this rhythm create? Does your writer repeat a certain kind of sentence structure? How many times? How does she vary that structure? Now copy the sentence rhythm of the passage by imitating, in order, the kinds of sentence structures your writer uses.

Practice: Sentence Rhythm

Choose a few sentence structures to practice. Write a paragraph in which you repeat one of the structures, then vary it by writing one or more sentences using a different structure. What do you notice in doing this? Read your paragraph out loud; how does the sentence rhythm sound to you? Try this practice again with different structures, if you're ready to do so.

Practice: Sentence Rhythm

Take a passage from your own writing and rewrite it, repeating some sentence structures and varying others. How does the passage sound to you now?

Think about the effect you want to create by arranging these different sentences structures. Do you need to change something to create the effect you want?

Rhythm and Sentence Length

As you do these practices, you are probably noticing that some of your sentences are short, and others are longer. Another way to play with sentence rhythm is simply to tune your ear to the relative lengths of your sentences, and to experiment with varying their lengths. Notice, for instance, in the following paragraph, how Conan Doyle makes use of sentences of different length:

> Mrs. Hudson, the landlady of Sherlock Holmes, was a long-suffering woman. Not only was her first-floor flat invaded at all hours by throngs of singular and often undesirable characters but her remarkable lodger showed an eccentricity and irregularity in his life which must have sorely tried her patience. His incredible untidiness, his addiction to music at strange hours, his occasional revolver practice within doors, his weird and often malodorous scientific experiments, and the atmosphere of violence and danger which hung around him made him the very worst tenant in London. On the other hand, his payments were princely. I have no doubt that the house might have been purchased at the price which Holmes paid for his rooms during the years that I was with him.
>
> —Sir Arthur Conan Doyle,
> *The Adventure of the Dying Detective*

Practice: Learning from the Pros

Find a passage from a writer you like and examine it for sentence length. Write down the pattern of short and long sentences, and then imitate that pattern.

Practice: Sentence Length

Write a paragraph or two, listening for repetition and variation in sentence length. Read your work out loud. How does it sound to you?

Try this technique to revise something you have written.

As you do these practices, I suspect you will notice right away that these techniques of creating rhythm through repetition and variation are powerful ones. Repetition can drive a point home or direct our readers' attention to something we want to make sure they take in. Variation keeps our readers' minds engaged, keeps them from becoming bored. Repeating and varying the length of our sentences, like the other techniques we've explored in this chapter, give our writing a musical quality, so that it affects our readers the way music does, making what we have to say more memorable. This technique can even enable us to affect readers emotionally, or physically: What happens in readers, for instance, when we give them one short sentence after another? What happens when we give them longer sentences?

The Rhythm of Sentences, Part 2: Making It "Sing"

This book rests on a fundamental belief: Words can make magic. Skillfully put together into sentences, words can transfer ideas and images from a writer's mind into the minds of readers—that, by itself, is powerful verbal magic. When we exploit the musical characteristics of language, we can make another kind of magic with our words: Through their sounds and rhythms, our words can "sing" to readers, and move them in the way music does.

So far, we've looked at how repeating and varying the elements of sentences can let us make rhythm and create various effects. Now let's look at creating verbal music from a different perspective: how to "make words sing." (Naturally, the sounds and durations of words contribute a great deal to their "singing"—but that's a subject for another book.) To explore "singing on the page," we return to word-groups.

When we talk about word-groups, we are talking about words that "go together," that make sense together. Usually what we mean by "word-group" is a phrase or a short clause; but sometimes we might be referring to a sentence fragment (incomplete sentence) or a very short kernel sentence.

When we talk about word-groups, we are also talking about the tiny pauses that we make before and after these groups in order to process them properly as we read and write and speak. Linguists call these tiny pauses in spoken language "junctures," by which they mean breaks in the flow of sound coming out of a speaker's mouth. These days, when many people speak very fast, it's harder to hear these junctures. That's why it's so important, as you read—and especially as you read out loud—to slow down: That way, your writer's ear can actually hear the junctures in the writing.

These tiny breaks before and after word-groups, then, are the way we mentally group words together as we speak, listen, write, and read. We might think of them as mental breathing spaces, where we pause momentarily to make sure we have taken in the meaning of one group of words before we move on to the next. Most of the time, our agile brains engage in this activity of making and processing word-groups without any conscious awareness on our part. When we want to make sure that our readers will gather our words into groups the way we intend—and when we want longer pauses between groups—we make use of punctuation to set off words and phrases, as free modifiers, clauses, and entire sentences.

If we want to "sing" on the page, we need to have a conscious understanding of word-groups because, to borrow a term from music, word-groups enable us to "phrase" our sentences—and the phrasing of a sentence, just like the phrasing of a line of melody, is one of the things that makes words "sing."

Singing always begins with breath, and breath is what shapes the phrases of a song. When a skilled singer phrases a tune, she makes a pause—a breathing place—before and after each group of notes; sometimes this pause is tiny, just the merest hesitation, while other times it can last for several seconds. The best songwriters know how to arrange words in a song so that the verbal phrases coincide with the musical ones, and singers can take their breaths in ways that give the verbal phrases maximum impact. Skilled writers know how to phrase their sentences in the same way.

The techniques we use for musical phrasing are the same ones we learned in earlier lessons: We can use words, phrases, clauses, and even entire sentences as elements we can "phrase" the way musicians phrase a melody. In earlier lessons, though, we were practicing using phrases and clauses (especially as free modifiers) in order to make meaning. All we're doing now is taking a different perspective on the same techniques of choosing and ordering sentence elements: We're focusing on how these techniques can help our writing "sing." Or, to put it another way, we're talking about how to let our writing breathe.

Now, not all written sentences breathe. Most sentences written by government bureaucrats, academics, corporate employees—even many journalists—don't breathe at all. That's because those writers "load the slots" of their sentences rather than create phrases. (See an example in Chapter 11, "The Limitations of Bound Modifiers.") Many writers of fiction and nonfiction don't know how to write in phrases either—and some of their books end up on the bestseller lists. But writing that breathes is alive; writing that does not is dead. The real masters of the art of writing always know how to let their words breathe and sing. They know that musical language gives pleasure to readers, and that readers who are experiencing pleasure will keep turning the pages.

When we want our own words to sing, we need to begin where singers do: with breath. As you read the following passages out loud, make sure that you are putting breath into the words. Try to experience each phrase set off by punctuation as a "unit of breath," so that you really pause when the punctuation tells you to. You will probably also find yourself making fractional pauses between some phrases not set off by punctuation, such as a string of prepositional phrases.

The Pros Sing

He had survived bombings and sinkings and shattered ships, only to bob up again, joking, indestructible, surviving to become one of the best-loved flag officers in the Service.

—Rosamunde Pilcher, "Spanish Ladies"

265

Iff shook his head and spread his arms wide. "Impossible," he said, "No can do, it's off the menu, don't even dream about it. Access to Gup City in Kahani, by the shores of the Ocean of the Streams of Story, is strictly restricted, completely forbidden, one hundred per cent banned, except to accredited personnel; like, for instance, me. But you? No chance, not in a million years, no way, José."

—Salman Rushdie, *Haroun and the Sea of Stories*

Opening her hands in a gesture of entreaty, Susan Carstairs let his hat fall, with a soft thud, upon the delightful blue carpet of their delightful dining-room. Until that moment neither of them realized she still held it. But now it dropped, rolled, vanished; and with the hat went her self-control.

—Margery Sharp, "The Girl in the Grass"

Why, thank you so much. I'd adore to.

I don't want to dance with him. I don't want to dance with anybody. And even if I did, it wouldn't be him. He'd be well down among the last ten. I've seen the way he dances ... Just think, not a quarter of an hour ago, here I was sitting, feeling so sorry for the poor girl he was dancing with. And now I'm going to be the poor girl. Well, well. Isn't it a small world?

—Dorothy Parker, "The Waltz"

He ... wondered why he had ever been fool enough to enter the place ... He might have known—he should have known—from the moment that he set his foot inside the door, that it would be just like any other wayside motoring hotel, only more so, where the soup came out of a tin, and the fish had been too long on the ice, and far too long off it, where the entrée was yesterday's joint with something horrible added to it, and the joint was just about fit to make tomorrow's entrée, where tough little cubes of pineapple and tasteless rounds of banana joined to compose the fruit salad, where fresh dessert was non-existent—in the heart of the country, in mid-August! but then it was forty-two miles from Covent Garden—where bottles of sauce stood unashamed on every table, and where the coffee—he looked down again at his half-empty cup, and felt for a cigarette to take away the taste.

—Cyril Hare, *Suicide Excepted*

Practice: Make It Sing

Remembering that each phrase is a unit of breath, write some sentences while repeating and varying sentence structures, using the list from "Repeating and Varying the Basic Sentence Structure," located earlier in this chapter. In this exercise, don't worry about which particular structures you are using. Rather, trust your trained writer's mind to give you what you need, and keep your ear tuned to the pauses that create the "phrasing" of your sentences. Relax, don't forget to breathe—and let yourself go! If you like, imagine that you are "singing on the page" as you write, saying (or even half singing) the words aloud as you put them down; let the music of the words lead. What do you notice in doing this?

Practice: Make It Sing

Now try writing some sentences while paying attention to the length of your phrases, clauses, and sentences. (This is just another way of considering phrasing.) Apply the principle of repetition and variation as you do this (that is, repeat and vary the length of your phrases, clauses, and sentences.) What happens when you try this?

Practice: Make It Sing

Examine a passage from a favorite writer (or the examples above) and note how the writer "phrases" sentence elements (single words, phrases, clauses, sentences). Try imitating his phrasing.

Practice: Make It Sing

Take a passage from your own work and revise it for phrasing. Try to "make it sing." How did that go?

Phrasing and Emphasis and Rhythm

Read the following sentence aloud and notice which word you stress: *I made a pie.*

Most likely you stressed the word *pie*, for English speakers have a predisposition to emphasize, in each breath unit, one particular word (more specifically, the stressed syllable of that word). Typically, in spoken English, the word in a sentence that gets the most stress comes at or near the end of the sentence: I made a *pie.*

Often, as we speak, we change this pattern to create a different kind of emphasis:

> *I* made a pie. (I did it, not someone else.)
>
> I *made* a pie. (I didn't buy it at the store.)

In writing, when we need to alter the natural emphasis in a sentence, we use italics, as in the sentences above. Italics are a typographical device to create emphasis; they are easy to use, but also easily overused. Instead of relying on typography, we can draw on our knowledge of syntactic structures and phrasing to create emphasis.

There are three places in a sentence where English speakers typically place emphasis or stress: at the end of the sentence, at the end of a smaller breath-unit (word or phrase or clause) within the sentence, and at the beginning of the sentence. Careful readers subvocalize as they read (which means that they unconsciously use speech muscles, but they don't utter sounds); skilled writers make sure to put the material they want to emphasize in the places that receive natural emphasis in speech. They know that, unconsciously, readers will be paying attention to these places and will be assuming that the material placed there is important.

Suppose we write this sentence: *We found a green and quiet place to rest, beside a stream.* If we want to emphasize the word *stream*, then this sentence construction works. But what if we want to emphasize *quiet?* Then we need to call upon our knowledge of syntax and phrasing to come up with a different sentence, perhaps something like this: *Beside a stream we found a place to rest, a place empty and green and quiet.* The meaning of the two sentences is virtually the same, but because the phrasing has changed, the emphasis is different, and so the effect on the reader is different.

Writers often make use of the words *it* and *there* as tools for creating sentence emphasis, enabling them to invert subject and verb to place the emphasis on the subject:

> In a hole in the ground, there lived a hobbit.
>
> —J.R.R. Tolkien, *The Hobbit*

In music, every note is not given equal stress; it's the way the stressed notes are repeated and varied that, among other things, create the rhythm of a melody. Generally speaking, in English, we emphasize content words (more specifically, the stressed syllables in these words); we rarely emphasize function words. When we learn how to phrase for emphasis, we call our reader's attention to particular words. At the same time, our phrases create patterns of stressed and unstressed syllables, which contribute to the rhythms of our prose.

Practice: Phrasing and Emphasis
Read the examples from "The Pros Sing" again, out loud, noticing how the phrasing leads you to emphasize certain words and not others. Imitate the phrasing and emphasis of one or more of these sentences.

Practice: Phrasing and Emphasis
Write some sentences, paying attention to how you can create emphasis through phrasing. Read your sentences out loud, asking yourself if the emphasis is on the right words. Revise the sentences if you need to.

Practice: Phrasing and Emphasis
Revise a passage from your work-in-progress for phrasing and emphasis.

Phrasing and Embodiment
While writing, have you ever had the experience of sensing, in a visceral way, your material? Perhaps, for instance, there's a tense feeling to the scene you are trying to write; or perhaps there's a sense of peacefulness. If you've had this experience of registering your content physically, you may also have struggled to find the right words to

transmit those physical sensations to readers. While word choice is, naturally, important here, phrasing provides you with another powerful tool to get your readers under your spell.

With phrasing you can guide the speed at which your reader (assuming you have a careful reader) moves through your sentences; you can, through the arrangement and rhythms of phrases, affect your readers viscerally. As we've just seen, careful phrasing (including where you place free modifiers) points your readers' attention towards the most important words and phrases in a sentence, giving those words and phrases maximum impact. In these and other ways, the way you phrase a sentence can help you do more than just transmit your meaning intellectually; it can help you embody what you have to say—that is, it can help you mirror through syntax the experience you are trying to convey.

Here's Sean O'Faolain presenting an old man's memory of an experience with a girl when he was a boy. Read this out loud, noticing how both the punctuation and the grouping of words without punctuation, encourage you to "sing" the sentences:

> He handed it [a piece of candy] to her with a smile; she at once popped it into her mouth, laughing at his folly. As they ambled along so, slowly, chatting and chewing, the donkey's hooves whispering through the fallen beach-leaves, they heard high above the bare arches of the trees the faint honking of the wild-geese called down from the North by the October moon.
>
> —Sean O'Faolain, "A Touch of Autumn in the Air"

What did you notice?

One of the things I love about this passage is the way O'Faolain makes us phrase the word *slowly*. Because we are forced by the punctuation to pause before and after this word, the word is emphasized, making it stand out. At the same time, because of the way O'Faolain phrases that part of the sentence, we, like the characters, are forced to slow down. In other words, the sentence conveys its meaning not only intellectually, but also actually *embodies* what it says.

Here's another example:

> The girl looked around to see if there was any water —a pool,
> even a puddle —in which to wash herself. Then she saw the
> well, and plumped herself down beside it.
>> At once a golden head came up, singing.
>> —Kevin Crossley-Holland, "Three Heads of the Well"

What do you think of the phrasing in these sentences? How does the
phrasing of the word "singing" and of the words "a pool, even a puddle"
affect you as a reader? To my ear, the way Crossley-Holland sets off the
word "singing"—especially the way he places the word at the end of the
sentence, where it gets emphasis—makes me feel I am experiencing the
head coming out of the well the same way the girl did: First she noticed
that it was golden, then she noticed that it was—amazingly!—singing.
Here, too, the syntax of the sentence embodies in words the particular
actions the sentence is conveying.

Passages like these demonstrate the power our syntactic choices have
to shape a reader's experience.

Now read the following passages (some of which you've seen before),
listening for rhythm, phrasing, and emphasis. Are there any places where
you feel that the syntax of a sentence is giving shape to experience in a
way that lets us share that experience?

> This morning all was quiet on Barrow Down. The war was
> over. The rabbits nibbled the dewy grass boldly, and the
> lark rose in the brilliant air, higher, higher on its spun-glass
> spiral of song, knowing nothing of peace or war, accepting
> joyously the bounty of another day.
>> —Mollie Panter-Downes, *One Fine Day*

> She had a real inspector's eyes: they worked into your con-
> science, sniffing out guilt and guile and drive, seeking give.
>> —Ian Rankin, *Knots and Crosses*

> It was the blue hour, dusk. All the colors in the room began
> to fade before the King's eyes. The red silk counterpane, the
> sheepskin rug, the yellow rushes on the floor, the sprigs of

silver birch: they all took on the dun-color of the cold stone walls. The kingdom of the day was declining.

—Kevin Crossley-Holland, *Havelok the Dane*

Then the creeping murderer, the octopus, steals out, slowly, softly, moving like a gray mist, pretending now to be a bit of weed, now a rock, now a lump of decaying meat while its evil goat eyes watch coldly.

—John Steinbeck, *Cannery Row*

During meals Fritz always answers the door, on account of Wolfe's feeling that the main objection to atom bombs is that they may interrupt people eating. Through the open door from the dining room to the hall I saw Fritz pass on his way to the front, and a moment later his voice came, trying to persuade someone to wait in the office until Wolfe had finished lunch. There was no other voice, but there were steps, and then our visitor was marching in on us—a man about Wolfe's age, heavy-set, muscular, red-faced, and obviously aggressive.

—Rex Stout, "Man Alive"

Practice: Phrasing and Embodiment

Use any of the techniques you have learned so far to practice writing sentences that embody an experience for your readers. You can invent sentences on a subject, or revise a passage of your own work, or imitate a passage by a favorite writer.

Phrasing and Voice

These days the concept of "voice" gets a lot of attention in books and workshops on writing; agents and editors claim that what they are most looking for is a "fresh voice." But what does "voice" in writing mean? Many writing teachers and literary critics apparently see a writer's voice as a function of her psychology; to access your voice, they tell aspiring writers, you must concentrate on digging deep inside yourself.

As I said earlier, I believe that this particular view of voice is wrong. Even more, this view can be very damaging to aspiring writers. It makes them concentrate on themselves, rather than on the work of writing. It places "voice" in the realm of the psyche, rather than where it belongs, in the realm of learning the craft.

John Fairfax and John Moat founded the famous Arvon workshops for writers in England. In their book, *The Way to Write,* they state unequivocally that a writer's voice is his individual use of language. Their words are worth hearing again: "It is only by working," they say, "by writing, by practicing the art long and regularly that a writer develops his ear; i.e., that sense which eventually enables a writer to *hear* where the power of the word lies and, ultimately, his own voice."

I completely agree with this view; that's why I wrote this book. Ultimately all the techniques presented here are designed to help you learn enough about the craft so you can develop your own style, your own voice.

One of the most important of these voice-building techniques is phrasing. As you read the examples given in this chapter, you undoubtedly could hear that they sounded different: There are different lengths of phrases and clauses, different patterns of structure. The same thing is true when writers create characters: Giving each person a characteristic rhythm of speech helps create that character's voice.

So I encourage you to keep tuning your ear to the way your favorite authors phrase their sentences, and to keep paying attention to your own phrasing as you write and revise. Eventually, as Moat and Fairfax make clear, this dedicated practice will lead you to your own distinctive voice on the page.

Practice: Phrasing and Voice
Choose a passage from a favorite writer and pay close attention to the way its phrasing creates voice. Now write a passage of your own, imitating that phrasing exactly. What do you notice?

Invent "voice exercises" for yourself. For instance, give yourself an assignment to write ten sentences, each of which contains two prepositional phrases, or try writing ten sentences that begin with kernels, followed by one or more single word modifiers. Try to feel the phrasing rhythms as you write. Then, as you read your sentences out loud, hear those rhythms, feel the emphasis.

Go back to any of the syntax practices from earlier in the book and do them with an ear for the music of your sentences, as well as their meaning.

TAKE TIME TO REFLECT

What has stood out for you in this chapter? Which techniques do you want to continue practicing?

SECTION 6

Using Your Power

CHAPTER 15

POWER AND RESPONSIBILITY

••

When we can take the green from grass, blue from heaven, and red from blood, we have already an enchanter's power—upon one plane; and the desire to wield that power in the world external to our minds awakes. It does not follow that we shall use that power well on any plane. We may put a deadly green upon a man's face and produce horror; we may make the rare and terrible blue moon to shine; or we may cause weeds to spring with silver leaves and rams to wear fleeces of gold, and put hot fire in the belly of the cold worm.

••

—J.R.R. TOLKIEN

THE DANCE OF WRITING

At the beginning of this book I talked about the two kinds of writer's mind: content mind and craft mind; I distinguished between large-scale craft and the craft of making sentences, the latter requiring a trained word mind. Although we have now spent fourteen chapters concentrating on training the word mind, you probably found, in practicing, that you sometimes came up with ideas and material you want to use for a story, or a poem, or an essay. For the purposes of practice, we separate the two minds, but they are naturally intertwined. As we write and revise, we switch back and forth between these two minds, one minute focusing hard on what we want to say, or on making a picture more vivid in our mind, and the next seeking just the right word to convey that thought or vision. As I have said earlier, this back-and-forth movement between content and craft reminds me of a dance, with first one partner leading, then the other. I find it quite miraculous that our two minds can partner each other in this way, moving so closely together that sometimes it seems our word mind is giving us ideas for content and our content mind is leading us to words.

As you now know, practice will strengthen your word mind so that it can collaborate well with your content mind and be an equal partner in the dance. (The same is true for practices that strengthen your content mind.) Practice will set you free to enjoy the experience of the dance of writing: that back-and-forth movement, the exhilaration of those moments when both partners are achieving the best they are capable of.

It's in such moments, when all our faculties are working well, and working together, that we can experience a sense of our power as writers, a confidence in our abilities, a feeling of mastery of our craft. After working through the exercises in this book, you have had, I hope, a few of these moments.

THE JOURNEY TOWARDS MASTERY

I hope, too, that you want to continue your journey towards mastery in making sentences. There's a lot to learn; and in this book I have presented only some basics. In the "For Further Reading" list at the end of the book you will find a number of resources to help you keep building your skills.

You will be able to make the best use of these resources if you think of your learning as an ongoing journey. Every expert, in any field, eventually becomes her own coach. You can do the same thing. Keep checking in with yourself to see which skills you need to learn or practice right now, then figure out which book or teacher to consult to help you learn those skills.

Here's a practice to help you become your own coach, one I encourage you to return to frequently. It will help you establish and stay on your own learning path.

Practice: Becoming Your Own Coach

I invite you now to take some time to think about this book from the point of view of your own learning journey as a writer. Use the freewriting (nonstop writing) technique, if you find that helpful, and let the following questions serve as a guide for your reflections.

What have you learned from this book? What can you do now with words that you couldn't do before? Make a list of all the skills you feel you now have. Mark the ones you especially want to keep practicing.

Next, make some notes to yourself about how you want to continue your learning journey. Where is your present "learning edge"—the place where you are on the verge of understanding something new, the place where you can see the road of your further learning unrolling before you? What do you want to know about writing now? What do you want to be able to do that you can't quite do yet? Make a list of the skills you need to work on.

Now consider this: How can you learn the things you want to learn? Are there books you might read? People you can talk with? Writers to study and learn from? Most of all: What are the practices you want to keep using regularly? Perhaps you might like to make a "learning plan" for yourself for the next few months.

As you do this reflecting, I hope you will keep in mind that becoming a writer is a lifelong learning journey. You don't have to "get it" all at once. I encourage you to take to heart these words the German poet Rainer Maria Rilke wrote to a young aspiring poet who had sought his advice: "Strive always to be a beginner."

I love that piece of advice because it reminds me that learning is cyclical, not linear. Just as a major league hitter takes batting practice almost every day, practicing the same moves over and over, so we writers can practice the same things every day, the same basics. We can go deeper, rather than further, in our learning, noticing new things, getting new insight into our own learning process and the nature of language.

PRACTICING IN THE WORK

Some years ago I heard the baseball player Sean Casey, then with the Red Sox, being interviewed by Joe Castiglione, the Red Sox radio broadcaster. Casey hadn't been playing much, and Joe C. asked him how he kept his skills sharp. Casey replied, "Even when I'm not in the lineup, I practice every day, I take my cuts in batting practice. I need to stay ready in case I get called into a game."

Like athletes and musicians, we writers need to practice, even when we're not engaged in a work-in-progress, so that we can keep our skills sharp, so we can be "in shape" when we want to (or have to) write a finished piece.

We can also see practice as something that we can do "in the work"—that is, as we are writing and revising our work-in-progress. Each writer needs to find his own way of practicing in the work. Many writers, for example, set aside all considerations of craft as they write a draft and instead concentrate entirely on what they want to say. Then, when they revise, they bring a well-trained craft mind to bear on the sentences and paragraphs they have produced. Other writers aim for the "dance" I described above, allowing content mind and craft mind to collaborate as they write and revise.

Yet another approach to practicing in the work is to select one or two craft skills and be aware of them as you write your story, poem, or essay. You might, for instance, say to yourself, "As I write this story, I'm going to concentrate on nouns," or "As I write this poem, I'm going to try to include interrogative and exclamatory sentences."

Perhaps you feel that setting such goals is too artificial, that it will interfere with your creativity. For the past several decades, most creative writing instruction has equated creativity with complete freedom. But the truth is that, in order to work at its best, our creative faculty *needs* limits.

Practice: Use Selected Skills in Your Work

Select one or two skills you have learned and focus on them as you write a short piece or a section of a longer work-in-progress. Afterwards take some time to reflect: How did this go? What did you notice?

If you find this practice useful, make it part of your repertoire. I also encourage you to spend some time thinking about other ways you might practice in the work, as you go about producing and revising your drafts. You can also practice in the work when you write e-mails or blog posts, business memos, reports, academic papers—or anything else.

Remember that while you will undoubtedly experience those moments when writing feels like a dance in which you cannot put a foot wrong, like all peak experiences, these moments are fleeting. Professional athletes and musicians spend hours every day in practice; their performances last only a few hours. If we see practice only as a way to improve our performance, we may be very disappointed when tomorrow's chapter does not go as well as today's. Practice, ultimately, is a way to live as writers, a way to be writers all the time, not just when things are going well.

As with most things, there is much about writing that we cannot control: whether ideas come to us when we need them, whether readers like our work, whether agents and editors deem it worthy of publication. But practice is something we can always choose to do, and when we make that choice, we receive many benefits in addition to the improvement of writing skills.

THE BENEFITS OF THE MASTERY PATH

Writing practice gives us an opportunity to do an activity we love anytime, anyplace. To produce a draft of a piece of writing we want others to read is a lot of work; it's a complex activity, like playing a complete game of basketball, so it requires a considerable amount of time, energy, and mental space. But to practice one particular writing skill—well, we can do that just about anytime we want, especially if we always have our writer's notebook nearby. Because our focus is narrowed to one specific aspect of writing, we can make use of tiny windows of practicing opportunity during our busy days: five minutes here, ten minutes there.

Such dedication to practice does more for us than build our writing skills: It improves our ability to concentrate. Every time we focus our attention on doing one specific writing exercise, we also give ourselves practice in an essential life skill: being aware of our attention and focusing it in a particular direction. As Ben Hogan, the world-class golfer, once explained, "While I am practicing, I am also trying to develop my powers of concentration. I never just walk up and hit the ball."[30] Just as Hogan then brought his improved powers of concentration to performance situations, so we can bring our honed attentional abilities to our work-in-progress. Just as important, in our world where distraction is a way of life, gaining control over our attention through practice is a skill that will serve us well in the world beyond writing.

Dedication to practice teaches us patience, as well. You have probably already discovered, in using this book, that sometimes you didn't understand a skill right away. Sometimes, on your learning journey, you probably felt you were stuck, not moving forward.

This experience may have made you feel very frustrated; perhaps you were tempted to give up. Perhaps you even said to yourself, "I'll never get this!" Or even, "I just can't write." These thoughts and feelings are very common when we take a learning journey. A certain amount of frustration, in fact, is an inevitable part of learning. That's because frustration visits us only when we try to do things we don't already know how to do. But if we do only those things we can already do, then we never learn anything new.

Those people who become experts in their fields are not those who are necessarily naturally gifted; they are those who don't give up in the face of frustration. Albert Einstein, for instance, once said, "It's not that I'm so smart, it's just that I stay with problems longer than most people."[31] It's that ability to stay with problems, to wrestle with the things we *can't* do, that distinguishes those who become masters in their field.

We also need patience for those times in our learning journey when nothing seems to be happening. George Leonard, a writer, teacher, and black belt in aikido, has called these times "the plateau," and he has written that, if we want to make progress at our chosen activity, we need to learn to love the plateau.[32]

Directing our own learning; dedicating ourselves to practice; persistence; patience: These are the characteristics of those who have chosen the path to mastery. We don't have to be born with these character traits, which are so important to success in life; we can build them through dedication to any practice, including writing.

Perhaps the greatest benefit we can derive from practice, apart from building our skills, is that writing practice is good for our brains. Even if we never get published, every time we do a writing practice, we are building the mental muscles in the parts of our brain that have to do with language.

Finally, and most important, when we dedicate ourselves to writing practice, we provide ourselves with a certain kind of pleasure: the pleasure of learning something new, the pleasure of moving towards mastery.

FROM PLAY TO DELIBERATE PRACTICE

I have said that practice is a form of play; and I have suggested that such play gives us pleasure. I have insisted on these things because so many people think of practice as mindless, boring drills to be avoided at all cost. For those new to practice as a learning path, there must be, I think, an immediate reward in the form of a feeling of satisfaction or pleasure.

It's also true, though, that the expertise researchers (see Chapter 2) insist that practice is not fun. They are talking about what K. Anders Ericsson calls "deliberate practice," which he defines as "considerable, specific, and sustained efforts to do something you *can't* do well—or even at all."[33]

Is this kind of intense practice necessary for writers? I suspect it is—at least for those who aspire to become outstanding. Certainly repetition is the key to learning skills, in any field; like athletes and musicians, aspiring writers need to practice their skills repeatedly, until they become second nature. Those who want to become experts also continually challenge themselves by combining skills, pushing their "learning edge" just a little bit further. You can do this, too. Once you've mastered a few of the techniques in this book, challenge yourself by inventing practices in which you use these techniques together: See, for example, if you can write with concrete words while also using bound modifiers; or try to write a compound sentence that includes free modifiers.

Another key element of deliberate practice is to compare what you have produced with a model of excellence. The elite performers Ericsson and his colleagues studied did this routinely, by comparing their own performance with the performance of people who had better skills. They would then examine their own abilities with a critical eye, assessing what they did well and what they still had to work on. It's fairly easy to do this kind of assessment in sports or music; it's a lot more difficult with writing. That's because there is no single standard for excellence in writing, nothing we can quantify the way we can count points scored or stolen bases, to be able to say, "This person's performance is the best." Still, I do think it's possible for writers to choose their own models of excellence. In this book, I have repeatedly invited you to learn from writers whose work you love. If you want to make more conscious use of the principles of deliberate practice, then use what you have learned to identify your chosen writer's skills. Then ask yourself whether you can do those things—or do them as well. If not, see if you can figure out exactly what your model writer can do that you can't, and then work on those skills.

Becoming a skilled writer takes time, lots of it. You may find yourself wishing that someone would just tell you exactly what you are doing wrong—or right. Perhaps at this point you will want to look for a teacher or a writing coach. People who want to be the best at what they do deliberately seek out coaches who can help them work on their weaknesses. At the same time, though, most top performers have learned how to coach themselves; they study their own work, identify the problems, and learn how to fix them. Even professional writers are always learning and developing their skills. As I mentioned in my first book, *How to Be a Writer*, Leo Tolstoy once happened to pick up one of his own early books at the house of a friend. After glancing through it for a few moments, he exclaimed, "Oh, this is terrible! *Now* I see how I should have written this!"

Perhaps you have the time, energy, and inclination to take your practice to more intense levels; perhaps you do not. Either way, though, if you develop the skills presented in this book to whatever extent you can, you will have gained power. As I said at the beginning of this book, mastery of diction and syntax enables you to wield a kind of magical power over the minds of your readers: to make them understand what you are saying; to make them see your visions, feel your characters' emotions, and be riveted by your story.

That's a considerable power to be able to wield. And when you possess this power—or any other kind—you will eventually be brought up against a vital question: How will you use it?

Power and Responsibility

As writers who can make use of the power of language, what is our responsibility? That's not a question that gets asked very often in creative writing workshops, but it's one I always ask my students. Very often, they are surprised by the question, and they reply, "My only responsibility is to express myself."

I understand why they give this answer: For quite some time now, writing instruction books and workshop leaders have told aspiring writers that creative writing is all about self-expression, with the emphasis on the "self." In the United States, we've lived through several decades where self-focus has been the norm in the culture at large, so it's no wonder that this attitude has made its way into the world of creative writing.

I think this is an unhealthy attitude, for many reasons, and so I invite you now to consider your writing skills in the light of how you can use them responsibly. For I believe that this responsibility inevitably becomes yours when you choose to put your writing out into the world. If you are writing only for yourself, then the matter of responsibility doesn't arise; but if you are going public with your words, then, I think, you need to consider their possible effect on other people.

So, for instance, will your words celebrate violence and hatred? Will they create nightmarish pictures—in Tolkien's words, will they "put green upon a man's face and create horror"? As soon as such questions are raised, some people inevitably raise the subject of censorship. So I want to make it clear that I am not laying down any rules about what you should or should not make public; I am, rather, saying that when you have acquired power, you ought to use that power in a responsible manner. I am inviting you to consider what *you* feel is your responsibility as a skilled writer.

One responsibility you might want to shoulder is that of using words with accuracy and clarity. Another might be to consider yourself as a caretaker of the English language. As the mass media continue to focus our attention on visual images rather than language, you might wish to take on the job of keeping alive and celebrating the richness of English diction and syntax. Finally, you might think about what you, as an educated writer, have to offer readers, about what you want to give them—or teach them—through the medium of the written word.

Practice: What Is Your Responsibility?
Do some thinking on the page, using freewriting, about what you consider to be your responsibility as a writer. How do you want to use the power with words you have now acquired?

MOVING ON

As we come to the end of this book, I hope you feel that your learning journey has been an enjoyable and productive one. I encourage you to remember that learning is a spiral, not a straight line, and that you can return to the practices in the book anytime you like to further develop your skills. In moving forward, you may also feel that now you are ready to consult some of the resources in the list that follows this chapter, or to find a teacher or writing coach. Whatever your next steps, I hope you will remember that the best thing about being a writer is that it provides a journey in lifelong learning.

May your own continuing journey be a fulfilling and joyful one.

FOR FURTHER READING

Expertise and Practice

Daniel Coyle. *The Talent Code,* Random House, 2009.

Geoff Colvin. *Talent Is Overrated: What Really Separates World-Class Performers from Everybody Else,* Penguin 2010.

K. Anders Ericsson, Michael J. Prietula, and Edward T. Cokely. "The Making of an Expert," *Harvard Business Review,* July-August, 2007.

Malcolm Gladwell. *Outliers: The Story of Success,* Back Bay Books, 2011.

George Leonard. *Mastery: The Keys to Success and Long-Term Fulfillment,* Penguin, 1991.

David Shenk. *The Genius in All of Us: Why Everything You've Been Told About Genetics, Talent, and IQ Is Wrong,* Doubleday, 2010.

Twyla Tharp. *The Creative Habit: Learn It and Use It for Life,* Simon & Schuster, 2006.

The English Language

Anthony Burgess. *A Mouthful of Air,* William Morrow, 1992.

Ian A. Gordon. *The Movement of English Prose,* Longman, 1966.

James Lipton. *An Exaltation of Larks,* Penguin, 1977.

Syntax and Style

Francis Christensen. *Notes Towards a New Rhetoric,* Harper & Row, 1967.

Francis Christensen and Bonniejean Christensen. *A New Rhetoric,* Harper & Row, 1976.

Richard Lanham. *Style: An Anti-Textbook,* Paul Dry Books, 2007.

Virginia Tufte. *Artful Sentences: Syntax as Style,* Graphics Press, 2006.

Virginia Tufte. *Grammar as Style,* Holt, Rinehart, & Winston, 1971.

Grammar Guides

Joseph C. Blumenthal. *English 3200: A Programmed Course in Grammar and Usage*, Harcourt, Brace, Jovanovich, 1962.

C. Edward Good. *A Grammar Book for You and I … Oops, Me!* Capital Books, 2002.

Martha Kolln. *Rhetorical Grammar,* 4th ed., Longman, 2003.

Michael Newby. *The Structure of English: A Handbook of English Grammar,* Cambridge University Press, 1987.

Patricia T. O'Conner. *Woe Is I: The Grammarphobe's Guide to Better English in Plain English,* Riverhead Books, 1996.

Patricia Osborn. *How Grammar Works: A Self-Teaching Guide,* John Wiley & Sons, 1989.

Other Writing Guides

Roy Peter Clark. *Writing Tools: 50 Essential Strategies for Every Writer,* Little Brown, 2006.

John Fairfax and John Moat. *The Way to Write: A Stimulating Guide to the Craft of Creative Writing,* St. Martin's Press, 1981.

Rudolf Flesch. *The Art of Readable Writing,* Collier, 1949.

Ursula K. Le Guin. *Steering the Craft: Exercises and Discussions on Story Writing for the Lone Navigator or the Mutinous Crew,* The Eighth Mountain Press, 1998.

Ursula K. Le Guin. *The Wave in the Mind: Talks and Essays on the Writer, the Reader, and the Imagination,* Shambhala, 2004.

Noah Lukeman, *A Dash of Style: The Art and Mastery of Punctuation,* W.W. Norton, 2006.

Frances Mayes, *The Discovery of Poetry: A Field Guide to Reading and Writing Poems,* Harcourt, 2001.

ACKNOWLEDGMENTS

My gratitude goes, first of all, to Virginia Tufte and Francis Christensen, from whose books I learned so much. I am very grateful, as well, to Heidi Hill, who has been a continuing friend to me and to this book. Marjorie Moon and Jan Nerenberg read early drafts of the manuscript and offered helpful suggestions. Tom Hallock kindly answered my many questions about the book business. Special thanks go to Ursula K. Le Guin, who offered support and encouragement at a time when both were missing from my life.

To write a book is one thing; to get it published, another. Jane Friedman (www.janefriedman.com) gave me suggestions and advice that set this book on its path to publication. Rita Rosenkranz extended a helping hand, then negotiated a book deal with consummate professionalism and unflagging good humor. My gratitude to them is boundless.

The good folks at *Writer's Digest* took the book through the editorial and publication process with their usual care; special thanks to editor Cris Freese. Bonnie Fortini, introduced to me just when I needed her skills, became my invaluable assistant.

Above all, I am grateful to my students in the Lesley University MFA Program in Creative Writing, and to my private coaching clients, especially Brenda Horrigan. Their enthusiastic response to the material in this book kept me going during the long and difficult time when I doubted the book would ever find a home. Now that the material is, at last, in book form, I hope it will give you, too, your footing on the mastery path.

You can find me at www.WhereWritersLearn.com, where I offer free writing lessons and am happy to answer questions.

NOTES

1. ... *to achieve extraordinary mastery.* Professor K. Anders Ericsson, quoted in Dodds, David, "E=MC2," *The Age,* 2006.
2. ... *what we demand of it.* David Shenk, *The Genius in All of Us,* p. 30.
3. ... *you become creative.* Pam Allen, *Knitting for Dummies* (For Dummies, 2002) p. 10.
4. ... *and his or her unique authority.* John Fairfax and John Moat, The Way to Write, p. 3.
5. ... *a signal traveling through a circuit.* Daniel Coyle, The Talent Code, p. 5.
6. ... *all circuits [can] grow.* Daniel Coyle, The Talent Code, p. 6.
7. ... *is precisely the way skills are built.* Daniel Coyle, The Talent Code, p. 80.
8. ... *work on their weaknesses.* Professor K. Anders Ericsson, quoted in Anna Patty, "Why Only the Right Kind of Practice Gets Anywhere Near Perfect," *The Sydney Morning Herald,* May 15, 2006.
9. ... *harder at golf than I did.* Quoted in Professor K. Anders Ericsson, Michael J. Prietula, and Edward T. Cokely, "The Making of an Expert," *Harvard Business Review,* July-August, 2007.
10. ... *some aspect of an individual's target performance.* From Gregg Schraw, "An Interview with Professor K. Anders Ericsson, *Educational Psychology Review,* Vol. 17, No. 4, December 2005, p. 397.
11. ... *Improvement is never effortless.* Professor K. Anders Ericsson, quoted in Shelley Gare, "Success Is All in the Mind," *The Australian,* January 24, 2009.
12. ... *a strategy they can fix.* Coyle, p. 87.
13. ... *prewired to imitate.* Professor K. Anders Ericsson, quoted in Coyle, p. 80.
14. ... *following the daytime of the hare.* Edward Field, Eskimo Songs and Stories (Delacorte Press), 1973, p. 7.
15. ... *the way we create the world.* Quoted in Lois J. Einhorn, The Native American Oral Tradition (Praeger, 2000), p. 3.
16. ... *consisting of a proton and a neutron.* The Random House Dictionary (Ballantine, 1980), p. 249.

17. ... *brings to the sentence.* Emma Darwin at www.thisitchofwriting.com, September 22, 2010.

18. ... *add other categories.* Some writers on grammar now consider that there are only eight parts of speech—they consider determiners to be a kind of adjective—while others identify twelve parts of speech. See R.L. Trask, *The Penguin Dictionary of English Grammar.*

19. ... *as close to the subject as possible.* Frances Mayes, The Discovery of Poetry: A Field Guide to Reading and Writing Poems (Harcourt, 2001), p. 28.

20. ... *very vivid mental picture.* Shirley Jackson, *Come Along with Me* (Viking, 1968), p. 239.

21. ... *the essential part of any sentence.* John Erskine, "The Craft of Writing," quoted by Francis Christensen and Bonniejean Christensen in *A New Rhetoric* (Harper & Row, 1976), p. 7.

22. ... *fact and fiction, prose and poetry.* Virginia Tufte, *Grammar as Style* (Holt, Rinehart, 1971) p. iv.

23. ... *about English prose style.* Dwight Bolinger, quoted by Virginia Tufte, *Grammar as Style,* p. 125.

24. ... *or a near-kernel.* Virginia Tufte, *Artful Sentences,* p. 24. I am indebted to Tufte for her explanation of kernels.

25. ... *which we call meaning.* Anthony Burgess, *Enderby* (Penguin, 1982), p. 406.

26. Summary of the Basic Sentence Patterns, adapted from Martha Kolln, Rhetorical Grammar, p. 16.

27. ... *may be called a value ...* Talcott Parsons, quote by Richard A. Lanham, *Style: An Anti-Textbook,* p. 106.

28. ... *is absolutely essential.* Virginia Tufte, *Grammar as Style,* pp. 39-40.

29. ... *the following roles (among others).* Nouns can also modify other nouns and be used in a noun series. For more information on these uses of nouns, consult your grammar book.

30. ... *just walk up and hit the ball."* Quoted in K. Anders Ericsson, et al, "The Making of an Expert," p. 4.

31. ... *longer than most people."* Quoted in David Shenk, *The Genius in All of Us* (Doubleday, 2010), p. 112.

32. ... *love the plateau.* George Leonard, The Mastery Path: The Keys to Success and Long-Term Fulfillment (Penguin, 1992), p. 15.

33. ... *or even at all.* K. Anders Ericsson, et al, "The Making of an Expert," p. 3.

INDEX

WD **WRITER'S DIGEST**

Is Your Manuscript Ready?

Trust 2nd Draft Critique Service to prepare your writing
to catch the eye of agents and editors. You can expect:

- •Expert evaluation from a hand-selected, professional critiquer

- •Know-how on reaching your target audience

- •Red flags for consistency, mechanics, and grammar

- •Tips on revising your work to increase your odds of publication

Visit WritersDigestShop.com/2nd-draft for more information.

CREATE MASTERFUL DESCRIPTIONS ON THE PAGE

Word Painting Revised Edition

REBECCA McCLANAHAN

The words you choose to describe a character, scene, setting, or
idea need to precisely illustrate the vision you wish to convey to
your reader. With *Word Painting Revised Edition*, you will learn
to develop your powers of observation to craft rich and evoca-
tive descriptions, discover and craft original metaphors and si-
milies, and weave effective description seamlessly through your
stories, essays, and poems.

Available from WritersDigestShop.com and your favorite book retailers.

To get started join our mailing list: **WritersDigest.com/enews**

FOLLOW US ON:

Find more great tips, networking and
advice by following **@writersdigest**

And become a fan of our Facebook page:
facebook.com/writersdigest